STORIES AND SUTRAS

TIMELESS LEGENDS • PRICELESS LESSONS

VIRAT CHIRANIA

PENGUIN BOOKS
An imprint of Penguin Random House

PENGUIN BOOKS

USA | Canada | UK | Ireland | Australia
New Zealand | India | South Africa | China

Penguin Books is part of the Penguin Random House group of companies
whose addresses can be found at global.penguinrandomhouse.com

Published by Penguin Random House India Pvt. Ltd
4th Floor, Capital Tower 1, MG Road,
Gurugram 122 002, Haryana, India

Penguin
Random House
India

First published in Penguin Books by Penguin Random House India 2022

10 9 8 7 6 5 4 3 2 1

This book is a work of creative non-fiction and is a collection of the Author's thoughts on historical and/or mythological figures. These essays are based on a variety of sources including published materials and the research conducted by the Author. For the purposes of narrative flow, certain creative liberties have been taken and a dialogue has been created, while trying to remain true to the essence of the stories. Each essay reflects the Author's own understanding and conception of such materials. The views and opinions expressed in the manuscript are those of the author only and do not reflect or represent the views and opinions held by any other person. The objective of this book is not to offend or hurt the sentiments of any particular individual, institution, region, caste, creed, gender, religion or community.

ISBN 9780143455349

Typeset in Bembo Std by Manipal Technologies Limited, Manipal

www.penguin.co.in

For

My Master
My eternal source of inspiration and love

Gurudev Sri Sri Ravi Shankar Ji

Contents

introduction

'You can't teach, not for at least the next four months! You need complete voice rest. We can't rule out a surgery either', said my doctor, with a plain face.

My world came falling apart. It took me some time to digest what I had just heard. For someone whose passion and profession are both one—teaching, this was the worst news I could hear. Four months without teaching would be four months without oxygen! I braced for impact.

I was advised to start off my four-month voice rest with a couple of weeks of absolute silence or 'maun'. I jumped at this idea and enrolled myself into two back-to-back advance meditation programmes by the Art of Living Foundation. Maun is an essential part of these programmes, and it was in one of those deep meditations that a memory surfaced from long ago; a WhatsApp message I had sent to myself.

When I finished the program and switched on my phone, I frantically searched for that message. And, fortunately, I found it. It was a random message I had written to myself while I was 30,000 feet up in the air on a Berlin–Mumbai flight a few years ago. *And then, this book was born.*

* * *

India is a land of stories. We are a story-obsessed people. As Muriel Rukeyser once said, 'The universe is not made of atoms, but of stories'. And the reason why amongst all the pre-bronze civilizations India is the only one that thrives vibrantly is because we continue to celebrate our stories.

I spent many years of my life travelling across India, working with students and young professionals and with people from all walks of life. In my interactions with them, I specifically remember asking many about what they know of Indian history. The responses I got were mostly very embarrassing. One common thread I noticed was that the lesser they knew about our true history, the lesser was the sense of pride in their roots. Once they discovered the mind-blowing heritage we have, their attitudes shifted. Not that I am an expert on Indian history by any stretch of imagination, but I thought I could at least share whatever little I know.

I also saw that in recent times, the curiosity of an average Indian towards our history and culture has skyrocketed. Their appetite for genuine Indian content is increasing, whether it is movies, social media or books. They want to know. They are all eyes and ears.

So, I decided to share stories of ancient Indian heroes in my own way. This book contains nine powerful stories that you might not know at all or might think you do, but believe me, there is more to them!

The stories I picked for this book are the stories that left deep impressions on me as an individual and as an Indian. My initial list contained twenty-one stories, and it was very difficult for me to bring it down to just nine.

These stories serve an important purpose—**Edutainment!**

The stories about Indian Superheroes are anyway ever inspiring and offer many goosebump moments. Once you hear/read them, they remain etched in your memory and in your conversations forever. But apart from their massive inspirational and entertainment value, they are a treasure trove of lessons for life.

We look at Lord Hanuman as the symbol of power and devotion, but do you know we can learn communication skills, negotiation skills and emotional intelligence from Hanuman? Chatrapati Shivaji Maharaj is synonyms with bravery and patriotism, but his life can offer amazing insights into how to run a start-up! This book showcases how Chanakya can teach us business strategy and the art of influencing, how Adi Shankaracharya can teach us spiritual leadership and how Kabir can teach us the power of messaging. Most people I met have never even heard the name of Rani Abbakka. She is one of the most unsung warrior queens of India. Do you know how Rani Abbakka from her tiny kingdom successfully defeated the Portuguese, which back in the day were the largest naval power of the world? We all know about the Indian freedom struggle, but do you know how Srinivasa Ramanujan fought an intellectual war of independence in the field of mathematics?

This book is an insight into India's ancient school of management and leadership. It's a like a mini MBA course taught by the original superheroes of Bharat. It has something to offer to everyone. It shares timeless legends and offers priceless lessons.

How to Read This Book

When I was writing this book, I felt that each character was talking to me, personally sharing their life story with me. And at the end of the story, I thought what I could learn from their lives. I request you do the same. Pause and ask yourself: What can I learn from this story? Please take a few moments for Swadhyay (self study), and write down your own personal learnings. Don't read this book from the intellect alone. Watch out for emotional responses and acknowledge them. If you can spring into action based on the learnings mentioned, you would have taken the impact of this book to the next level!

Note to the Reader

Book readers are a special species. You, my friend, belong to an elite club. Keep reading and spreading the cheer.

When I wrote my first story during the four-month period of voice rest, I never thought I would come this far. But miracles happen. What you hold in your hands right now is a slice of my life, which is just like me, uniquely Indian and utterly global. I am very happy that you found this book or vice versa. Thank you for taking the time to get to this book. I shall eagerly wait for your feedback (Refer to the Connect section at the end of the book).

I hope you enjoy reading this book as much as I enjoyed writing it!

Love and light,
Virat

* * *

PS: For those who are still wondering what on earth was in that WhatsApp message, it contained the raw idea of this very book. So, the next time you get an intuitive flash of an idea, write it down somewhere.

gratitude

I feel immensely grateful for

Gurudev—They say when the time is right, the guru finds you. Thank you for finding me; for crafting for me a life, which I couldn't have imagined better.

My luck, to be born in India—To this romance called Bharat!

Mom and Dad—For all their sacrifices and unconditional love, for the upbringing they gave me despite the challenges they faced. Also, gratitude to my ever-loving sisters and their families.

My wife, Jhalak—For being the anchor of my life. Words cannot do justice to the gratitude I feel for you.

My beta readers (alphabetically)—Ami Patel, Aruna Rajagopal, Nakul Dhawan, Prateek Khandelwal, Priya Subramanian, Rajat Khot, Swami Purnachaitanya,

Smitha Murthy, Shreyans Mehta, Shreyasi Walia, Yashaswani Sharma. Thanks for your invaluable and detailed feedback. Thanks for showing faith in me early on. The book stands in its current shape because of you!

The awesome team at Penguin Random House India—Aparna Kumar, Shreya Punj, Meru Gokhale, Shaoni Mukherjee, Akangksha Sarmah, Vijesh Kumar and many others behind the scenes.

My illustrators—Shiladitya Bose and Shubhadeep Roy (the cover design dudes from Doodle Nerve) and Adriraj Paul, Vinay Brahmania, Hitharth Bhatt, Gauri Gupta, Pankhuree Shukla and Vaishnavi Gaikwad.

All the writers and content creators who preserved our true history, our culture and our scriptures.

My team, which is more like my family. You are the pillar of strength in everything I do, not just this book. You know who you are. You are the reason why I got this far.

1

Bhishma Vadh

'But you can neither defeat him nor kill him'

With slow chants from the Saam-Veda reverberating in the atmosphere, with measured steps and a zillion thoughts in his mind, Bhishma walked up and down his royal canopy. Dressed in his trademark white dhoti and angavastra (stole for men), sporting a long white beard, he was planning the strategy for the war tomorrow. It would be the tenth day of the epic battle of Mahabharata, which was being fought between the Kauravas and the Pandavas at Kurukshetra. Bhishma was the senapati (commander-in-chief) from the Kauravas' side. It was almost the second prahar (unit of time) of the evening, and the last platoon of soldiers was returning from their basic dinner at the campfire. The stronger the army, the more ordinary the food! Bhishma had already finished his sandhya-vandanam (evening prayers) and taken his simple meal.

Suddenly, his personal guard came at the tent door and said, 'Pitamah, Pandava Prince Yudhishthira and the mighty Arjuna wish to see you'. 'Pitamah' was the title most commonly used to address Bhishma. It meant grandfather. Bhishma was stunned to hear that the enemy, if he could call them that, was at the door on a battle night to meet him, but he was seasoned to not show his feelings on his face. 'Send them in', commanded Bhishma.

Yudhishthira was the eldest brother of the five Pandavas and the leader of the opposition. He was considered the epitome of righteousness and wisdom. He entered first, followed by Arjuna. Bhishma's eyes fell and rested on Arjuna's face alone. In the mighty world-renowned warrior, the critically acclaimed best archer on the planet, the one who was considered undefeatable even by the gods, all Bhishma saw was his little grandson, the Arjuna he had cuddled in his arms and mock-wrestled as a child, the Arjuna who would not eat until Bhishma fed him with his own hands every single night! A teardrop tried to slide itself down Pitamah's eyes, but he forced it back in with a deep breath.

'Pranam Pitamah', said the brothers in unison as they joined their palms in a namaste and bent to touch Bhishma's feet to take his blessings.

'Vijayi Bhava', (may you be victorious) came out of Bhishma's mouth instantly and naturally. Here he was slaying thousands of enemy soldiers every single day, and yet from his heart, the blessing he gives them is for their victory!

'Pitamah', said Yudhishthira, 'I am sorry but I request you take back this ashirvaad (blessing) of yours'.

'Putra (son), great men do not take back what has been given once, even if it's a blessing. Don't disrespect my blessings; accept them'.

'How can we, Pitamah', spoke Arjuna this time, 'when we know that the person standing between us and victory is you!' Arjuna shook as these harsh yet true words came out of his mouth. Bhishma took a moment to register what he had just heard.

'Truth be told, you are right dear Arjuna. I do stand between you and your victory. And neither my defeat nor death is possible'. It was a well-known fact that Pitamah Bhishma had the rarest boon of Icchha Mrityu or death by will. This meant that unless he himself willed it, he could not be killed, and this made him invincible. Bhishma had access to more divya-astras (divine weapons) than any warrior in history. He had managed to stalemate his own guru, Lord Parshurama. He was truly unconquerable.

'We know, Pitamah. And that is why Vasudev suggested we come and meet you', said Yudhishthira.

A big smile ran across Bhishma's face as he exclaimed 'Vasudev! So, it's Vasudev who told you to come and meet me tonight'. The smile grew bigger, and Bhishma's eyes twinkled at the mere mention of the name 'Vasudev', the name of his beloved lord, the omniscient Supreme Divine who was in his eighth avatar on the planet, the Maha Vishnu himself. In his current human avatar, the lord had manifested as Krishna or Vasudev and was presently playing the role of Arjuna's charioteer in the Mahabharata war. So, technically, Vasudev was Bhishma's enemy. And just a few hours earlier in the battlefield, tired of Bhishma's carnage of the Pandava army, Vasudev had almost broken his pledge to not pick up a weapon in this battle and had raised his Sudarshan Chakra (Krishna's spinning discus weapon) to kill Bhishma.

'I still can't take back my blessings', Bhishma was saying when Arjuna interrupted him, 'But, Pitamah . . .!' Bhishma glared at Arjuna.

'Cut my arrows, dear Arjuna; I will be very pleased. But never cut my words! Leave this task for Duryodhana.' Duryodhana was the eldest son of the Kauravas and the embodiment of ignorance and ego. Unfortunately, Bhishma was the chief of his army.

'Pardon me, Pitamah', Arjuna instantly apologized.

Bhishma continued, 'Go and tell Vasudev that I cannot take back my blessings. Anyway, even without my blessings, He very well knows that in the end, victory shall kiss his feet alone. For wherever He stands, victory comes there'.

यतः कृष्णस्ततो धर्मो यतो धर्मस्ततो जयः

(Where there is Krishna, there is Dharma. Where there is Dharma, there is victory)

'Pitamah, you have always shown us the right path, the path of dharma. You have taught us to speak the truth and be fearless. This war is for re-establishing dharma and for the welfare of residents of this glorious nation. But this war seems to have no end. If this war continues, the entire Kshatriya race (clan of warriors) shall be eliminated from the planet. We need to bring this endless destruction to a conclusion. To that effect, oh worship-worthy father, we must secure victory, and for that you must be defeated. We ask you in the name of the holy

Ganges, please show us the path to our victory and your defeat, oh saintly grandsire', said the Pandava brothers to their beloved grandpa.

What a great moment in history this was! A grandson asking his own grandfather to share the secret that will bring about the latter's defeat and death in the battlefield. And what does the grandfather and the chief of the enemy army do? He smiles and says:

'Listen, my dear grandchildren. There is only one way to defeat me. If a woman comes in front of me, I shall not lift my bow anymore! And then it will be quite straightforward for Arjuna to eliminate this weaponless old man!'

It is said that gods and angels gathered in the heavens that moment to bestow flowers of respect on Bhishma, for only the purest of souls can willingly show the path to their own death for the larger good of mankind.

As Yudhisthira and Arjuna departed from Bhishma's canopy, the only question in their mind was: how can a woman enter the battlefield? That's against Kshatriya dharma or the law of the warriors! Their puzzle was only half-solved.

* * *

It was late in the night, but Krishna was wide awake, anticipating the Pandava brothers to come straight to him to discuss Bhishma's peculiar statement. As always, he pretended he didn't know anything, and as the brothers narrated their conversation with Bhishma, they asked him, 'Vasudev, how can a woman enter the battlefield? History shall never forgive us if we break the code of conduct for a war'.

'You are right', said Krishna, 'a woman cannot come into the battlefield. But which code or law can possibly stop Prince Shikhandi from facing Pitamah Bhishma?'

'Prince Shikhandi?' exclaimed Arjuna. 'With due respect, oh Krishna, our brave brother-in-law Shikhandi may be half-male, but he is still a man'.

'He is a man for you and I, oh Arjuna. But believe me, Pitamah shall only see the late princess Amba in him. And as soon as Pitamah sees Shikhandi, he will drop his weapons', concluded Krishna.

'Are you sure'? asked Arjuna. Krishna looked at him and smiled.

Arjuna smiled back, apologized and hugged Krishna. That's the problem in having God as your friend. You sometimes forget that He is God!

'Let me tell you a story', said Krishna. 'Gentlemen, take a seat'.

> Many years ago, on the banks of the Ganges, lay the holy kingdom of Kashi. The king of Kashi had three beautiful daughters named Amba, Ambika and Ambalika. The then young and brave Prince Devvratta (the birth name for Bhishma) abducted the three daughters to bring them to his brother as wives. When Amba shared that she was in love with another prince, Devvratta respectfully sent Amba back to her lover,

but the lover then refused to accept Amba. Amba came back to Devvratta and asked him to marry her, but Devvratta had already pledged celibacy. Insulted, hurt and with nowhere to go, Amba went to Bhishma's guru, Lord Parshurama and asked him for justice. What unfolded was a fierce battle between a guru and shishya (disciple), between Lord Parshurama and Bhishma, and in this fight, Devvratta brought his guru to a stalemate. Continuing to burn intensely in the fire of revenge, Amba performed a long, uninterrupted tapasya (purification/meditation process) to please Shiva, the Mahadev (Lord of all lords). Shiva, pleased with Amba, appeared in front of her and asked her for a boon, and in response, Amba said:

'Mahadev, the most important piece of jewellery a woman wears is her respect, and Bhishma has stripped me off it. Bless me so that I shall be the cause of his death, even if I have to take multiple births for this'.

'*Tathastu*' (so be it) said Mahadev and disappeared into space.

The same Amba, in this lifetime, is born as Prince Shikhandi, with the sole purpose of ensuring Bhishma's death. Shikhandi knows who he or she is. So does Bhishma.

'Tomorrow', said Krishna to Arjuna, 'request Shikhandi to ride with you on your chariot'.

* * *

It was a unique morning. The sun seemed to be running late, as if hesitant to start the day. Somewhere, it knew this day shall be remembered for eons to come. And it would not be a very happy memory. Rise it had to, for that was its dharma. Everyone was playing their dharma in this battle. To each his own. There are moments when history decides to turn a page, and no power in the world can change that, let alone the sun. Today was one such day.

Shikhandi sat on his bed romancing the morning dew. He had not slept at all the whole night. He didn't want to. He wanted to fully live every moment leading up to the day. This was the sun rise he had waited on for a very, very long time. He took a scented bath and an unusually long time to get dressed, carefully adorning his armour like a bride adorns her wedding gown, picking his lucky war armlet like a child picks his favourite toy. He had an elaborate festive breakfast, unlike a war meal.

He suddenly heard footsteps leading to his room, and a smile ran across his face. He intuitively knew who the visitor was going to be. Standing with his back to the visitor who was entering, Shikhandi said, 'Welcome, oh mighty Arjuna. Welcome'. And before Arjuna could recover from the absolute shock he was in, Shikhandi added, 'The answer to your request is *yes.*' He turned and smiled, enjoying the ghostly look on the great archer's face. And, so, that day in the battle, for the very first time in his life, Arjuna did not ride on his chariot alone. With him rode Shikhandi. And with them rode Yama himself (the God of Death).

Bhishma had not slept at all either. He kept thinking about the choices he had made in life, about all the pratigyas (pledges) he had taken — I shall never marry; I shall never become king; I shall unquestionably protect whoever sits on the throne! He had been carrying the weight of these promises for many decades now. He was tired. After ages, he had taken time out to visit his mother, the great river Ganga. He had relieved his servers (the cooks, caretakers, cleaners) from the curse of slavery and had given them rich gifts to start their lives afresh. He insisted he would not need their services from that evening onwards. He knew something they didn't. He was packing for a very long, hard journey, and material comforts wouldn't be of any use on this trip. And, so, that day in the battle, Pitamah Bhishma, the son of Ganga, rode on his chariot alone . . . for the last time!

And then the conches roared their heavenly sounds announcing the start of the day's battle. Krishna blew his famous Panchajanya, Bhishma his Shashank and Arjuna his Devdutta (names of their conch shells, all having a unique, identifiable sound). Like a hungry lion, Bhishma unleashed himself on the Pandava army. He kept tearing through the enemy ranks, and within no time, the grandsire created a cemetery of dead bodies, broken chariots, fallen horses and deceased elephants. Using the celestial Agniastra (a special weapon that could shoot hundreds of fire-lit arrows simultaneously), Bhishma delivered to death thousands of infantry and cavalry soldiers without even a scratch on his body.

Seeing the fire-lit arrows in the sky, Krishna identified the location of Bhishma's chariot and manoeuvred the wheels towards Bhishma.

They were now face-to-face. Two of the greatest warriors the world had ever seen. A grandfather and a grandson. Two men who loved each other more than their own selves. Both bound by their own definitions of dharma. Both ready to kill and die for protecting their definition. For a moment, memories of his childhood spent in Pitamah's lap flashed in front of Arjuna's eyes: his heart sank, his lips went dry, and his Gandiva (his bow) slipped an inch from his hand. But then he recalled the lessons from the Bhagvad Gita — lessons that Krishna had taught him at the beginning of the battle:

सुखदुःखे समे कृत्वा लाभालाभौ जयाजयौ।
ततो युद्धाय युज्यस्व नैवं पापमवाप्स्यसि

Fight for Dharma.
Hold pleasure and pain, gain and loss, victory and defeat as similar. If you fight like this, you shall incur no sin.

Bhishma saw Shikhandi standing with Arjuna, and true to his word, he immediately dropped his bow and arrow. He stood tall with a smile on his face. As eager as Shikhandi was for his revenge, so was Bhishma to repay his karmic debt to the late Amba and release his soul for its onward journey. Both had a strange kind of impatience.

Arjuna pulled his arrow back, ready to shoot. Mentally and silently, he bowed down to his beloved Pitamah and asked for forgiveness. He looked at Krishna. Krishna nodded. And then Arjuna did what he thought he would never be able to do! He shot his grandfather. The arrow struck Bhishma like a thunderbolt, pierced through his skin and muscle, tore through his heart and emerged from the other side of his body, drawing thick blood on to Bhishma's chest. Shikhandi exploded in joy and made no attempts to conceal his happiness. But the rest of the battlefield skipped a heartbeat. Everyone stopped their combats and stared at Bhishma. They could not believe their own eyes!

And then, Arjuna released the second arrow. And then the third. Tears trickled down Arjuna's face as the grandsire's body looked like a dartboard. With every arrow drawing his blood, Bhishma would say *Ayushman Bhava* (may you live long) to Arjuna. Arjuna was now shooting with eyes closed and crying inconsolably. He kept firing. Pitamah, still standing, kept taking the blows like a mountain. Shikhandi kept smiling.

And then he fell. When not even two fingers worth of distance was left between the arrows on his body, he fell. The oldest and most senior warrior of the Kuru dynasty fell. And he fell like the Himalayas had fallen! Suspended mid-air on a bed of arrows, he fell from his chariot. The Pitamah had fallen.

Time stopped still. The battlefield froze. Loud cries of lamentation and disbelief echoed in the air. Warriors from both sides ceased fighting, laying their weapons down in respect as per the truce protocol. The gods and the holy spirits appeared in the heavens and showered flower petals at Bhishma's feet. The sounds of conches, bells and drums filled the sky. The clouds poured a cool drizzle, and the atmosphere was filled with sandalwood fragrance.

Bhishma lay fallen but not defeated. His body was covered in blood, but his face glittered with serenity and peace. He still had full command over his senses. Bhishma looked majestic lying on the bed of arrows. This was a true hero's bed. The Pandavas and Kauravas surrounded him with joined palms. Arjuna sat like a statue, holding the grandsire's feet in his hands. His tears had dried up, but his sorrow was beyond comprehension.

'Water', said Bhishma. 'I need water'.

The kings immediately brought many pitchers of water, but Bhishma declined them and said, 'He who has given me this bed of arrows shall give me the holy water too'. Arjuna understood his Pitamah's request and picked up his Gandiva. He placed upon it the Parjanya-astra (Parjanya is the deity of rain) and pierced the earth with it. Instantly a fountain of water sprung up and quenched Bhishma's thirst.

'Son, I also need to rest my head'.

Arjuna picked up his Gandiva again, chanted a sacred mantra before he released the arrow, and manifested a headrest of arrows befitting the hero's bed of arrows.

The sun was now beginning to go feeble. It had seen more than it wanted to. The armies had gone back to their camps, but the kings and the family members still stood around Bhishma, in disbelief and grief. For a long time, Pitamah kept his eyes closed, as if in deep samadhi (equanimous meditation). Then he finally opened his eyes and spoke:

> Listen, my Kaurava and Pandava sons and grandsons. Ten days of this brutal war have gone by. Death has consumed millions like a forest fire consumes clueless trees. Behold this sight of countless corpses, a feast to the vultures and hyenas. Hear the unbearable screams of the widows and the orphaned babies. To what avail, I ask? To own a piece of land and a title? For power at the cost of progeny? Is it worth the price?
>
> There is still time. Stop the war.
>
> Keep aside the ego and the revenge and know at the end of it all, only death shall be victorious.
>
> Remember — a war has no victors, only losers on both sides.
>
> The choice is yours.

Bhishma closed his eyes again.

* * *

Pitamah Bhishma lay on the bed of arrows for fifty full days. He finally chose to leave his body on the first day of Uttarayan, the auspicious time when the sun moves to the northern run. He left his body only after fulfilling his pledge of seeing his land, Hastinapur, in safe hands.

While on his death bed, on Krishna's request, he narrated the secrets of ruling a kingdom and the qualities of an ideal king to Yudhisthira. Bhishma also narrated the Vishnu Sahasranaama, a famous Sanskrit hymn with a collection of 1,000 names of Krishna, which is popularly chanted across India even till this day.

With Lord Krishna's blessing, Bhishma attained moksha (liberation).

KEY TAKEAWAYS

1. Put Aside Your Ego and Ask for Help

When the goal is clear and the commitment is strong, leave no opportunity to create a win for yourself. Arjuna has to win at any cost. It's do or die for him. Too much is at stake. Nine days of the war have gone by, and countless causalities have been suffered. Too much time, effort and money has been invested in this project already. The debts are high, and the board of directors is asking for results. There is no turning back now. The stakeholders need to see progress else they might cancel the next level of funding. The team needs to see hope. Arjuna needs to win not just for himself, but for his team, for the trust his team members have put in his leadership.

And so, he goes and asks Bhishma to show the way for his defeat. *This is revolutionary*. We think a hundred times before we ask even our friends for help because our ego comes in the way. Arjuna on the other hand does not hesitate in asking his 'enemy' for help. Such is his commitment towards his goal that he sacrifices his ego and is ready to face public shame if it solves his problem. Would you call a rival company and ask how they are meeting their sales targets even when the economy is crashing? Would you ask a colleague who you see as competition to help you with your presentation? When you yourself are one of the best in the class, would you ask the class topper how to solve that difficult problem?

What is more important for you — your image or your goal?

And what if you were in Bhishma's shoes? Would you do the same if your enemy or competitor asked you for help? The answer is not simple but worth thinking about.

Manthan

Pause. Introspect. Express.

Think of a situation in which you should have and could have kept your ego aside and asked for help. How did it unfold for you? What can you learn from that incident?

2. Go to Battle Anyway. Don't Give Up Before You Begin.

At the outset of the war, the Pandavas know that Bhishma has the shield of *Icchaa Mrityu* and it's pointless to fight him. They also know their army is smaller compared to the Kauravas'. Yet they go into the war. Because they have faith that if their path is that of truth, then some unknown doors will open up and solutions will emerge. Destiny favours the brave. If you don't even go into the marketplace, knowing that the competition is stronger, you will never know if you could have toppled the enemy. So what if the class topper is appearing for the same interview, so what if the global industry leader is bidding for the same tender, so what if you face the tournament's strongest team in the knockout round itself — *go into the battle and give your best. Wait for your moment. The Shikhandi can appear anytime.*

3. Get a Guru

The game changer here for Arjuna is his coach and guru — Lord Krishna. The most important lesson from this story and from life itself is – find your coach/your guru/your guide. Your guru will know secrets you don't. You mentor has access to information you don't even know exists, and information is power. Only Krishna knows the secret of Shikhandi in connection with Bhishma. And he advises Pandavas to use it just at the right time. With the right guide, even Bhishma can be defeated; the most difficult exam can be cracked, the most complex relationship issue can be solved, the seemingly impossible negotiation can be won.

We all experience ups and downs and highs and lows in life. But with a guru/coach, it is easy to navigate through these highs and lows, because the guru is greater than the highs and lows.

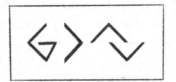

The Guru Is Greater Than Highs and Lows

Manthan

Pause. Introspect. Express.

Do you have a Krishna in your life — personally and professionally?

If yes, hold on to that person very closely. If not, pray to the universe to send you one. And if you do have a guru, listen to what your guru says.

4. Pass the Baton Willingly

Life is about timing. It's time for Bhishma to retire but he is holding on to the 'death by will' boon and sticking to his pledge which protects the cruel Kauravas. Ultimately his grandson has to kill him for new times to start.

The founder of the family-run business (or say a political party) has the **Icchha-Retirement** boon. The new generation can see that the business is doomed, the current sets of staff members are unprofessional and unethical and yet the old founder insists on protecting the old people and old practices. The grandson is capable of running the business, but the grandfather is blinded by commitments made in the past that have now become a burden. In his heart, the grandfather actually wants to let go and retire but is somehow not able to make the move, till the grandson forces it. And that is why Bhishma gives away the secret to his own death, for he knows internally that in his defeat lies his freedom. This is **Business Kshetra** and the **Corporate Mahabharat**. It happens every day in the joint family-run businesses or big corporations. We see the same trends in politics, sports and businesses where the captain/founder/grandfather does not retire willingly at the right time.

Learn to let go gracefully

* *Read the **TEDex** learning from the Adi Shankaracharya story*

5. The Dilemma of Dharma

For the cause of dharma, Arjun has to kill his own family members. It's a very difficult choice — to pick doing what is right over what is convenient. This is the ultimate dilemma. For the larger good of the organization/business/team, you sometimes have to let go/fire your own relatives/friends/co-workers who are not performing or are becoming obstacles on the path of progress. *This is not personal — it's the call of duty.* Arjuna does not carry the guilt of killing Bhishma. In fact, not killing Bhishma would have been sinful.

Pray for the courage to pick:

- **the right over the convenient**
- **dharma over adharma**

every single time.

6. Don't Make Impulsive Promises

Be very careful of the promises you make in the early stages of your life, business, relationship or career.

Bhishma in his youth was very impulsive and almost arrogant because of his limitless powers and took many vows of sacrifice (celibacy, unquestionable allegiance to the king etc.). He took a lot of pride in these pledges. But this pride was misplaced. These very vows became his chains and forced him to take the side of the Kauravas, of adharma. And even when he should have broken his vows, he unfortunately did not.

Don't make rash investments and promises in your youth when the business or career or a new relationship is growing. *These commitments become burdens later.* Remember, your past will haunt you. The contracts you sign, the people you hire, work for or make business partners, the liabilities or expenses you keep adding, the abuse you do to your body or resources — all of it comes with a price tag later. *Think long term. Times can change.* And if you feel an earlier vow is now causing your destruction, have the courage to change it. Remember, wise men say, only fools rush in.

Don't make impulsive promises

Manthan

Pause. Introspect. Express.

Think of one commitment/promise you made many months/years ago that has now become an obstacle on the path of your dharma. Do you need to edit/improvise it?

7. Find Your Shikhandi

When you need a knife, a thousand spoons will not help.

The unique character of this story is Shikhandi.

Till the ninth day, the war is neutral, maybe slightly in favour of the Kauravas. Suddenly, on the tenth day, after Bhishma's fall, the odds are heavily in favour of the Pandavas. Everything changes. And the person responsible for this sudden shift is Shikhandi. And yet no one knows or cares much about Shikhandi before the tenth day, or even after the tenth day. He is the showstopper just for one day.

First of all, a leader needs to know each team member in depth. You must have the minutest piece of information about not just their current life (role) but their past life (previous work experience, track record) also. You need to know which team member should be used at what point. What Shikhandi can do, no one else can. When you need a knife, a thousand spoons will not help. When you need a Shikhandi, a thousand kings and warriors will not help.

And Shikhandi just needs to stand with you, not even really fight. Arjuna does the fighting bit. Shikhandi is that team member who carries a unique advantage that can't be logically traced to any effort. It's not a core competency. In this case, the advantage is gender. In other cases, the advantage could be a particular name/surname, knowing a particular language, being a member of a particular community or even some physical attribute. The advantage is random and difficult to explain. But the advantage is irrefutable and must be leveraged at the right time.

But you need a Krishna to make this move. Shikhandi in the hands of Duryodhana is a waste.

When you need a knife, a thousand spoons will not help.
Find Your Shikhandi

Manthan

Pause. Introspect. Express.

- If you are leading a team — do you know your team members in depth? Are you by chance overlooking a particular skill/advantage a team member can provide?

- If you are being led — does your leader know your competency and background story in detail? Can you make a skillful attempt to let your leader know more about you?

* * *

Saraansh

A summary of learnings from this chapter

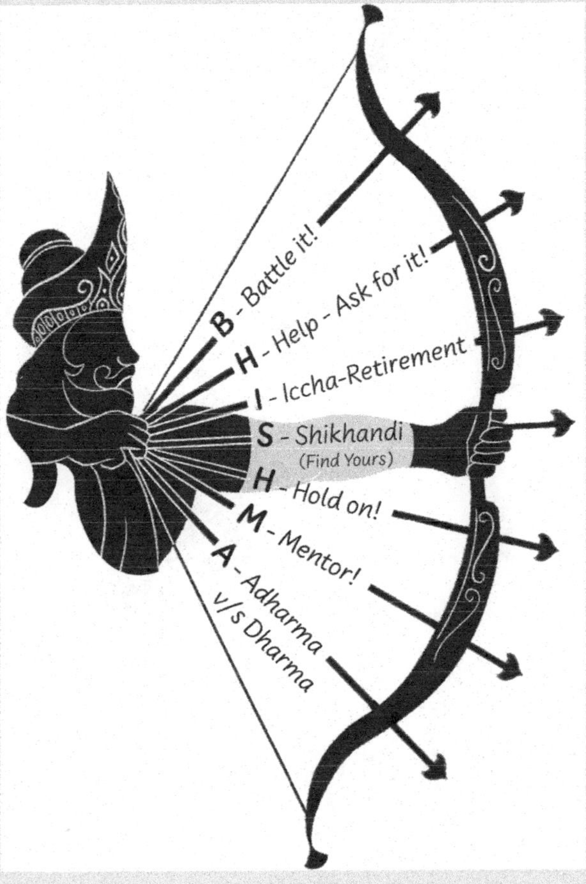

2

Jai Bhavani

'How do we get the Mountain Mouse out of hiding?'

'The time has come now for Swarajya (self-governance). Tomorrow, we shall conquer the Torna fort'.

The room fell silent. They looked at each other and then at the sixteen-year-old boy in front of them. His head was tilted up towards the sky, reflecting the heights of the Sahyadri mountains in his eyes. The sun lit up his face with the glow of a thousand stars. His aura expanded to cover the whole space of the room and beyond. They knew life will never be the same again. In that one moment, the boy stepped into manhood.

This was the birth of a leader the world shall remember for eternity. This was the birth of a legend. This was the birth of Chhatrapati Shivaji Maharaj!

The next day, sixteen-year-old Shivaji led a small group of soldiers and surprise attacked the Torna Fort from their least guarded wall, the one along the mountain slopes, a tactic they would use frequently in the years to come. The fort was captured. The Bhagwa (the trademark orange Maratha flag) flew victoriously over the blue skies marking the beginning of a new era. Chhatrapati Shivaji Maharaj was not just a warrior king. Chhatrapati Shivaji Maharaj was an era.

Seated at his mother Jeejabai's feet in the sprawling veranda of their ancestral house back in Pune, Shiv'ba (as he was affectionately called) was narrating with enthusiasm the details of the Torna victory.

'What is it that you have on your mind Shiv'ba?', Jeejabai asked, sensing the unsaid from her beloved son's story. Without batting an eyelid, Shivaji instantly replied, '*Swarajya*'!

'Maa Saheb, this land is ours. Why should a firangi (foreigner) rule my land? Does Maa Bharati not have a worthy son to rule her people and bring back her glory? Every time I look at Maa Bhavani in the temple, I feel she is asking me to fulfil my dharma! You have always shared with us the stories of Mahabharata and Ramayana. Lord Krishna says in the Bhagvad Gita:

यदा यदा हि धर्मस्य ग्लानिर्भवति भारत
अभ्युत्थानमधर्मस्य तदात्मानं सृजाम्यहम्

(Whenever adharma rises on the planet, I shall come again and again to re-establish dharma)

'Aurangzeb is the epitome of adharma. I am not Lord Krishna but if I don't stand up in this fight for dharma, I shall never be able to forgive myself. Swarajya is the purpose of my life, the love of my heart, the reason of my birth'.

'I pledge to you, Maa Saheb, to Maa Bhavani and to Maa Bharati, that I shall give my country the Swarajya it deserves! Till Shivaji lives, the sons of this soil shall rule Bharat. The Bhagwa shall fly over the Sultanate of Delhi, I pledge'!

Jeejabai had tears in her eyes. She hugged her son tight and blessed him.

And so began the rise of the great Maratha empire, which would one day go much beyond the borders of Maharashtra and cover most of India! In just a short span of eight years after the Torna victory, Shivaji Raje captured forty forts and became a formidable power, challenging the Mughals and the Adil Shah empire of Bijapur. He consolidated the Marathas and got them together under one umbrella. He revised the tax collection system and secured his borders. His subjects were happy and worshipped him like God. He became famous for his justice and patriotism. His growing power was the biggest threat for the Bijapur Sultanate ruled by Adil Shah.

Shivaji Raje had to be stopped. And there was only one man who could do this. The bravest and the fiercest general of the Adil Shah army. The man who could fight lions with his bare hands, who had led countless expeditions bringing glory to his emperor. The one man whose name evoked more fear than his giant battle-scarred body.

Subedar Afzal Khan

Badi Begum, Adil Shah's mother, the de facto queen and ruler of the Adil Shahi Bijapur empire, summoned Khan into her personal chambers in the dead of the night. In a soft yet powerful voice, she said,

'Capture or kill him. At any cost'. With a cold stare, she handed him his marching orders.

'InshaAllah' (Allah willing), Khan whispered back, a wicked smile running across his face. This was the opportunity he was waiting for. This would be his journey to eternal fame. He was confident of his victory.

The mighty Afzal bowed in front of the queen and left. He was to set out immediately but secretly. No one was supposed to know about his movements yet. On the other side, someone had sniffed out his plans even before they began taking shape.

* * *

'It's us against the mountains tonight', said Prabhat to his friend, Vayu. Vayu nodded and looked in the direction of the Sahyadris. In times like these, Prabhat could only depend on Vayu's speed and strength, for Vayu was known in the whole Maratha Empire as the Ashvaraaj — the king of horses! As Prabhat swung on to the saddle, he touched his side jacket lightly to ensure the scroll was intact. The scroll had to reach Shivaji Maharaj before the break of dawn. Those were his orders.

'*Jai Bhavani*', roared Prabhat and gave a tilted kick-start breaking Vayu into a gallop. And so they tore through the forests and the streams and just as the first rays of Surya Devta (the Sun God) bathed the Pratapgadh fort golden, they entered the fort city where Shivaji Raje was currently camping. Prabhat was one of the most trusted members of the spy wing of the Maratha Empire, the backbone of Shivaji Raje's war and administrative strategies. There were thousands of spies spread across the empire and many were placed in the enemy kingdoms too. The accuracy and speed with which these brave spies collected secret information and brought it to their leaders was mind-boggling. There were constant attempts by the enemy to identify and buy them out or capture them and make them talk, but like all soldiers in Raje's army, the spies pledged unwavering allegiance till death to their God-like king, Shivaji Maharaj.

Although the guards at the fort recognized Prabhat, the protocol demanded they validate his identity with the customary passcode verification.

'Identify yourself', said the guard in a stern voice.

'Kaalratri', said Prabhat softly. (Kaalratri was one of the names of Maa Bhavani, the fierce goddess worshipped by the Marathas. The passcodes kept changing frequently and the spies were duly informed about the same). The spears gave way and Prabhat was soon taken to the royal meeting room of Shivaji Maharaj where his presence was eagerly awaited.

Maharaj opened the scroll, his heart beating faster every moment. The contents of the scroll could have a life-changing impact on him and his troops, and possibly the whole Maratha Empire. In beautiful Devanagari (ancient Indian script), the shiny black ink carried a very inspiring poem.

A mixture of a frown and a smile spread through Raje's countenance.

The men in the room could not hold their curiosity anymore and came close to have a look at the scroll. They were puzzled and righty so. The most puzzled, in fact shocked, was Prabhat! He rode the entire night without resting for a moment to deliver an urgent and critical message to Maharaj — and all the scroll contained was a poem!

'What do you all see?' asked Maharaj, spreading the scroll on to the table. 'Just a poem? Read it again'. And so the men read it again! And they read it one more time. And yet, they couldn't see what Shivaji Raje saw!

'Now instead of reading the lines horizontally word by word, read the poem vertically down with just the first two letters of the first word of each line'. Their eyes broadened in amazement at the utter brilliance of the poem! It now read

'*The Subedar of Bijapur is on his way. Be ready.*'

The Subedar of Bijapur was none other than the mighty Afzal Khan. As the sound of his name echoed in Raje's ears, it brought forth strong memories of his father and brother. It was Khan who had played a key role in the killing of Raje's brother and the imprisonment of Raje's father. A wave of hatred and rage stirred through Raje's veins.

That Afzal Khan was on his way to capture Shivaji Maharaj meant only one thing — this was war!

Raje curbed the storm of emotions in his mind and said in a calculated voice,

'Find out more details about Afzal Khan's army, weapons, his speed of travel and route. And put all the killas (forts) on high alert. Activate the spies. I want every piece of information possible. Get Naik on the job. I want him to handle this personally'.

Bahirji Naik was a dark-skinned, tall, slim man who had been personally trained by Shivaji Raje in the art of deception and information gathering. Naik was the head of the intelligence network. He could speak Marathi, Hindi and Urdu fluently and knew the terrain like the back of his palm. It was said that even when the wind lost its way in the forest, it would seek directions from Naik! A few weeks later, he stood in front of Maharaj and the inner circle of trustworthy ministers.

'Maharaj, Afzal Khan moves with a large and strong force. We estimate around 10,000 infantry soldiers and around 5,000 cavalry warriors', said Naik.

'What about cannons?' asked Maharaj.

'A ballpark of fifty long- and short-range cannons. Add to it fifty odd elephants.'

'Hmnn . . . he moves heavy and hence he moves slow. Where do we stand?' asked Maharaj, looking at Netaji Palkar, the commander-in-chief of Raje's army.

'We have at best 4,000 men, about 1,000 cavalry and twenty cannons', said Netaji Palkar.

'Maharaj, there is no way we can win against them in the open battlefield', remarked Moropant, a close confidant of Shivaji Maharaj.

'We will not go to them on the open plains of Wai. We will make them come to us in the hills and jungles of Pratapgadh. We will do this our way', said Maharaj.

* * *

Back in the Afzal Khan camp, there was growing impatience to draw Shivaji Raje on the open battlefield.

'Huzoor, there is one way to get the mountain mouse out of hiding', said Sayyed Banda, Afzal Khan's personal bodyguard and a battle-hardened warrior.

'Mountain Mouse' was a name given to Shivaji Maharaj by Aurangzeb because of Maharaj's famous Ganimi Kava (guerrilla warfare tactics of hide and fight in the mountainous terrain). What the Mughals thought was a shameful mocking name to insult Shivaji, he took as a war title with pride. Mooshak or the mouse is the vaahan (vehicle) of Ganesha, the elephant god dear to the Marathas and worshipped with zest and pomp. Ganesha is the lord who removes obstacles from the path, and currently the biggest obstacle in the path of Swarajya was the Mughal Empire in general and Afzal Khan in particular.

'What is it?' asked Afzal Khan, desperate now to fulfil his mission of capturing Shivaji.

'We must hit where it hurts him the most. The Marathas are ardent devotees of Goddess Bhavani and

Lord Vitthala. We must destroy their temples. This will enrage them into coming out and fighting!'

Afzal Khan liked the idea and so began the mindless, cruel devastation of all the temples that came along the way of Afzal Khan's army, including the Tulja Bhavani temple and the Vithoba temple at Pandharpur, which were major pilgrimage sites for the Marathas. Innocents were killed, women were raped and temple treasures were plundered. But this backfired on Afzal Khan. Instead of Shivaji Raje coming out for open battle, what this did was unite the smaller Hindu forces that were scattered till now, on the side of Shivaji Maharaj and against Afzal Khan. Afzal Khan now reached Wai hoping Shivaji would finally fight him. Shivaji Maharaj of course had no such plans. But he did have other plans. He always had a plan. And not just one, generally two or three back up plans as well!

'Sayyed, call upon Krishnaji Bhaskar', said Afzal Khan one day.

Krishna Bhaskar was Khan's loyal advocate and minister and also a well-respected Brahmin in the Hindu community.

'Salaam Huzoor', said Krishna Ji as he stood before Afzal Khan.

'Krishna Ji, I want you to go to Shivaji and invite him to meet me. The little monster is scared to fight us in open battle so I will deliver him to Allah in a personal meeting.'

Shivaji Raje met Krishnaji Bhaskar deliberately inside a Devi mandir. (temple). Krishna Ji was welcomed by putting a chandan tilak (sandalwood mark) on his forehead and after he bowed down to Maa Durga's idol, he was offered the holy panchamrat (a mixture of five ingredients – milk, honey, ghee, curd and sugar offered as prasad (devotional offering) in temples). For a moment, Krishna Ji forgot that he worked for the Mughals. That is exactly the emotion that Shivaji Maharaj wanted to plant.

'My dear friend, please tell me what I can do for you', said Raje, addressing the enemy's envoy as a friend.

'Oh revered king, I come to you with a message from my lord, the mighty Afzal Khan. My lord would like to meet you in person and negotiate a deal that can create a win-win situation for both sides', said Krishna Ji.

'You have stolen the words from my tongue', said Raje. 'Even I would like to meet the great Afzal Khan and sign a truce, for I don't want to cause mindless bloodshed. Anyway, my army cannot match his and I know that'. Krishna Ji smiled.

'But I have a two conditions', continued Raje. 'First — we shall meet weapon-free. Just Afzal Khan and I'. Krishna Ji was listening carefully. 'I will come with ten of my men. Afzal Khan can come with ten men too. One bodyguard shall stand outside the meeting tent while nine others wait at an arrow's shot length from the tent.'

Raje continued, 'Second, we shall meet at the foothills of Pratapgadh fort. I have not been keeping too well and so would like to request Khan Saheb to do me a favour and cut down my travel pains'.

Krishna Ji Bhaskar thought for a while and then said, 'On behalf of Afzal Khan, I give my consent to this proposal oh great king. With your permission, the meeting can be arranged on the fifth tithi (lunar calendar day) of the ascending moon next month' and rose to leave.

'Krishna Ji, this is a Hindu speaking to another Hindu brother. We are inside the Devi's abode right now. Tell me — what is Khan's plan?' Krishna Ji was shocked to hear this question straight to his face. His Hindu roots would not allow him to lie inside the temple and Raje knew that. 'I don't know my lord's exact plans oh king, but Mughals are known to value victory over code of honour. That's all I can say', and he left without giving another chance for a dialogue.

'I want an urgent meeting with the inner circle. In my chambers, right now', announced Raje.

* * *

The chants kept getting louder as the holy smoke filled up the whole ambience. There she stood in all her glory — Devi Maa Bhavani herself. Dressed in bright red garments, with the sun as her crown and the stars as the beads of her celestial necklace, the depth of the oceans in her compassionate eyes, holding the trident, the lotus, the conch and the rotating discus in her multiple arms, an epitome of limitless power and motherly love. Tears of gratitude ran down Shivaji Raje's face, as he sat at her feet, hands clasped in prayer to his source of eternal devotion.

'Oh Divine Mother, my life is fulfilled at your darshan (sight). Please bless me and be by my side forever', said Raje.

'Shiva, my child. **I reside in your sword**. Use it for the protection of dharma. Move forward without fear. Victory shall be yours!'

Shivaji Maharaj sat up with a jolt and slowly opened his eyes. He took some time to adjust to the darkness of his bedroom. He could still feel the divine presence in the room. The lingering fragrance could still be sensed. His heart was beating fast as he tried to replay what he had just seen. His mind did not want to believe it was a dream. He smiled and glanced on his right, where a beautiful idol of the Devi was illuminated mildly by a small oil diya (lamp). The first rays of the sun were breaking in. A new dawn was ready to welcome the world again. Today would be a significant day.

As he shared the vision he had seen in the wee hours of the morning with his dear ones, a wave of renewed confidence and commitment to move forward for the sake of Swarajya spread through the entire Maratha army. This new divine boost was much needed to raise the spirits of the soldiers to fight the army of Afzal Khan, which was more than three times the size of the Maratha army.

Shivaji Maharaj finished his prayers and had a light meal of gudbhaakri (jaggery and traditional Maharashtrian bread) and got ready for the meeting with Afzal. He gave detailed instructions to his commanders and went over the expected sequence of events and the contingency plans again.

Shivaji Maharaj's mind was already in the shamiana (canopy) where the meeting would happen. It was as if he could already visualize the upcoming event in great detail. He knew Afzal Khan could not be trusted and he wanted to be prepared for all possibilities. And so, he decided to wear a steel armour under his shirt and a metal helmet under his turban. The protocol was to meet weaponless but there was no guarantee that Afzal would respect the arrangement. And so, Raje used a weapon specifically made for occasions like this, his trademark waagh-naak (tiger claws). This weapon was designed to consist of beautiful diamond rings on the top but sharp curved nails on the inside, much like tiger's claws. On curling the fist, one could only see the delicate rings on the top while the claws remained hidden. Raje also carried a concealed bichwa (dagger) under his left sleeve.

The master of deception that he was, no one could get the slightest hint that Shivaji Maharaj was armoured and loaded. As was his ritual, he spent a few moments praying to Maa Bhavani and reminded himself of her promise. He touched Jeejabai's feet and marched out of his palace.

* * *

Shivaji Maharaj was late and that was deliberate. Afzal Khan reached first and chose to wait inside the royal shamiana constructed for this special meeting. Raje's delay irked him and got him restless — exactly what Raje wanted. The Maratha advance party reconnoitered the venue and ensured there was no one inside the shamiana except Afzal Khan.

Shivaji Maharaj walked into the shamiana like an emperor. Sayyed Banda and Jiva Mala, the bodyguards of Afzal Khan and Raje respectively, waited right at the canopy's entrance. Afzal Khan stood up, exposing his mountain-like body. Shivaji Maharaj was at least 1.5 feet shorter than Khan and much leaner in physique.

'Greetings, Shiva. Welcome', said Khan in his naturally loud voice.

'Greetings, Khan Saheb', responded Raje. Both men were still standing.

'We meet as friends today, not enemies in war. Come, let me embrace you to mark a benign beginning of our new friendship', said Khan smiling and opening his arms, inviting Shivaji Maharaj.

Maharaj moved forward cautiously yet confidently. His expert peripheral vision assured him of no sudden movements from any side. He kept his eyes locked with Khan's and had a customary smile on his face. They embraced, Shivaji Maharaj reaching up only till Khan's shoulders. Maharaj was well aware that the Mughal custom was to hug thrice changing sides each time. Just when the second hug was about to finish, his intuition bells rang loudly inside his head.

And then it happened.

Before the third hug could conclude, in one swift move, Afzal Khan twirled his left arm around Raje's neck and held him tight in a captive body lock. Using his right hand, he took out his hidden dagger and stabbed it with all his force on Raje's back. To his utter shock, the blade refused to pierce through Raje's body because of the steel armour under his shirt.

With lightning speed, in a counter-attack, Shivaji Maharaj opened his left fist and struck hard with the tiger claws into Afzal Khan's torso. Afzal shrieked as the metal pierced his skin, turning Maharaj's left palm blood red. This loosened Afzal's lock on Maharaj's neck. Shivaji Maharaj thrust himself away to make room. In a split second, before Afzal Khan could comprehend what was going on, Shivaji Maharaj used his right hand to pull the hidden dagger from under his left sleeve and struck its blade up straight into Khan's stomach. Khan howled in agony as blood fountained out from his ruptured abdomen. Maharaj pulled out his dagger and rammed it brutally once again, twisting the blade as it cut through Afzal's skin, tissue, muscle and intestines. Clutching his stomach, Afzal Khan collapsed heavily on the ground.

The screams from the shamiana tipped off Sayyed Banda and Jiva Mala instantly. Shivaji Maharaj turned just in time to see the sword of Sayyed raised over his head. Sayyed had a clear shot at Maharaj. But just as

Sayyed brought his sword down on Maharaj's head, Jiva Mala managed to push him, unbalancing Sayyed and taking away the force of his blow. The sword hit Shivaji Maharaj on the head but once again, Maharaj was not hurt since he was wearing a metal helmet concealed under his traditional cloth turban. Fate did not give another chance to Sayyed as Jiva Mala struck him down in one clean move of his sword, taking the last breath out of his body. Shivaji Maharaj acknowledged Jiva with a quick nod of appreciation.

Afzal Khan, in the meantime, managed to get up on his feet, almost holding his hanging intestines and ran towards his palanquin. The kahaars (men who carry the palanquin) quickly stretched him out on the plank and started to run away from the shamiana. But Sambhaji Kavji dashed off behind them and quickly caught up with the running kaahars. Without giving Afzal Khan any time to react, Kavji lifted his sword and beheaded Afzal Khan, and blood spurted all over his face. He then lifted the severed head and carried it away like Maa Durga carried the severed head of the demon Mahishasur after killing him. Thunderous cries of *'Jai Bhavani, Jai Shivaji'* echoed in the atmosphere.

The mighty Afzal Khan had been killed! This was unprecedented.

But there was not time to celebrate yet. The chief was slain but the battle still had to be won.

'Quick, at the cannons. Shoot the double sound signal', ordered Shivaji Maharaj to his men.

The Maratha troops hiding in the Javali forests around Pratapgadh were ready and waiting. As soon as they heard their pre-decided double cannon signal, they unleashed their men from different sides on the unsuspecting and unprepared Afzal Khan army.

Moropant led the Maratha infantry towards the left flanks of the Adilshahi troops. The suddenness of this attack at such close quarters made them lose their ground and the artillery tanks failed to provide the desired cover for the Mughal soldiers. With the troops completely exposed, the Maratha cavalry slaughtered them mercilessly in an all-out attack. The Adilshahi cavalry retreated and this was exactly what Netaji Palkar was waiting for. He pursued the retreating forces and massacred them before they could join the larger Mughal reserves waiting at Wai.

Horror spread in the Adilshahi camps at Wai on hearing the news of the fall of their commander and the raging Maratha army charging towards them. The Mughal army retreated towards Bijapur but were chased and killed by the unstoppable Maratha troops. Raje's men captured more than twenty forts within the next few days.

The victory was historic and it's in times of victory that the character of a king is tested. The wounded Mughal soldiers were given medical treatment as per their rank. The women and children, as a policy, were treated with respect and sent back to their homes while the men were taken in as prisoners of war. Afzal Khan himself was buried as per Islamic customs, and chivalrously

Shivaji Maharaj had a tomb constructed at the foothills of Pratapgadh for his fallen opponent.

Shivaji Maharaj was clear with his fundamental ideology — *once the enemy is dead, so is the enmity.*

Swords of honour and war medals were presented to the soldiers who had shown exemplary courage in the war. Families of the martyrs were granted lifelong pensions and disabled survivors were given suitable jobs in the kingdom.

* * *

The echoes of Shivaji Maharaj's unparalleled victory over Afzal Khan were heard till Delhi. Aurangzeb woke up to recognize the size and audacity of this new threat from the Deccan.

In the years to come, Shivaji Raje became Chhatrapati Shivaji Maharaj and ushered in a new era of Bharat's history. He won countless battles and innumerable hearts and laid the foundation of hindiva swarajya (independent governance based on the principles of Hindutva). At its peak, the Maratha Empire stretched from Bengal in the east to Afghanistan in the west, and from Kashmir in the north to Kaveri basin in the south, an area of approximately 250 million acres.

Aware that he would need a strong navy to control the west coastline of India, which was then dominated by global naval powers like the Portuguese, Chhatrapati

Shivaji Maharaj invested in building a modern naval force and thus came to be called the 'Father of Indian Navy'.

A journey that started with a lone dreamy-eyed, lion-hearted sixteen-year-old boy, with three odd forts and 1,000 odd men, transformed into a legendary empire with an army of over 1,00,000 men and more than 300 forts. The seed of Swarajya that was sown by Chhatrapati Shivaji Maharaj in the sixteenth century blossomed into a flourishing grand tree. The Marathas remained a formidable power till the eighteenth century.

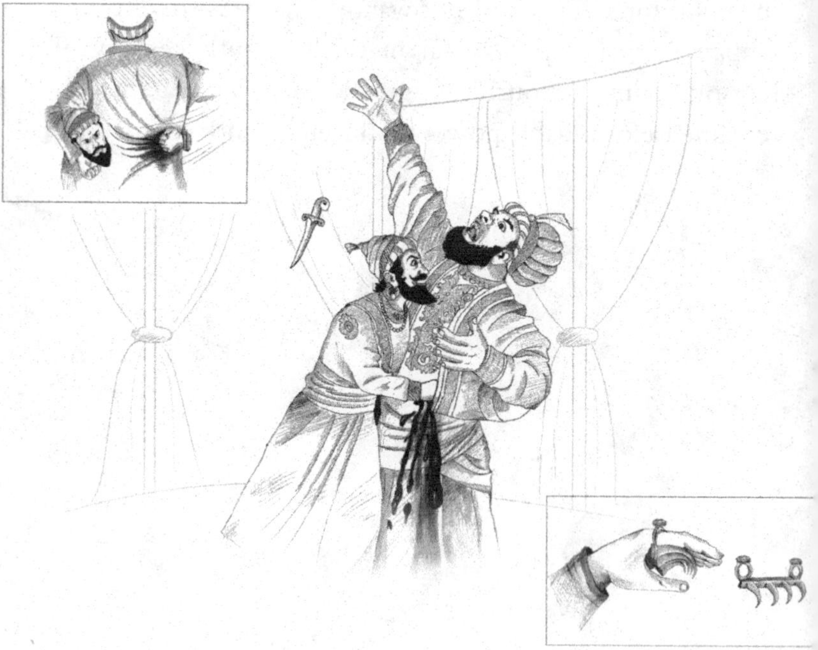

KEY TAKEAWAYS

1. Start Small but Start Today

Shivaji Maharaj started at sixteen. He had very little resources, no formal training on running a kingdom, no great backups or powerful connections, not even a steady army. He was basically a start-up. Maybe a start-up with some seed capital or basic funding, but nothing more. He also could be seen as an ' intrapreneur' (someone who works in a big institution but operates like an entrepreneur).

The most important lesson is right here — Start Small but Start Today! Shivaji Maharaj does not wait for the ideal market conditions or a godfather. He launches. He takes the first step. Most people don't. And therein dies the Shivaji inside them.

Repeat in your mind:

Start Small but Start Today

It could be a small project (professional or personal) that you want to take up, it could be a habit pattern you want to change, it could be some social service/seva that you want to do, it could be starting your yoga practice, it could be starting your blog, it could be anything. Don't wait for the perfect day. Start today.

Write Down Below Two Things That You Will Start Today

1. ______________________________

2. ______________________________

* * *

2. What's Your Dream?

And although Shivaji Raje does not have much support, he has what every great entrepreneur/leader has. He has a dream, an idea, a passion. He has a very strong sense of purpose. And that is 'Swarajya'. The young dreamy-eyed entrepreneurs or aspiring leaders or emerging sports stars believe in their ideas with every cell in their bodies. They do not want to be rich or famous or powerful — those are by-products. All they want is that their dream comes true. And they want their dream to benefit the masses — to solve a problem — to make a difference and to bring peace and comfort to mankind! It's not a selfish pursuit. And they are willing to go to any lengths for that Hence their unique and unconventional style of war and leadership and their huge appetite for calculated risks. ***Blind risk is called gamble. Calculated risk is called strategy***. There is definitely madness but there is a method to this madness. But the most important lesson is: Shivaji Raje dares to dream.

Dare To Dream

Manthan

Pause. Introspect. Express.

Write your dream. Visualize it. Describe it. What is your dream for yourself/your organization?

3. Transfer Your Dream

And the great leaders, whether in business, politics or the social sector has the unique ability to transfer their dream onto a million eyes and make their mission the peoples' mission! That's what Shivaji Maharaj did with natural ease. His dream of 'Swarajya' became theirs. He invoked god-like worship amongst his subjects and deep fear amongst his enemies.

So, the second learning is to

Transfer Your Dream

4. Teamdom

But know that no dream comes true unless you create a winning team to achieve that dream. So, the third step is to

Remember

Create a winning team

because

A dream works when a team works

Manthan

Pause. Introspect. Express.

Do you have a team? Can you start building one? If you have a team, can you grow it? What should you do so your team is as motivated as you?

* * *

5. The Start-Up Called Shivaji Raje

This start-up called 'Shivaji Raje' is challenging the industry leaders, the multi-nationals, the Adil Shahs and the Aurangzebs, by a clear disruptive innovation strategy. That strategy is called *'Ganimi Kava'* or 'Guerilla Warfare'. And this innovation is born because of a burning demand in the market for a product, which is basically an oppression-free, unified Hindu nation, not governed by invaders. This product is fuelled by an ideology called 'Swarajya', and Shivaji Raje is currently the only person claiming to offer this product! People want this product and while the big giants are sleeping, Shivaji Raje is giving it for free in return of long-term brand loyalty.

Here is another lesson from Shivaji Raje in advertising/sales:

Sell the ideology, not the product.
Talk about the '**why**' more than the '**what**'

If people connect with the ideology, they will automatically buy the product. The advertising heads of smart companies highlight their belief, the ideology, the identity, not the product directly.

Shivaji Raje's endeavours are dangerous of course, but a start-up has little to lose and lots to gain, so the odds of the risk are in their favour. With every small victory of the Marathas, the brand value and market evaluation of the start-up increases. Soon, the giants wake up and try to do the easiest thing first — offer to buy it out. The sturdy and confident start-ups don't sell early since they know their prime time is yet to come. They are not tempted. Soon the start-up gets its major venture capitalist funding and is now a publicly listed entity. Game on.

And with every fort that Shivaji Raje's men conquer, the stock value keeps increasing. It's now a threat to the biggest players in the space. The Afzal Khan attacks with all his might, backed by the grand Bijapur empire. It's the fight or flight moment. The game is dirty now.

* * *

6. Fight, but on Your Terms

Shivaji Maharaj fights, but on his own terms. The underdog has the best chances of victory when he changes the very rules of the game. He calls Khan to Pratapgadh (in the forest and the hills) instead of going to Wai.

He avoids what is strong, He attacks what is weak.

A fundamental strategy in both war and business.

Afzal Khan's huge army, cavalry and cannons are rendered useless in the mountains. His key advantage is nullified. In fact, Khan's strength now becomes his burden since he cannot move fast. Shivaji Maharaj's army had full-time and part-time warriors. He had even trained farmers to become soldiers. When there was no war, the part-timers would go back to their farms and freelance jobs. A start-up uses contractors, freelancers and interns effectively. Less staff. Shared office spaces. The start-up sells online instead of brick-and-mortar stores. No additional overhead expenses. Digital marketing over expensive newspaper and TV ads. New ideas of 'maximum profits, minimum overheads'.

Minimalistic. Powerful. Revolutionary.

Shivaji Maharaj at 5.5 feet stands in front of this mountain of a man, the giant called Afzal Khan. Khan is almost 7 feet tall. In their embrace, Shivaji Maharaj only reaches up to Khan's shoulders. Anyone who does not know what Shivaji Maharaj is made up of, would put all their money on Khan winning this combat. But Shivaji Maharaj outsmarts Khan on several accounts. First, he understands the psyche of his opponent. He knows Khan will breach the code of trust and attack him. So he wears the armour under his kurta and the helmet under his turban. If Shivaji Maharaj had given into over confidence that day and assumed that since Khan had invited him for a negotiation, he had the upper hand, it would have cost him his life. He has two hidden weapons to attack with — the tiger claws (baagh-naak) and the dagger (kataar).

Go to every important meeting like a Shivaji-Khan meeting, overprepared not under.

Never underestimate the opponent. Afzal did that and paid a price.

Shivaji Raje has deep emotional wounds on account of Khan. Khan had killed his brother and imprisoned his father. But Shivaji Raje does not let his emotions take his focus away. He keeps his mind in the present moment and operates with ***courage, not rage.***

**Business or Battle, don't get swayed away by emotions.
Act based on intuition and intelligence, not mere emotion.**

* * *

Shivaji Maharaj's 4S Blueprint

Strategy — Speed — Surprise — Skill

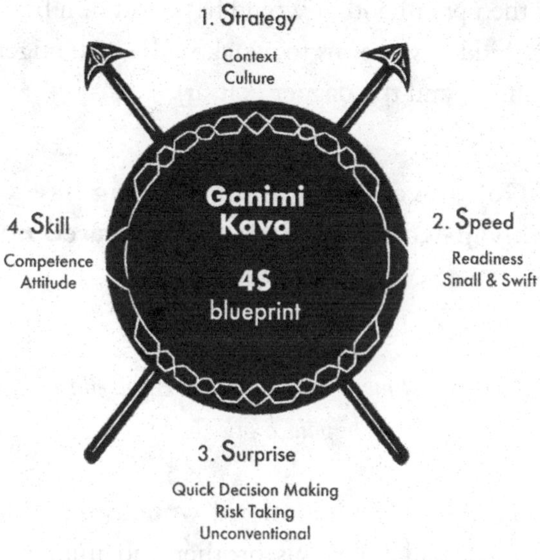

Shivaji Maharaj is an expert on **Strategy.** One of the key components of his strategy is *context*. By context we mean the set-up, we mean factors like weather, terrain, deception, access to reserves, tactics, intelligence etc. The second important aspect of his strategy is *culture*. The famous management coach Peter Drucker says, 'Culture eats strategy for breakfast'. Well Shivaji Maharaj understood this hundreds of years ago and built his strategy in tune with the culture of his organization.

The second pillar of his war blueprint is **Speed.** Because his army is small and he has trained them to be always battle-ready, he uses speed as an advantage over size. Even in personal combats like the one with Khan, he uses speed to cover up for size. Most people read the equation wrong when they assume size is the only advantage, Small allows for speed and for improvization, big doesn't. In today's world, the speed with which you adapt to changing market conditions is critical to your survival.

Because he is quick in decision making and has an unconventional thought process, he almost always has the element of **Surprise**. He catches his enemies off-guard and keeps them guessing. His surprise style works also because his men know how to keep their plans secret. If secrecy is not guaranteed, surpises might become shocks.

The last pillar in Shivaji Maharaj's blueprint is **Skill**. He trains his men for both *competency* and *attitude*. He leads by example and sets very high standards of skill. Quality control is strict and skill is rewarded.

The small business, the start-up, the struggling artist, the weaker sports team, the underdog – they have to come up with their own customized 'Ganimi Kava 4S blueprint' if they want to succeed in the war out there.

Manthan

Pause. Introspect. Express.

Do you have a 'Ganimi Kava' strategy for yourself/your team/your company? Can you create one?
Can you anticipate a probable 'Ganimi Kava' strategy from your opponent/competition?

* * *

7. Information Is the Currency of Power

It was so in the sixteenth century, and it is today. Invest in developing your intelligence network. Invest in people. Invest in research and development. One of the top reasons for Shivaji Maharaj's success was the superb spy network he had built and the accuracy of the intelligence reports he received. In an era of no tech gadgets, sitting at the top of Raigadh fort he knew exactly what the movements of the opponent army thousands of kilometers away were. Hence his attacks hit the target. Almost always.

Your information source is invaluable if it is (ironically) a:

F.R.A.U.D.

Fast. Relevant. Accurate. Unique. Dependable.

Manthan

Pause. Introspect. Express.

Do you have access to important information needed for your success? Are you keeping yourself abreast of with the latest and the greatest in your field? Have you spent time, money and effort cultivating human and machine sources that are F.R.A.U.D?

* * *

If we want to grow in life, we have to rename problems as challenges, as opportunities to grow. That's what Shivaji Raje did. He broke his own mental barriers and proved that he was bigger than the problem. His life teaches us this simple mantra —

You Are Bigger Than Your Problem!

* * *

There is a small Shivaji inside you. And there are moments when the gigantic problem called Afzal Khan is standing right in front of you, that too with hidden weapons!

Manthan

Pause. Introspect. Express.

Think of an Afzal Khan-sized problem in your life right now.
What will you do? Come up with a strategy —
How will the Shivaji Maharaj inside of you beat the Afzal Khan?
Write down your plan.

* * *

saraansh

Summary of Learnings from this chapter

1.
Start Small but Start Today

2.
Dare to Dream — Transfer Your Dream — Create A Winning Team

3.
A Dream Works When A Team Works

4.
Sell the Ideology, not the Product (the *why* more than the *what*)

5.
Fight on your terms (*avoid what is strong, attack what is weak*)

6.
Go to every meeting like a Shivaji-Khan meeting. Overprepared, not under!

7.

Courage, not rage!

8.

Business or Battle, act based on intuition and intelligence, not just emotion!

9.

Make your own Ganimi Kava strategy, your 4S war blueprint! Shivaji Raje's was — Strategy, Speed, Surprise, Skill

10.

Information is power

11.

Create information sources that are F.R.A.U.D. Fast. Relevant. Accurate. Unique. Dependable.

12.

You are bigger than your problem.

13.

Blind risk is called gamble. Calculated risk is called strategy.

3

Kabir Vaani

Kahat Kabir Suno Bhai Saadho . . .

The sunrays took the first dip in the holy Ganga. It's only Ganga that can purify even the virgin rays of the sun. The sunrays, in turn, painted the waters a shiny golden — a game they had been playing for centuries. The ghaats (river side steps) woke up lazily and pandiculated to another beautiful morning in the holy city of Kashi. Soon there would be a million people on their steps leading to the Ganga.

Neeru was rushing through the narrow pathway alongside the river, a tad late for his namaz (prayers in Islam) at the local masjid (mosque). As he was about to take the final turn to the mud road leading away from the river, he suddenly froze at what he saw. In a small basket, on the waters touching the lowest step of the ghaat, lay a beautiful baby boy, eyes closed as if enjoying the first boat ride of his life! Neeru was magnetically drawn to the baby and picked him up in his arms gently. He looked around to see who the baby belonged to. There was no one in sight. Neeru waited for a long time. He had a strong voice inside his head telling him the baby had been abandoned and he should take him home. Maa Ganga, as if she had heard Neeru's voice, nodded smilingly. Neema, Neeru's wife, was thrilled to see the little boy and instantly fell in love with him. With a lot of love, they named the child Kabir (great in Arabic).

Little Kabir grew up around the 'khatarr khatt khatarr khatt' noise of the weaving machine of his father, one of the oldest julaaha (weaver) families of the city. One day, his father told him to go to the rangrez (the cloth-dyeing person) and get the cloth he had woven dyed.

'Chacha (uncle), my father wants this cloth dyed', said Kabir, handing rangrez chacha the piece of cloth.

'Wait, my child; first, let me finish what I am doing. Have a seat', said the old man.

Kabir sat down on the broken stool, legs dangling in air. Suddenly the old man's wife walked into the room and almost screamed seeing Kabir sitting there. 'Ya Allah, why have you shown me a kafir's (infidel) face in the morning?'

'Chachi, I am Kabir, not Kafir', said Kabir innocently, assuming the old woman had got the names mixed up.

'You are a kafir, wretched boy! Born to the non-believers, that too unethically!' yelled the woman. (It was believed that Kabir was born to a Brahmin widow)

Kabir sat there stunned and shaken. Tears rolled down his cheeks. He was too young to understand who a kafir is, but he felt as if someone had drawn the air out of his lungs. His ears went numb. His whole body was shivering. And at a very young age, he was unfortunately introduced to the feeling of being hated. With a heavy heart and still crying, he ran home and, on the way, accidentally bumped into the local temple pundit (Hindu priest). When Pundit ji looked at Kabir's face, he shouted, 'Watch who you touch, you impure soul! I will have to take a cleansing bath again now! Shiva Shiva Shiva'!

Pundit ji left, cursing Kabir under his breath as he walked away. Kabir stood there frozen, even more hurt and insulted. He could no longer see or hear anything. The world was blurred.

What mistake of his was he being punished for? What do soul and kafir mean? Why does he not get the love and affection that other children get? Why is he not allowed to enter the mosque like other children? Several questions flooded his mind.

As he grew up, the fuzz of questions became stronger. When he tried to ask his parents, he was scolded and discouraged to even voice them, let alone get answers. So, he decided to ask his questions to anybody and everybody and started talking his thoughts out loud in the form of his two-line poems which were later called dohas or saankhis. Poetry and songs came naturally to him, from somewhere deep within. Kabir never went to school. He was life-schooled. He learned how to weave from his father and would try to help him make ends meet.

'Go and sell this cloth at the bazaar, Kabir', said his father Neeru one day. Hearing this, Neema came rushing in and with joined palms said, 'Kabir, my dear, please don't argue with people about your religion and caste'. Kabir winked and said, 'I don't argue at all, mother. If a Hindu asks me, I say I am the son of a Hindu Brahmin and if a Muslim asks me, I say I am the son of Neema, the musalman'. Neeru didn't find this funny. In a stern fatherly voice, he said, 'Sell the cloth at some good price. Don't give it away to some needy for free like last time and ensure you don't get in trouble'! The last part was a standard instruction for Kabir whenever he left the house.

Kabir nodded and lifted the multicoloured thaan (bundle of cloth) on his shoulders. Humming his favourite tune, he set out to the bazaar. On the way stood the old masjid with the red bricks, showing how badly they needed some repair. As Kabir was passing by, he heard the maulvi (Muslim priest) climb to the top of the mosque and sing aloud the azaan (prayers) facing the direction of Mecca (the holy shrine of the Muslims).

'Allah-Hu-Akbar (Allah is the greatest)

Ash Hadu Anna IllahaIllallah' (I bear witness that there is no other God but Allah)

Something spontaneously popped up in Kabir's head and not holding himself back, he sang:

कंकर-पत्थर जोरि के, मस्जिद लई बनाय,
ता चढ़ि मुल्ला बांग दे, का बहरा भया खुदाय?

(With some stones and pebbles, a mosque was built. The Mullah shouts the Lord's name from the top of the mosque — has the Lord gone deaf?)

All the people in the mosque were enraged and hurled curses at Kabir for this blasphemy. Kabir took each abuse as a compliment and continued walking, singing even louder with each step. He now reached the bazaar only to realize that it was an unusually crowded day. Upon inquiry, he learned that a new idol for the Devi temple was being established today with a grand ceremony. Hundreds of pundits stood in disciplined rows with plates full of flowers, chandan (sandalwood) and diyas (earthen lamps). Thousands of devotees waited patiently to get the first glimpses of the magnificent marble idol. There were separate sections for each caste. The higher castes stood up and close for the best view and the lower ones were shrugged away in the corners behind. Some castes were entirely banned from the ceremony. A group of pundits observed Kabir trying to come close to the temple walls and yelled, 'You low-caste julaaha. How dare you come close to the temple? Even your shadow is a bad omen for the Devi. Move away, you insect!' Kabir smiled and started singing:

पाथर पूजे हरि मिलै, तो मैं पूजूँ पहार
घर की चाकी कोउ न पूजै, पीस खाए संसार

(If you can meet the lord by worshipping a stone, I would rather worship the mountain. No one worships the stone flour mill (chaaki) in the house, which gives us food.)

'You foolish pundits! You worship a statue of stone, which a human has made and yet you abuse a human being that God has made?' Seeing this argument between Kabir and the pundits, a crowd gathered. Crowding up to watch an argument is an age-old pastime found in nearly all societies since time immemorial. The innate curiosity for random situations and people seems to be supremely high in the human DNA.

'The Devi you worship, the Jagdamba Jag Janani is the Universal Mother and hence my mother too. Question her caste if you want to question mine', said Kabir. And then he didn't speak again. A few angered men came from behind Kabir and one of them struck Kabir with a stone straight on the back of his head. Hot blood oozed out of Kabir's scalp as he went down on his knees, the thaan falling off his shoulders.

'He thinks he can say anything about our gods and nothing will happen! Today we shall show him the wrath of the Devi. Kill the bastard!' And this announcement was enough to give the others the license to assault Kabir. As Kabir was beaten black and blue, the crowd watched.

साधो, देखो जग बौराना,
सांच कहूं तो मारन धावै, झूठे जग पतियाना

हिन्दू कहत हैं राम हमारा, मुसलमान रहमाना,
आपस में दौऊ लड़े मरत हैं, मरम कोई नहिं जाना

(Oh seeker, look the world has gone mad. If I say the truth, they assault me. If I lie, they trust me.

Hindus say Ram is theirs. Muslims say Rehman (Allah the all gracious) is theirs. They fight and die over their religion but neither understand the true essence.)

At the very moment that Kabir was being lynched at the bazaar by the Hindus, Maulvi sahib from the masjid had reached the kotwal's (sheriff) office to lodge a complaint against Kabir and was presently asking for Kabir's head to be severed off.

But Kabir was destined to live a very long life.

जाकों राखे साइयां, मार सके ना कोय
बाल ना बाका कर सके, जो जग बैरी होय

(The one who is protected by the Almighty cannot be killed by anyone. A single strand of his/her hair cannot be hurt even if the whole world becomes his/her enemy.)

* * *

Kabir recovered from the injuries, but his heart remained wounded. He was more determined than ever before to find his answers and to find them fast. He had heard from the sadhus the glory of Sri Ramananda Ji, a revered saint who lived on the Panchaganga Ghaat. Kabir approached his ashram but as expected, was shooed away because of his low caste. But he was not going to take no for an answer.

People say that Ramananda Ji goes for a dip in the Ganga at the Brahma Mahurat (auspicious time 1.5 hours before sunrise) every morning. I will just lie down here at these narrow steps. He will surely stumble upon me when he comes. I will find my mantra.

The next morning, before the sun broke the spell of darkness on the world, Ramananda Ji came down the ghaat unaware of Kabir lying on the steps. As soon as his leg touched Kabir, instantly what came out of his mouth was 'Ram Ram'!

'Ram'! The word echoed a million times in Kabir's ears.

Kabir jumped out of joy. To him, this was his sacred initiation. In his heart, Kabir had already accepted Ramananda Ji as his guru. This was the moment he was waiting for. He felt goosebumps through his entire body. He suddenly saw a flash of bright light. The ball of light engulfed him and took over him completely. He felt a breeze of fresh air filling up his whole being with a unique fragrance. He felt transported to another land and his heart expanded beyond his body. He felt as if the skies were embracing him. It was surreal. He was there but he was not. Kabir felt as if there was a power that loved him, and this power will always protect him. This power did not care if Kabir was of low caste or a kafir. He was no longer anaath (traditionally an orphan but literally someone without a guru/lord). He now had a guru, a naath! He now had a path. He felt his questions melting away and clarity dawning.

गुरु गोविंद दोउ खड़े, काके लागूं पाँय
बलिहारी गुरु आपने, गोविंद दियो मिलाय

(Both the Guru and God stand in front of me — whom should I bow down to first? Definitely the Guru, since the Guru made me realize the God)

As the sunrays lit up the Ganges and the ghaats, Kabir felt he was born again. It was a new day for the world and a new life for him. He finally knew who he was. He started dancing and singing:

चदरिया झीनी रे झीनी
के राम नाम रस दीनी
चदरिया झीनी रे झीनी

सो चादर सुर नर मुनि ओढ़ी, ओढ़ के मैली कीनी
दास कबीर ने ऐसी ओढ़ी, ज्यों के त्यों धर दीनी
चदरिया झीनी रे झीनी

(Kabir compares the body to a sheet of cloth. This body and mind are coloured in the colour of the Lord. This body is a gift and yet people, whether ordinary men, evil men or saints, have stained the sheet. Kabir returns the sheet unstained, as is.)

* * *

Kabir, by now, had many Hindu and Muslim friends since the only common denominator for friendship was poverty. They liked Kabir, they loved his poetry and the message in his poetry. There was Bashira — the water sprinkling guy, Raidas — the cobbler and a gifted poet himself, Sena — the guy who did nothing and everything and Pipa — the barber, to mention a few. None of them could read or write. All of them could feel what Kabir felt.

So one day, while Kabir was hanging out with his buddies, something took over him and he announced, 'From tomorrow, we shall start our own satsang (sitting together and singing devotional hymns and discussing wisdom)'! The whole group fell silent.

Our own satsang? How, where, why?

'Great. Now I shall surely achieve my dream of getting arrested by the police', laughed Sena.

'I will definitely come for the satsang, along with my bags and baggage. There is no way my mom will keep me in the house after this', remarked Pipa.

'This is the best idea ever Kabir. Where shall we do this? You have a spot in mind'? asked Raidas, already imagining the sight of sitting together and singing bhajans (devotional songs).

'Let's do it in the early morning, so that people can carry on with their jobs in the evening,' said a more pragmatic Bashira.

'Where? Right here, at the beginning of the ghaat', said Kabir, pointing to one corner of the street touching the ghaats.

'But the pundits cross through this street Kabir. They will be offended if we sit in their path', objected Sena.

'Well then, they will have to change their path. Or else they will keep bathing in the Ganga the whole day', laughed Kabir. (It was believed that if you even see a low-caste human, you have to cleanse yourself again by taking a dip in the Ganga.)

न्हावे धोवे से हरी ना मिले, जो मन का मैल न जाए
मीन प्यासी जल में रहे, धोवे बांस ना जाए

(Holy baths cannot make you meet the Divine unless the mind is purified.
The fish is constantly surrounded by water, yet remains thirsty and her bodily odour remains forever.)

And so, Kashi saw a morning that would change the way the story of the city would be told for generations to come. Never again would Kashi or Banaras be mentioned without the mention of Kabir.

That morning, Kabir broke an age-old unsaid rule. He took away the monopoly of the pundits and the mullahs. He challenged the dominance of religious institutions out in the open. He redefined the socio-religious fabric of his era. He gave a voice to the poor and the scorned. He started a public movement. And he did it all just with his ektaara (single-string Indian guitar) and his songs.

The backdrop of the pundits bathing in the Ganges with temple bells ringing, the azaan going off somewhere far away and the sight of ash-smeared yogis from the Gorakhnath ashram practicing sun salutations inspired Kabir's evergreen words:

मोको कहां ढूंढे रे बंदे, मैं तो तेरे पास में
ना मैं मंदिर ना मैं मस्जिद, ना काबे कैलास में
ना मैं जप में, ना मैं तप में, ना मैं बरत उपवास में
ना तो कौनो क्रिया कर्म में, नही जोग बैराग में

खोजी हो तो तुरत मिलु मैं, एक पल की तलास में
कहत कबीर सुनो भाई साधो, मैं तो हूं विश्वास में

(Where do you keep searching for me oh human,
I am so close to you,
Neither in temples, nor in mosques,
not even in Kaaba or Kailash,
Neither in any religious rituals nor in practice
of yoga and renunciation,
If you long for me with passion, you can
realize me in a microsecond,
Says Kabir listen oh seeker, I reside in faith alone.)

There was one group of people who would sit right at the back of the satsang and fanatically try to memorize the words and the tunes. They came from a niche community. A very powerful community with thousands of loyal members. They were the beggars! And so, within a matter of a few days, all the streets and the bylanes of Kashi were reverberating with Kabir's songs and saankhis, much to the frustration of the pundits and the mullahs. The harder they tried to shut him up, the louder his dissent became.

But the beggars were not the only ones listening keenly. There was another group. Unfortunately, they were the spies of the emperor, Sikandar Shah Lodi. The matter was reported to the emperor immediately with a special note of displeasure signed by Shah Takki, the religious advisor to the king who was supremely upset at the open insults to Islam in Kabir's songs.

The next day, Kabir was summoned by the emperor.

* * *

'Bow down to the Sultan', said the guards as Kabir stood tall in front of the emperor in the royal courtroom, completely disinterested in the whole affair. 'This head bends only in front of the Lord', said Kabir in a clear, confident voice.

'Are you insane? Bend and offer salutations before the Sultan gets angry', nudged the guards again.

'I won't. You can break me but not bend me'.

The royal court was shocked at this defiance. Sultan decided to ignore it and in a loud, kingly voice said:

'Listen julaaha, are you a Hindu or Musalman?'

'Neither and both'

'What kind of a foolish answer is that? Do you believe in Islam?'

'Of course, I do.'

'Then why don't you offer namaz and keep Roza?'

'You think offering namaz and keeping Roza alone makes one a Muslim. That it pleases Allah more than being a good human?'

दिन में रोजा रखत हैं, रात हलत हैं गाय
ये तो खून वो बंदगी, कैसे खुसी खुदाय

(If you worship the God by fasting for Him during the day and yet kill and eat an innocent cow in the evening — do you think you can truly please God?)

'You are disrespecting Islam and its customs', screamed the Sultan.

'Do you even understand Islam? If yes, then tell me who is right — the Shias or the Sunnis or the Sufis? If there is one Allah alone then why is there a conflict between His children? In the conquest of power, have we not seen one Muslim kill the other in the past? I don't believe in idol worship but what kind of a brave king destroys temples and pieces of stone? (It was believed that Lodi, like most other Mughal emperors, destroyed thousands of Hindu temples)

Said Lodi,

'You speak like a fakir (ascetic) or a sanyasi (mendicant/monk) but I don't think you are one! You are just a hypocrite! You have a profession I hear. You sell cloth for money! Tell me, what is it that you really want? Ask me and it shall be given but you have to accept Islam and stop your satsangs. I am the Shah, the Sultan. Ask whatever you desire. Do not hesitate.'

'Listen Oh Sultan, I don't want anything. And that is why I am a very dangerous man. I live free, internally and externally. Allah takes care of me every moment.'

चाह गई चिंता मिटी, मनवा बेपरवाह
जिनको कछु नहि चाहिये, वे साहन के साह

(Devoid of desires and worries, my mind is cool and carefree.
The one who does not want anything is truly the
king of the kings.)

Know that the true Sultan is Allah alone. You have unfortunately become a victim of maya (illusion). You think you are the Sultan; you are in control! Break the bubble of your imagination and realize that you will die one day. Sultans have come and gone. So will you! So why this arrogance and blind hunger for power? Smilingly, Kabir sang:

मत कर माया को अहंकार, मत कर काया को अभिमान
काया गार से कांची
हो काया गार से कांची, रे जैसे ओस रा मोती
झोंका पवन का लग जाए, झपका पवन का लग जाए
काया धूल हो जासी

ऐसा सख्त था महाराज, जिनका मुल्कों में राज
जिन घर झूलता हाथी
हो जिन घर झूलता हाथी, उन घर दिया ना बाती

(Don't be proud of your body and your imaginary powers for they are weaker than clay. They are just like dew drops. One tiny gust of wind is enough to destroy the body and its possessions. There was once a mighty Sultan who had conquered many countries. Elephants (riches and powers) would be his slave. Today, no one even lights a tiny lamp at his grave/home.)

आए है तो जायेंगे, राजा रंक फ़कीर।
इक सिंहासन चढी चले, इक बंधे जंजीर।

(If you are born, you will die — whether you are an emperor, a beggar or a fakir. Some will go on the throne and some in shackles, but everyone will surely go.)

The royal court fell in a deafening silence. The Sultan was shocked and enraged. His eyes burned with anger and his heart was beating fast. This was the first time someone had dared to speak or rather sing the naked ultimate truth to his face and made him look so tiny and inconsequential. Hiding his internal quiver, he decided to shoot the messenger instead of focusing on the message.

'Kill the kafir. Get him out of my sight.'

Kabir was still smiling. He who can smile on the face of death is willed to defy even Yamraj (the God of Death). And as he left the court, he sang in his trademark style:

निर्भय निर्गुण गुण रे गाऊंगा
जीत निसान घुराऊंगा जी
उल्टी पवन चढ़ाऊंगा

(Fearless, I shall sing glory of the attributes/qualities of the one who is beyond attributes. [Nirgun — beyond the three gunas as per Hindu scriptures — Sattva, Rajas and Tamas.]
I shall wave the flag of victory,
I shall make even the wind blow in reverse.)

What unfolded were fifty-two attempts (Baawan Kasni) to torture and take Kabir's life but to everyone's shock and his clan's joy, Kabir miraculously survived every single attempt of murder. They tied his hands and legs and threw him in the Ganges, but the river returned him to the shores alive. They threw him to be crushed by wild elephants, but the beasts refused to charge. And the more they tried and failed, the stronger Kabir's legend grew and the faith of his followers became unshakable. Now Kabir began to be revered as a saint and fakir with divine powers. Kabir became 'Kabir Das'. Ultimately, the king's cowards burnt Kabir's little hut, that too on his wedding night.

* * *

Loi walked into the burnt hut in her new bridal gown. Except a small corner that still had a roof, there was nothing left of the already dilapidated cottage. Kabir saw the saved corner and danced out of joy.

'Oh my Ram. You saved me a corner so we can sleep tonight in the shade! The whole hut could have been burnt. But you are ever so compassionate!'

Suddenly, he heard a sobbing voice. His joy was broken to see Loi, his newly wedded wife, her face covered with her palms, crying like a small child.

'I didn't know my father has wedded me off to a mad fakir! He didn't even ask my consent. Look where I have come!'

'Loi, what is on your mind? What do you desire?'

'I liked someone in my neighbourhood. The merchant's son. In my mind I had already taken him as my husband.'

'Oh! I didn't know this Loi, or else I would have never married you. But now that you have shared your desire, I promise you that you will have your way. Let's go meet him right away. Let me gracefully hand over to him what is rightfully his.'

Loi couldn't believe her eyes and ears. This was beyond her wildest imagination. Indeed, this was a mad fakir but with a giant heart! She experienced a rush of love and hope but didn't show it on her face.

'Are you sure'? she asked hesitantly.

Kabir laughed. 'Of course. What is the big deal in this? Life is a game, Loi. Let's go before it starts raining again'.

As Kabir and Loi stepped out of their razed 'palace', only within a few steps, Loi suddenly stopped. She pulled Kabir's hand, turned and dragged him back to the burnt hut.

'Loi? What happened? Loi! Loi?'

'I am not going anywhere Kabire. I shall stay here. As your wife. As your life partner.'

'But you love the merchant's son right? He will keep you happy Loi. I have nothing to offer you', said Kabir, looking at the condition of his cottage.

'You have a clean heart Kabire. It's very rare to find. Huts can always be rebuilt. My father has knotted me to you under the oath of togetherness, with the sacred fire as the witness. I shall respect this oath forever', said Loi as she hugged him tight, tears rolling down her eyes.

* * *

The wheel of time rolled on. Kabir's popularity grew by leaps and bounds and the satsang now shifted to his repaired home. Although his students tried to take the load of weaving off him, he insisted on continuing to be a karma-yogi (believer in the yoga of action). Kabir now had a son called Kamal and a daughter called Kamali.

One day, a great Vedic scholar from south India, Pundit Sarvananda came to meet Kabir. He had travelled the length and breadth of India and defeated everyone in Shastraarth (debate over holy scriptures). His final conquest had to be Kabir. So, carrying a bullock cart full of the holy texts, he approached Kabir's house. On the way, he felt thirsty and also needed exact directions to Kabir's humble hut. He saw a girl near a well. Drinking water from her earthen pot, he thanked and politely asked her:

'Where is Kabir's house'?

The girl looked at him and then at the cart full of books and replied:

कबीर का घर शिखर पर, जहाँ सिलहली गैल
पाव न टिके पीपली का, पंडित लादे बैल

(Kabir lives at the peak. The road to the peak is very slippery. Even an ant slips — let alone a pundit with a bullock cart of books.)

Sarvananda was amazed with the little girl's poetic verse. But he did not understand the symbolic meaning of what she said. He thanked her again and proceeded.

That little girl was Kamali.

When Sarvananda finally met Kabir and challenged him to a debate, Kabir joined his palms and said, 'I am an illiterate weaver, oh saint. I have neither interest nor appetite for bookish arguments. Please consider yourself victorious'.

Sarvananda was not satisfied by a verbal defeat and demanded Kabir give this to him in writing. Kabir said:

मसि कागद छुओ नहीं, कलम लियो नहि हाथ

(I have never touched a piece of paper, ink or pen in my life.)

So Sarvananda himself wrote out a victory certificate: 'This is to testify that in the debate, Sarvananda won and Kabir lost.' Kabir happily gave his thumb impression on the letter, fed Sarvananda with love and bade him farewell. Back to his weaving machine, he started weaving and singing with joy:

पोथी पढ़ पढ़ जग मुआ, पंडति भया न कोय
ढाई आखर प्रेम का, पढ़े सो पंडति होय

(Reading books, no one becomes a scholar/wise. If only you can read and live one short word — love — you would probably become a scholar.)

After a long travel, Sarvananda returned home and with pride showed the letter to his mother, announcing he had finally conquered even Kabir. When he opened the letter, in his own handwriting, the letter read:

'This is to testify that in the debate, Sarvananda lost and Kabir won!'

Sarvananda skipped a heartbeat. He instantly realized his small-mindedness and Kabir's obvious divinity, which he had failed to recognize in his arrogance of mastering the scriptures. He went back to Kabir and became his disciple for life.

* * *

Only a lit lamp can light more lamps. Kabir realized he needed to light many more lamps and save many confused souls. So he started travelling far and wide with his simple message of love, devotion and peace over mindless religious extremism. Wherever he went, miracle stories followed him. He met kings, saints and commoners alike and created a movement that spread across the country.

Kabir intuitively knew his time was short now. And, so, he decided to take his last trip — from Kashi to Maghar. It was believed that those whose souls leave their bodies in Kashi attained heaven and those who die in the cursed town of Maghar were sure to go to hell. And so, Kabir decided to do with his death what he did with his entire life — break with the orthodoxy and show the new way. Just to die, he went to Maghar.

का कासी का मगहर भैया, राम हृदय बस मोरा।
जो कासी तन तजै कबीरा, रामे कौन नहिोरा

(Kashi or Maghar —doesn't matter, for Ram resides in my heart. If I will get heaven only by the virtue of dying in Kashi, then what was the point in worshipping Ram my whole life?)

The last moment was here. There was a wave of peace and contentment in Kabir's heart. Time for the ultimate union had come. People around him were weeping but Kabir couldn't be happier. Lying alone in his bed, waiting, he heard faintly the conversation between his disciples:

'He is a Hindu. We must arrange for a royal funeral pyre for the last rites.'

'Don't be stupid! The whole world knows he is a Muslim, raised in a Muslim weaver family. We have to bury him.'

'Muslim? Through his life he sang praises of Ram, and at the time of his death you want to suddenly make him a Muslim? Did he ever do the namaaz?'

'Oh c'mon. You call yourself his student and you don't even know that the "Ram" he praised was "nirgun" and not the Ram in the temples! He criticized idol worship and led a movement against the caste system. Which Hindu would do that?'

'It will be the pyre my friend, no matter what you say.'

'We will bury him respectfully, come what may.'

The irony of the game of life and death, the certainty of the grip of maya (the all-pervading illusion) on humans, stood laughing to Kabir's face. Kabir laughed back having known and realized the ultimate truth.

The doors opened and Kabir's disciples eagerly walked in, praying to their own version of God for extending their beloved teacher's life a little more. They were shocked at what they saw.

There was no Kabir. Just a bunch of flowers on the bed.

* * *

KEY TAKEAWAYS

There are very few men who can change your entire life in four lines. Kabir was one of them.

If Kabir was alive today, there would be at least a hundred court cases on him.

Unmistakably, the strongest personality trait Kabir demonstrates is fearlessness!

1. Be Fearless

He stands in Kashi — the epicentre of religion in India and challenges the authority of the religious bodies (of both Hindus and Muslims) and their doorkeepers. He is the individual against the institution, he is the kafir against the king, he is the present thought challenging past rituals, he is the lone freedom fighter against the entire East India Company, he is the Abhimanyu inside the chakravyuh (special military formation) and he is the new age IT start-up challenging the malpractices of the giants. *He lays the foundation of the new normal.*

And he irritates and irks the establishment even more since he is untrained for this exhibition of intellectual, social and spiritual supremacy. He has never been to school or read the holy scriptures. For once, the establishment can swallow the bitter taste of defeat at the hands of a learned one — but for a low-caste julaaha to thrash them at their own game is humiliation at a different level. He is the homeschooled beating the Ivy League graduates; he is the Pele from the slums thrashing the uptown soccer league players; he is the rural folk singer outperforming the classical gharana (school of music) artists. He represents the downtrodden, the poor, the unfortunate, the so-called sinners. *He is their hope.* He does not set out to do any of this but ends up doing all of it.

Kabir is fearless.

2. Be the Change

Kabir is not an activist. He is a reformer and a devotee. His rebellion is not fuelled by dharnas (protests), angry riots and violence. His movement is propelled by faith, devotion and selflessness. He is not constantly in a negative complaint mode but rather in a positive reform mode. He proves that the proverbial pen is mightier than the sword. He is a part of the solution. He leads by example. He becomes the change and shows how it's done. This attitude is something we need today in the era of activism and protests.

3. Go Viral — The Power of Right Messaging

Kabir's message went viral. That too entirely organically. You know how? Because thousands of people suddenly started sharing his poems and songs. Who were these people that were sharing his messages without even knowing him or having ever met him?

It was the network of beggars — one of the most widely spread net of information disseminators. And they did it for free! It started with the ghaats of the Ganges, then spread across the whole city of Kashi and then travelled far and wide across the cities and hinterlands of northern India.

Beggars were forbidden to chant the holy mantras. They anyway never understood Sanskrit. They were also not classically trained to sing in difficult metres. Kabir's saakhis or dohas were just perfect for them. They were in the local language. They were short. They could be sung in a very simple metre. And they were super relevant and impactful. Perfect combination for a viral message. Influencers, are you listening?

For a message to go viral, it has to be:

UBER

Useful – It must add some value to me

Brief – It needs to be short and crisp

Easy – It needs to be simple. Easy to understand and implement

Relevant – It must be relevant to me and the current times

UBER Check

Run an 'UBER' check on your messaging (social media or work emails) before you shoot it out. The 'UBER' check can be useful for all kinds of messaging.

4. Never Give Up (Always Give Up)

Kabir's determination is legendary. His focus and clarity on his goal is exemplary. His house is burnt down, he is lynched publicly, he is rejected by all the gurus, the emperor orders a series of ordeals for him to go through, and yet, he stands firmly committed to his goal. No negotiations there. Kabir never gives up, or rather he always gives up — he surrenders his actions to a higher power! And that's the source of his strength.

In a song dedicated to Kabir by one of his students, Dharam Das, with reference to his commitment to his path for finding the divine, it is said, 'I can climb the most difficult peak, I can even throw away/sacrifice this physical body (or die trying) in order to merge with my beloved'! That is the level of commitment Kabir makes. (Any guesses which song this is? It's a rare one. Write to me at virat.chirania@gmail.com with your answers).

Never Give Up
Always Give Up

Are you ready to go through whatever it takes to meet your goal? Where do you draw strength from for your commitment?

5. Be Spiritual; Focus on the Essence

Kabir teaches us the difference between religion and spirituality. Gurudev Sri Sri Ravi Shankar Ji gives a beautiful example where he says, 'Spirituality is the banana and religion is the banana skin. We have thrown away the banana and are fighting over the skin'. Kabir focused on the values more than the rituals. He focused on spirituality more than religion. This is probably the approach we need in these times of global conflict.

6. Kabir for You and Me

Kabir is talking to you and me. Initially when you read Kabir you might feel he is talking about someone else. But without a doubt, he is talking to you and me.

Kabir challenges you. Kabir forces you to stop and think. He says, 'Hey you, the person reading this, I am talking to you'. He challenges our hypocrisy, our insecurities, our fears, our foolishness, our ignorance. He asks you difficult questions and does not let you off the hook easily. He shows you the mirror. Kabir grows on you. *The way to relate to Kabir is to read each doha and reflect on how it applies to your life.* A lot of learnings and realizations then reveal themselves.

7. Hands-on Experience

Kabir's wisdom is not borrowed, it's his own. He only speaks from his experience and hence is so sure of what he is saying. He does not speak of heavy theoretical concepts or bookish knowledge. He keeps it simple.

तू कहता कागद की लेखी, मैं कहता आँखिन की देखी।
मैं कहता सुलझावन हारि, तू राख्यौ उलझाई रे।

(You speak of the written word. I only speak of what I have seen with my eyes. I speak to solve the mystery. You keep it entangled and confusing)

He observes life very keenly and learns from it. In that sense, his approach is very modern and scientific. He is the scientist in the lab of life conducting experiments with his mind. Kabir removes all the middlemen — the pundits, the mullahs and he removes all the other crutches — the books, the scriptures — and approaches the divine directly based solely on his observations and experiences.

Manthan

Pause. Introspect. Express.

Do we attempt to get our own experiences in life/profession or are we satisfied with borrowed, bookish knowledge?

More Gems

जात न पूछो साधु की, पूछ लीजिये ज्ञान।
मोल करो तलवार का, पड़ा रहन दो म्यान

साधु ऐसा चाहिए, जैसा सूप सुभाय,
सार-सार को गहि रहै, थोथा देई उड़ाय।

(Don't ask the saint his caste/religion/gender, only ask for the knowledge. Value the sword and ignore the scabbard. We need saints who are like grain cleaners. They keep the good stuff and remove the waste.)

Kabir is a proponent of meritocracy and equality. To him, all that matters is the wisdom/knowledge the person is carrying and not the outer appearance/gender/name/degrees etc. A lot of the time people tend to accumulate degrees but not knowledge, information but not intelligence. Kabir suggests we ignore the outer shell and focus on the real stuff inside.

Merit Over Appearance

* * *

Consider the following verse by Kabir:

पहला तो गुरुजी हम जनम्या पीछे बड़ा भाई
धूम धाम से पिता रे जन्म्या सबसे पीछे माई

राम के नाम रे पकड़ो रे भैया छोड़ो नी मूरखाई
कहत कबीर सुनो भाई साधो मूर्ख समझ ना पाई
बेर चलया मेरा भाई

ये उलट वेद की बानी रे
कोई ज्ञानी करो विचार

It translates to:

First I was born and then came my elder brother,
With celebrations, then my father was born, and in the end,
my mother.

Hold on to the name of the Lord, let go your foolishness
Kabir says, listen oh seeker, the foolish don't get it.
Time is slipping away, brother.

This is the upside-down voice of the Vedas,
The wise ones need to examine!

This is a classic example of a lesser known style of Kabir's poetry called **'Ulat Baansi'** or **'Ulat Baani**', which means **'Upside Down Speech'.**

Kabir challenges us to think outside the box, to recognize the not so obvious, to go beyond the constructs and constraints of logic. He gives us a fresh new perspective to live life and to understand the abstract world of the divine. In this, his poetry does not make sense. And that is the beauty and purpose. Why should everything make sense?

Why should all experiences be measured and explained by a logical yardstick? Can life and the experiences of subtle energies in deep meditations truly be captured in logic and words alone? Why does the mind struggle with that which is beyond logic? To meet the divine, you have to kill the mind. He reminds us that time is slipping away, so don't waste your time trying to make sense of this temporary world and its nuances but rather focus on the divine (which means living a useful, meaningful spiritual life).

The Ulat Baansi forces your mind to clear the clutter of existing logic and experiences and then approach life with a new mind where anything is possible. There are many other examples of his Ulat Baansi verses that are available for us to enjoy.

It is interesting to note that a similar example is found in the Bhagvad Gita when Bhagwan Sri Krishna speaks of the upside-down tree with its roots in the air and branches hanging downwards. Symbolically, this tree reminds us that our roots should be established in the divine consciousness and not in the material world.

Manthan

Pause. Introspect. Express.

Do you always want to 'make sense' in whatever you do/say/write? Are you comfortable when your logic is broken? Can you do something today that is illogical and does not make sense?

* * *

निंदक नियरे राखिए, आंगन कुटी छवाय,
बिन पानी, साबुन बिना, निर्मल करे सुभाय

(Always keep a critic close to you. Without water or soap, this person will cleanse your nature.)

This is a profound piece of advice for all of us. Keep one person close to you who has the freedom to criticize you. Typically, we keep such people away and we tend to surround ourselves in a bubble of adulation. If we want to succeed and lead in life, we need to learn how to handle criticism and we need quick, fearless feedback coming in.

Keep a critic close by!

Manthan

Pause. Introspect. Express.

What happens to your mind and body when you face criticism? How do you handle it? Do you think you can handle criticism well? Do you hold a grudge against the person who criticizes you? Do you have one such person who can freely criticize you?

* * *

ऐसी वानी बोलिए मन का आपा खोए
औरन को सीतल करे आपूही सीतल होए

(Your speech should be such that it takes you beyond ego. Your speech must bring peace and calm to yourself and to others who listen to it.)

Human beings are gifted with speech. Are we really aware of what comes out of our mouths? Do our words bring violence and agitation or peace and hope in others? One of the biggest achievements is to have a say over your speech.

* * *

Decode

Take a shot at decoding the following dohas yourselves before you Google them

नैहरवा हम का न भावे
साई की नगरी परम अति सुन्दर, जहाँ कोई जाए ना आवे
चाँद सूरज जहाँ, पवन न पानी, कौ संदेस पहुँचावै

माटी कहे कुम्हार से, तू क्या रौंधे मोय
एक दिन ऐसा आएगा, मैं रोंधुगी तोय

Saraansh

Summary of Learnings from this chapter

1.
Be fearless

2.
Be the change

3.
The secret of viral messaging

4.
The UBER check
U: Useful; B: Brief; E: Easy; R: Relevant

5.
Focus on the essence

6.
Hands-on experience

7.
Merit over appearance

8.
Keep a critic close by

9.
Don't be bound by your logic

10.
Purify your words

11.
Never give up (always give up)

4

Chanakya

Uthistha Bharatah

(Rise, oh India)

'Winning a war with bloodshed is the lowest form of political art'

The Back Story

It's roughly 300 years before the birth of Jesus Christ. Bharat is the richest and one of the most advanced civilizations on the planet. In Bharat's most powerful kingdom called Magadha, a special boy named Vishnugupta is born. He is also called Chanakya, named after his father Chanak. He grows up to become a teacher at the prestigious Takshashila University in Gandhar (present day Afghanistan). Everything is going smoothly till a short, brave Greek king called Alexander decides to invade Bharat . . .

Characters

Chanakya* aka *Vishnugupta: The kingmaker, the teacher, the hero of our story

Chanak: Chanakya's father, a teacher in Magadha

Chandragupta Maurya: Student of Chanakya, the emperor of Bharat, the founder of the Maurya Dynasty

Alexander: The Greek invader King, a world conqueror

Ambhi: The king of Takshashila

Dhanananda: The king of Magadha

Sharangrao, Akshay, Nipunak: Chanakya's students and Chandragupta's classmates

Amatya Rakshas: The Prime Minister of Magadha

Sinharan: Commander in chief of Ambhi's army, later Commander in chief of Chandragupta's army

Philipus: Greek Governor of India on behalf of Alexander

He stood there alone in the river facing the rising sun, palms joined at his chest. The waters were unusually cold today, but his mind was somewhere else.

'Aum Adityaya Namah' (Salutations to the Sun) — the chant continued under his breath. Vishnugupta finished the ceremonial bath, neatly tied his shikha (tuft of hair) over his shaved head and walked slowly towards his modest hut. Today was a very special day. There was an air of excitement and nervousness in the whole atmosphere. Takshashila University was getting dressed for its annual convocation. Thousands of young men dashed around doing the last-minute preparations. The campus looked gorgeous with big oil lamps, orange flags, decorated banana leaves and shiny yellow marigolds all over.

Tucked away in the beautiful valley of Gandhar, Takshashila University was one of the most illustrious jewels in India's crown. Reputed as the first and the largest formal university of the world, Takshashila attracted more than 10,000 students not just from all over India but from all corners of the globe, including China, Babylon, Persia, Greece and far east Asia. This was the place where great men like Panini (Father of Sanskrit) and Sushruta (Father of Surgery) had graduated from. Although education was almost free, only the brightest minds got admissions after a rigorous selection process. Vishnugupta was brighter than most.

The students sat dressed in their bright yellow dhotis and an angavastram, colour coded to their fields of specialization — white for those graduating in Ayurveda, ochre for Vedic Studies, red for Warfare, green for Alchemy, maroon for Metaphysics and so on. Takshashila offered more than forty specializations to its students. Vishnugupta sat wearing a purple angavastram. He was the only one wearing purple. His classmates were confused, but they were too busy to ask him the reason for this anomaly.

'And now we come to the most unique announcement of the day', said the Kulapati (Chancellor) after having finished his inaugural speech. 'This has never happened in the history of our university before. Today we have a student amongst us, who like you will graduate, but unlike you will not leave the campus. He shall now stay back with us as a professor! To this august assembly, I am pleased to present our very own Vishnugupta, or rather Acharya Chanakya, the youngest faculty member in the Department of Economics and Political Sciences!'

Amongst a thunderous applause, Chanakya walked to the dais and looked at the prestigious body of students and teachers in front of him. A few seconds ago, he was a student and now a teacher. In one moment, everything had changed. He cleared this throat and spoke thus:

> A classroom is where a nation is created, its where men are born. Men born in my motherland are truly fortunate, for India is indeed the promised land where

> the heavens and humans unite. Bharat is the birthplace of human civilization and the lap in which science and spirituality play and display the illusions of matter and spirit. As we graduate today, let us remember our first duty is always towards our country.
>
> Today, we go back not as progeny of a particular family, practitioners of a particular profession or residents of a particular state of India. We go back as Indians, and we pledge to protect the ideology of an united India till our last breath. It is not enough that you are proud of Mother India. *The real question is — is Mother India proud of you?*
>
> Aum Shanti Shanti Shantihi.

He stood tall as the assembly hall burst into tears, claps and slogans of *Jai Maa Bharati* (Hail Mother India). Behind him, inscribed on the top of the building read the eternal words:

| स्वदेशे पूज्यते राजा विद्वान सर्वत्र पूज्यते |

(The king is worshipped only in his kingdom, but a wise scholar is worshipped everywhere.)

* * *

Alexander raised his right hand signalling the army to a halt. Dressed in his royal blue war outfit and a red fur helmet, he looked like a Greek god. He was short but had the shoulders of a giant, the shoulders that carried the weight of winning almost the whole world.

Alexander turned back once to look at his men. They stood there, at their leader's command, 50,000 of them, in disciplined formations. They had marched all the way from Greece, across Egypt, Mesopotamia, Persia and were now approaching the Hindu Kush, the end of the known world. They had conquered every inch of land on the way. The famous Indus Valley Civilization was their final pursuit. And they were now standing at the doors of the mighty Indian subcontinent.

And unfortunately for India, they knocked, and the doors were opened for them. A royal walk-in, just like that. Ambhi, the cowardly king of Takshashila, begged for an alliance with Alexander, so that they could together overpower his neighbouring arch-rival, the mighty Porus. The news of Alexander's entry to conquer India and of Takshashila's fall spread rapidly. It reached the Gurukul (Takshashila University) too.

It was the darkest prahar of an almost moonless night, the time Chanakya loved the most. He made his best moves in darkness. The darkness hid his ugly pockmarked face and his crooked nose. It hid his unfortunate past that was buried in the busy lanes of Patliputra (present day Patna), the capital of the Magadha Empire, where he was born. He decided it was time to go back to his hometown. The only way India could be saved from Alexander was if Magadha intervened, for Magadha was the strongest empire in India and boasted of an army twice the size of Alexander's. Magadha could keep India free from the Greek invasion.

There was one problem though — Dhanananda. The king of Magadha was a lost cause, hopelessly sunk into carnal pleasures, oblivious to the slow degradation of his subjects and the rampant corruption in his bureaucracy, disinterested in discussions of welfare and nationalism. He was also the reason why Chanakya's father, Acharya Chanak, was dead. And yet, Chanakya was going to go and ask him for military help to stop Alexander. It was always India first for him.

* * *

Patliputra stood decorated and festive as if welcoming Chanakya. It was the day of the Gyan Sabha (knowledge symposium). Students and scholars from across India would debate on the deepest theories of the scriptures and the victorious would be handsomely rewarded by the emperor. As a professor from Takshashila Gurukul, Chanakya aka Acharya Vishnugupta had a special invitee pass to the conference.

'What is the basis of sukha (happiness)'? asked the debate convener in a rapid-fire round to one of the delegates.

'Dharma', replied the delegate. (Dharma is duty/ rightful path and not merely organized religion.)

'What is the basis of dharma?'

'Artha.' (wealth/means)

'And the basis of artha?'

'Rajya.' (state/nation)

'Who is the ideal raja?'

'Lord Ram and hence his utopian rule, Ram Rajya. The one who sacrifices his personal happiness, treats his subjects as his master and himself as nothing more than a public servant, the one who has control over his five senses, is the ideal king. The ideal king is actually a royal sage.'

'Am **I** not the ideal king? Am **I** not the incarnation of Lord Ram himself?' interrupted Dhanananda much to the shock and fear of the assembly. The obvious answer would have angered the king. And so, they all kept silent. At this moment, Chanakya rose from his seat and walked into the middle of the court room, his fearless gaze fixed on Dhanananda. He wore a simple dhoti and only his janeu (the sacred thread of the Brahmins) to cover his torso. But he wore the glow of the Vedas on his face and the light of knowledge in his eyes.

'No, you are not Lord Ram. You are Dhanananda, presently the caretaker of this great country only on behalf of its citizens.' Fire poured out of Dhanananda's eyes as he glared at the Brahmin standing in his court, challenging his authority.

'An ordinary teacher who expects alms from me has the audacity to talk to me like this!'

'There is no such thing as an ordinary teacher. *Teachers are always extraordinary*. The teacher cradles in his lap creation and destruction alike. Teachers are the kingmakers. And if my teachings have power, I shall create kings who shall feed and protect me.'

'Then why have you come begging to my court?'

'I came not to beg but to warn you. Listen oh king, a Greek war hero by the name of Alexander, having conquered the whole world, now has his eyes on our motherland. The cowardly Ambhi has already made an alliance with him. Magadha alone has the military power to stop Alexander and save our nation from this invasion. India needs you oh king. Save India from the Greeks!'

'Don't lecture me on India and warfare, stupid Brahmin. Leave now and I shall spare your life.'

'Dhanananda, wake up from your slumber. Takshashila is compromised today. Tomorrow it will be Magadha and then the whole of India. This is the moment you can make yourself immortal in history. Else, you shall be cursed to rot in hell forever.'

'Who are you anyway? How dare you curse the mighty Dhanananda in his own court? Throw this ugly animal away into the dungeons or slay him right here! Let me challenge the holy scriptures today by sacrificing a Brahmin!'

'I am Chanakya, the son of the saintly Chanak who you killed by misuse of your state power. But for you, today I am Yama (death).'

Dhanananda was shocked! Chanak's face flashed in front of his eyes. Although a few decades had passed by, it seemed like yesterday when he had crushed the rebel Chanak.

'You wretched rat! You survived! I should have killed you along with your father.'

'You absolutely should have. Learn this lesson, king — *always pay the loan to the last penny and eliminate the enemy to the last trace.* Always. That is what I intend to do with you!'

'Pray for your life right now Brahmin. Guards, kill the bastard.'

As Dhanananda's men drew their swords and approached Chanakya, Amatya Rakshas (the noble prime minister of Magadh) stood up and screamed just in time, '*Brahmano Avadhyaha*! (a Brahmin is exempt from death penalty) Let him go'. Dhanananda gave a nasty stare to Amatya Rakshas but didn't oppose his order. The swords went back into the scabbards and the guards caught Chanakya by his shikha and started dragging him out.

'This is your end Dhanananda — mark my words. I pledge, I shall create a king who will unite and rule the whole land mass of India. I pledge I shall expunge you. And I pledge I shall keep my shikha unknotted till you are destroyed completely', screamed Chanakya as the guards dragged him out of the court and threw him on to the streets. His words kept echoing in Dhanananda's ears and the empty corridors of the palace.

* * *

His feet automatically took him towards the river where he used to play with his friends. As he took the familiar turn on to the mud road, he saw a group of teenagers playing. Vishnugupta felt nostalgic. He went closer to get a better view. A make-believe courtroom drama with guards, attendants, ministers and the common people was unfolding. Sitting on a rock throne was a sharp-looking young boy wearing a royal turban with a morpankh (peacock feather) tucked in.

'Hail the mighty King Chandragupta, the benevolent emperor of Magadha', said one boy, playing the announcer while two other boys made drum sounds with their mouths.

'Open the case', announced the king.

Two young men marched forward.

'Samrat (emperor), this shameless human is a thief. I bought his well last week. Now he tells me that he only sold me the well and not the water in the well. So, I have to pay money if I want to use the water. Give me justice oh king.'

'Hmm. Well, he is right my dear fellow. He only sold you the well. And yet he keeps his water in your property. So, from now he shall pay you rent for keeping his water in your well', chuckled Chandragupta. The young man jumped with joy. 'No one goes without justice at your court! More power to you', he cried as he saluted the king on his rehearsed exit.

Chanakya had a smile on his face and a thousand possibilities exploding in his opportunist brain. He suddenly, playfully stepped forward into the court and with joined palms said:

'Victory to the Samrat! Please help this poor Brahmin'. The kids got scared, feeling their drama might have offended an elderly Brahmin and ran away. Chandragupta kept sitting on the throne unperturbed and said, 'Pray tell me what you need, oh learned scholar'.

'Samrat, for me to perform my yagnas (fire rituals) as per the holy scriptures, I need the Panchagavya — milk, ghee, curd, gaumutra (cow's urine) and cow dung cakes. Hence this poor Brahmin needs a cow', explained Chanakya.

'Granted', said Chandragupta.

'Oh king, I have neither cash nor kind to pay and yet you are giving me a cow. At this rate, you will empty the rajkosh (royal treasury)', objected Chanakya, trying to test Chandragupta.

Instantly, Chandragupta replied, 'My dear Brahmin, this cow is in fact been given to you to protect the rajkosh! You perform yagna only as a ritual but fail to see the cosmic law governing the very concept of yagna. Each being has to play their role so that the universe functions in harmony. This creation is based on interdependence. Remove one screw from the machine and the entire set-up collapses.

अन्नाद्भवन्ति भूतानि पर्जन्यादन्नसम्भव:
यज्ञाद्भवति पर्जन्यो यज्ञ: कर्मसमुद्भव:

The Bhagvad Gita says — all beings evolve and get nurtured from food. Food in turn comes from the rains. Rain comes from the sacrifice/yagna. Sacrifice/yagna is rooted in actions/duty prescribed as per the Vedas.

If the Brahmins of my kingdom are not able to please the Devatas (higher subtle powers) with their prescribed rituals, my land shall be cursed by the divine powers. There shall be no rain and hence no crops. This would starve the farmers and the markets would crash. There will be an economic crisis and tax subsidies will follow, which will indeed bleed the treasuries. This would mean budget cuts for defence and the army would be weakened. News would spread and my enemies would surely take advantage and attack us. My kingdom would be there no more and I shall no longer be the king! Hence, by giving you this cow, I am in fact saving my empire and the well-being of my people.'

Chanakya kept staring at Chandragupta in awe.

'What is your name young man'? asked Chanakya in a serious tone.

'Chandragupta Maurya.'

'Don't you know you are supposed to add your guru's and father's names in your introduction?'

Chandragupta's eyes welled up and his head tilted downward. With a shaky voice he said,

'Arya (respected one), I have neither a father nor a guru. I wanted to study but all the gurukuls in Magadha rejected my candidature since I am of a low caste. I told them I would sit far away and listen to the lectures, but even then they disapproved.'

'I will not allow another Eklavya (an ace archer from the Mahabharata who suffered because he didn't find a guru) to go down the lanes of history. From this very moment, I am your guru, Chandragupta', said a resolute Chanakya.

An overjoyed Chandragupta touched his guru's feet. This was his second birth. He was no longer anaath (without a guru/guardian).

'*Uthistha Bharata* (rise oh India)', blessed Chanakya.

* * *

'War elephants'! exclaimed a stunned Alexander.

He tore across the ranks of his army to go right in the front. He got a full view of the massive army that waited on the other side — the army of the legendary King Porus.

His eyes flared in amazement and shock. In the countless battles he had fought most of his adult life, he had never seen a sight like this! There they stood, the humongous beasts, rising several feet up, covered in shiny metal armour, mounted by specially trained warrior mahouts (elephant riders) with long spears and arrows. There were thousands of them lined up like an impenetrable wall. And when they roared their thunderous trumpets, it terrified the Greek horses and sent shivers down the soldiers' spines.

But Alexander was both brave and battle smart. He quickly changed his strategy to negate the advantage of the elephants and attacked Porus with all his might. It was a bloodbath on both sides, ending indecisively. Although Alexander claimed an unsubstantiated victory, this battle over the river Hydaspes (present day Jhelum) was the closest Alexander ever came to death and defeat in his life.

Soon after this battle, as an aftermath, Alexander faced a mutiny from his army. His men refused to take his orders to march forward into the Indian heartland. Alexander was obsessed with the idea of conquering India, the last frontier known to mankind, the land of rare riches and even rarer rishis (saints). He tried to tempt his army with the limitless bounty they would loot and the eternal fame they would achieve but his men were tired and homesick. They had travelled thousands of miles from home and fought incessantly for the last eight years. They saw no purpose in this never-ending war. And when they heard of even bigger armies with more combat elephants lying on the other side of the Ganges, they persuaded their ambitious king to return home.

Disappointed to have failed in his mission of world conquest, Alexander reluctantly ordered his troops to head south and take the sea route back to Persia while he chose to travel by land.

On the way out, pretty much like on his way in, he crushed and killed as many as he could. *Alexander was brave, but hardly great.* He butchered weaponless priests and hung their dead bodies on trees in full public view. His men always looted the cities they conquered and raped the women. Even little children were not spared.

Alexander appointed his close confidant Philipus as the Shatrap (Governor General) of India with headquarters in Takshashila, with the assurance he would return after a few years. Each conquered kingdom was left to Greek generals to administer and rule and thus maintain a strong Greek empire in India.

Before Alexander the Brave left India, his last desire was to take with him a few rishis and ascetics and learn the eternal wisdom of the Vedas from them. To his utter shock, the rishis refused to go with him. He tried to bribe them and scare them but nothing worked on these sages. One day, Alexander himself went to convince a sadhu (monk) who was meditating in the forests. Alexander got off his horse and walked up to the sadhu. The sadhu sat there like a statue, lost in the bliss of samadhi (deep meditative state).

'What are you doing'? asked an iimpatient Alexander.

The sadhu slowly cracked opened his eyes and said, 'Well before you interrupted me, I was bathing in the bliss of infinity'.

'What are you doing?', asked the sadhu.

'I am on a mission to become the first man to rule the whole world', answered Alexander.

They both looked at each other. Each thought the other was insane. The sadhu closed his eyes again and said,

'Oh, ignorant king, you have travelled miles away from your home in vain. You carry the blood of innocents on your hands. You are not a world victor but a disruptor of world peace. Whether you believe in them or not, the laws of karma will make you pay for your actions.

And since your ego clouds your intelligence, let me tell you a secret — even after having conquered the world, when you die, you will only own as much of this earth as required to bury your body!' Saying this, the sadhu burst into loud laughter that echoed in the forest.

Alexander shook from his head to toe. The sadhu's words pierced him like an arrow through his heart. No one had ever spoken to him this way. The ultimate truth was impossible for him to digest. All his global victories seemed meaningless.

Alexander the Brave left India a defeated man.

* * *

It was late in the night, a time Chanakya loved. A cool autumn breeze was beginning to envelop the quiet streets of Takshashila. They had gathered around the massive yet delicately carved marble statue of Maa Saraswati in the central library building, the iconic tower of the Takshashila Gurukul. It was a secret meeting. Present in attendance were the Kulpati (Chancellor), the board of trustees, the president of the student council and Chanakya aka Acharya Vishnugupta with his core team of disciples — Chandragupta, Sharangrao, Nipunak and Akshay. All ears were waiting for Chanakya to share why he had summoned this urgent meeting.

'Alexander's troops have conquered all the small and big republics and may soon penetrate deeper into the heartland.

Alexander may return with a more powerful army and a stronger resolution to conquer India. Takshashila is the place where the Yavan (Greek) flag fluttered for the first time, thanks to our cowardly king Ambhi. Hence, this has to be the first place to commence the auspicious ceremony of making India Greek-free again.'

'You are planning to conspire and rebel against your own king'? asked one of the trustees.

'Fighting against invaders is called an independence struggle not a conspiracy', corrected Chanakya instantly.

'But we are a gurukul, not the government or a political outfit. These matters are for the king to think and act on. Ours is the path of non-violence', said one of the academicians.

'If the king fails to protect his people and his borders, the teacher will do it. What the government fails to do, the gurukul will. The scriptures we teach proclaim:

अहिंसा परमो धर्मः धर्म हिंसा तथैव च

(Non-violence is the highest dharma. So too is violence in service of Dharma.)

'If education cannot respond to the challenges put forth by the invaders today then that education is worthless. A teacher is successful only when he/she is capable of building a character based on human, nationalist and spiritual values in every individual of the nation. Gurukuls do not just give a degree; they train our young men for manhood.

The invaders, in due course, will take over our educational institutes and then our entire culture. They will re-write our history their way. Today, India stands attacked but not defeated. Till the time we can protect our sanskriti (culture), we will not be defeated. What has hurt us the most is not the evil actions of the invaders, but the non-action of our own country men. The hands that hold the book can also lift a sword! If we can't save this soil, what is the point of education? I refuse to see my mother get insulted in front of my eyes. I still have blood in my veins, not water. What about you?'

The room felt silent. It was almost impossible to resist getting convinced by Chanakya. He had vaak siddhi — the power to influence by words and manifest his speech in reality. It was unanimously decided that the gurukul would lead the independence struggle against the incumbent Greek government and Acharya Vishnugupta would be the orchestrator of this freedom war. It was also clarified that the Acharya shall not expect any monetary help from the board and the students' participation would be voluntary. This was enough for the Acharya. He was confident of his plans.

* * *

Many years had passed since the day Chanakya met Chandragupta for the first time. Chanakya had brought Chandragupta with him to Takshashila and secretly taken a resolve to anoint him to the throne of Magadha, thereby fulfilling his commitment to expunge Dhanananda. His unknotted shikha reminded him of his pledge every single moment.

Over the last several years, Chandragupta had undergone rigorous training befitting the making of a worthy king. His day began at the break of dawn with physical exercise and combat training. This was followed by meditation and Vedic chanting. After a break, the routine resumed with classes on subjects such as economics, politics, languages, mathematics, law and strategy. Then it was time for horse riding, archery and wrestling. Post lunch, the classes resumed with the study of ancient scriptures and spiritual discourses. Evenings were for warfare tactics, debates and martial arts. Post dinner it was time for a walk with Chanakya, recapping the day's learnings and trying to survive the arrows of difficult questions that Chanakya would fire to test his learnings. This was also the time when Chanakya would personally guide him and share his vision for the future. It was then time for retiring his exhausted body with prayers and chants of gratefulness, and somehow stealing a few hours of sleep, never more than five. The next day was a repetition.

There was another part of Chandragupta's training that he was not even aware of. This was a secret only Chanakya knew. Every day, Chanakya added small doses of poison in Chandragupta's food. Chanakya was far-sighted. He knew that Chandragupta's future enemies would try to poison him to death, and one cannot dig a well when the house is already on fire. So, in order to make his body immune to poison, Chanakya administered extremely calculated measures of poison to his body every day. In the years to come, Chandragupta would be immune to poison.

He now stood a tall, handsome man with broad shoulders and muscular arms, an aristocratic face, a poised yet sharp mind and most importantly, a heart full of love for his motherland. Chandragupta was ready for Chanakya's mission.

'Have you planned our next move Acharya'? asked Sharangrao while they all gathered around the bonfire. The Acharya added a fresh set of incensed mango twigs into the flames and said:

'Vishnugupta does not act without a plan, even in his dream! We need to create an army. Just the combat-trained students from the gurukul shall not suffice in fighting the large troops of Philipus and the Greek governors in other states.'

'But we don't have a kingdom. How will we raise an army'? asked Akshay.

'Well, what do we do when we want a house built or furniture made'? asked Chanakya.

'Hmm. We hire masons and carpenters', replied Akshay hesitantly.

'Exactly. So, when we want to fight a war, we hire fighters', explained Chanakya. 'We shall create an army of mercenary soldiers'! (Mercenary soldiers were trained warriors who fought only for money. They had no political or geographical loyalties).

'And where shall we get the funds to pay them? The gurukul has clearly denied us funds', remarked Chandragupta.

'*We will crowd source*'! answered Chanakya. The group was stunned. As usual, they waited for their Acharya to explain.

'This is not our personal war. This is for the freedom of our motherland. And every single citizen has to be a part of this fight. Why should we keep all the merit to ourselves? Let's not be that selfish. We will make this a mass movement, a people's movement!' The group had goosebumps envisioning what was coming their way.

'Sharangrao — you will lead the awareness campaign and funds collection. Chandragupta — you will raise and train the army. Nipunak — you will create a network of student spies in our state and all the neighbouring ones. Akshay — you shall be my personal secretary and additionally handle communication with heads of other republics so we can spread the fire we light in Takshashila all the way to the Magadha borders. We have very little time on our hands. Tomorrow, we launch our campaign. Sleep well boys. '*Jai Maa Bharati*'. Saying this, Chanakya walked away from the group for a lone stroll. The boys didn't sleep though. They got to work the very moment the Acharya left.

The next day, like every day, thousands of gurukul students went to beg for food from the city's householders. But today, they begged not just for food but blessings and support for their brothers who were ready to lay down their lives and make the ultimate sacrifice for the motherland. Chanakya had told them, 'You are going to interact with the lady of the house. Remember, her currency is not money. Her currency is emotion. Stir the right feeling in her and she will stir the ocean for you'. The students made the women the champions of their cause and received tremendous support emotionally, financially and, of course, gastronomically. The students also got in touch with other gurukuls and student bodies and got them on board. Soon the flags were up, the torches were lit and the masses were out in marches against the Greeks and anyone who supported the Greeks. The uprising had begun.

India was witnessing its first ever independence struggle.

In the meantime, Chandragupta secretly met the one man he needed the most — Simharan, the ex-commander-in-chief of the Gandhar army, who had been expelled by Ambhi. Humiliated and purposeless, the independence struggle was his chance to bounce back and die for his country with honour. He was already a hero amongst the mercenary forces and with him joining Chandragupta, their army soon had thousands of battle-trained warriors. The mercenary soldiers were so inspired by Chandragupta's speeches that they did not even ask for any remuneration. In fact, they were keen to finally fight for a cause and not just coins. 'Oratory is a priceless skill for a public leader', recalled Chandragupta from his evening walks with Chanakya. Apart from the military support, their invaluable contribution was to discourage and scare their fellow mercenary soldiers who fought for the Greek army and cause confusion and mistrust amongst their troops. Mistrust in the enemy camp is a powerful tool in war — Chanakya would say often.

And then one night, when Philipus was least aware of the looming threat, Chandragupta attacked his camp and went straight to eliminate the top leader of the Greek forces — a high-risk, high-reward strategy. He knew if he managed to get Philipus out of the way, the other Greek governors and their entire army in India would lose their steam and the empire would begin to crumble. And that is exactly what happened. Philipus fell and the news spread like wildfire. The already activated spies in various republics spread a mixture of facts and lies to ensure the morale of the Greek soldiers plummeted, and Chandragupta mercilessly attacked all the Greek camps that existed in Gandhar and other northern areas.

The final nail in the Greek coffin was the sudden news from Persia that Alexander the Brave was dead! He had succumbed to an unidentified illness in Babylon. India was now free from the Greek invaders. The first half of the mission was complete. There were celebrations in the Chandragupta camp. Chanakya did not believe in celebrations. He, however, did not spoil the party for the boys.

* * *

Chanakya was out on a pre-dinner walk with Sharangrao. They chose to walk to the hillock on the backside of the gurukul to try their luck at catching a beautiful sunset. As they passed a few huts where some of the university staff lived, they saw a woman saying something very animatedly to her little son. They stopped to catch a seemingly interesting conversation.

'You are foolish! Who asked you to eat the hot khichdi (an Indian food dish) straight from the centre? You must always eat from the cooler sides first and then move towards the center'! scolded the mother, compassionately blowing air on the slightly burnt fingers of her child. Chanakya froze in his tracks. The lady's remark hit him like a thunderbolt! Unknowingly, she had taught him a priceless lesson in strategy. He remembered a line from the scriptures, *'To the degree you are awake, everything around you brings you knowledge'*!

Chanakya turned back and walked briskly to his kutir (cottage). Sharangrao quickly followed, still imagining the pretty sunset they never saw. 'Assemble in my chambers right now. Dinner can wait', he instructed Sharangrao as he closed the door.

Those who obey, learn to command.

They obeyed their Acharya's instructions 100 per cent. As a result, they had blossomed into fine leaders themselves. Chandragupta, Sharangrao, Nipunak, Akshay and Simharan sat with their eyes closed and their awareness on the breath. This was the normal practice when they waited for the Acharya. This kept their minds relaxed and focused in the present moment, a pre-requisite to be able to grasp the Acharya's unconventional thought process.

Chanakya emerged from his personal room and came to the meeting chamber. He sat down cross-legged on his bamboo aasan (seat) on the floor and chanted 'Aum' three times, a protocol he always followed when opening a meeting.

'It's time to claim Magadha. Our strategy shall be two-fold. Injure from inside and attack from outside.

Our ultimate goal is not just to capture Magadha but to bring the whole of Bharat under one rule as a single nation. Magadha is the first step. Patliputra is the centre of Magadha's power and politics but as I learnt today, we don't grab the centre directly; we start off with the edges.

Chandragupta — you, along with Simharan and your present troops will march towards Magadha. On the way, you have to win the allegiance, either by negotiation or by force, of all the smaller republics, incorporate their armies into yours and station your forces outside Magadha borders. I will correspond with the kings of Kaikey, Myanmar, Mallayrajya, Kalinga etc. and make them our allies.

The bigger challenge would be to break Dhanananda and his empire from within. I have a plan for that as well. Tomorrow, I leave for Patliputra. I shall keep sending you further instructions from time to time. Come, let's pray together for blessings from Maa Bharati', saying this, Chanakya invoked the Devi.

* * *

She dimmed the lights and lit the sandalwood incense sticks. The gentle drizzle outside added the perfect air of romance to the room. The royal suite of the pleasure garden was reserved for the finest display of sensuality and passion and she was a master at her craft. Dressed in a revealing dark blue sari, she had let her wet hair hang loose over her right shoulder. She delicately poured a glass of exquisite wine for her special guest tonight, the young prince, Dhananandaʼs son and the future king of the Magadha dynasty. She sipped the wine, looked deep into his eyes and then brought the glass to his thirsty lips. He gulped it down in one shot. Throwing the silver glass aside, he grabbed her from the waist and pulled her on top as he lay down on the rose-petalled bed.

She climbed over him, her ivory skin glowing in the dark. She bent over with her bosom on his chest, her silky hair on his face and locked lips with him in one long, wet passionate kiss. He surrendered completely into the arms of this celestial creature, experiencing a supreme state of carnal bliss.

Seconds later, he was dead.

She stepped back and watched with satisfaction as blood oozed out of his discoloured lips and his unblinking eyeballs kept staring at the roof. She checked his pulse to be sure her victim was lifeless. She then quickly took off the diamond ring from the princeʼs right hand, dipped it in a special ink and pressed it hard on the paper scroll. Putting the ring back where it belonged, she cleaned the stains and tied the scroll on her waistband. Like a smooth cat, she jumped out of the window and disappeared into the darkness. One hour later, bathed and changed into fresh clothes, she sat in front of her master — Chanakya.

The girl sitting in front of Chanakya was not a ganika (courtesan) the prince had mistaken her for. She was a Vishkanya, a trained poison damsel. Chanakya had a created an army of deadly female assassins called the Vishkanyas. Their training would begin in childhood. Chanakya's secret services would identify little girls, typically from modest families and with a horoscope that predicted early widowhood. They would be administered a carefully crafted concoction of poisonous herbs in small doses every day. Those who survived the initial training were graduated to higher dosages. By the time they were in puberty, they were completely immune to the deadliest poisons on the planet, including bites from the most venomous snakes, and their own bodily fluids were highly poisonous. They were now lethally toxic and ready for the kill. Such was the legendary skill of the Vishkanyas that just one kiss with minor exchange of saliva was enough to knock dead the strongest of men! Sometimes, they administered their fatal blows through carriers such as alcohol or food, and other times, a cobra-bite kiss.

In this case, the Vishkanya responsible for the prince's death was personally trained by Chanakya. She was one of his best with 100 per cent strike rate. She didn't have a name. Just a code. Taking the scroll from her, he asked her to rest. Although he was very pleased with her work, he didn't praise her. Chanakya never praised his best pupils. He opened the empty scroll and started writing a fake message.

* * *

The scroll reached its desired destination, the Prime Minister of Magadha (Amatya Rakshas). The letter was addressed to the commander-in-chief of the Magadha army. It stated the alliance between the prince and the commander-in-chief and detailed the preparations for the elimination of the Prime Minister. Chanakya carefully planted a mistake because of which the scroll accidentally fell in the hands of the Prime Minister. The royal seal of the prince's ring confirmed the undoubtable authenticity of the message.

Parallelly, the brilliant spy network that Chanakya had created in Patliputra informed Dhanananda about the murder of his dearest son and framed the innocent Prime Minister as the mastermind of this conspiracy.

Patliputra was frying in the fire of a civil war the very next day. The prince's and the Prime Minister's loyalists were up in arms, killing and exposing each other. And in the middle of this internal conflict and state of anarchy in the kingdom, news reached Dhanananda that Chandragupta had reached the Magadha borders with a massive army. An all-out attack could be expected anytime. The prince dead, the unstable king in mourning, the Prime Minister in revolt and a civil war raging in the country created ideal conditions for Chandragupta to challenge the might of Magadha.

In such a sensitive condition, Chanakya's final move on the chessboard was to convince a reputed Buddhist monk who was very dear to the king to advice him to willingly take up sanyasa (renunciation) and leave the running of the kingdom to the young and dynamic Chandragupta. As per Chanakya's guidance, the monk further convinced Dhananand to get his daughter married to Chandragupta as a political alliance, to ensure the safety of the royal family. This, in turn, ensured that Chandragupta would not be seen as an invader but rather welcomed by the masses of Magadha as their new monarch.

Without getting a single soldier killed, Chandragupta was invited to grace the throne of Magadha.

He remembered what Chanakya had once told him:

'Winning a war with bloodshed is the lowest form of political art!'

* * *

Chanakya walked unannounced into the personal chamber of the new emperor of Magadha — Chandragupta Maurya. Chandragupta jumped with joy and dismissed the meeting he was holding. He touched his Acharya's feet with the same joy and respect that he had the very first time when he had found his guru, his Acharya.

Today, in a grand ceremony, taking oath on the holy scriptures, he had been coronated as the emperor of Magadha, the most powerful kingdom in Asia and one of the largest in the whole world — all thanks to the short, dark Brahmin who stood in front of him. Chanakya was pleased to see the morpankh (peacock feather) embellished crown on his student's head. Chandragupta was relieved to see his Acharya's shikha finally knotted!

A teardrop rolled off his cheek and touched the feet of his Acharya. Chanakya held Chandragupta by the shoulders and lifting him to his feet, said in his trademark style:

'*Uthishtha Bharata* (Rise oh India). This is the day Maa Bharati has waited for. It's time to weave India into one single nation — Akhanda Bharat! And for you to achieve that goal, I have a special gift for you.'

'Oh, what is it Acharya'? asked Chandragupta with childlike enthusiasm.

Chanakya brought forth a beautifully gift-wrapped case and presented it to Chandragupta.

'Go ahead, open it', said Chanakya.

Chandragupta slowly and delicately opened the wooden case and took off the silk cover, his heart beating rapidly. When he realized what he held in his hands, he had goosebumps all over his body.

On a dark-red hardbound cover lay the gold-inscribed words which read 'Artha Shastra'.

This was what the Acharya had been working on for the past several decades. This was the distilled essence of everything Chanakya had thought and taught his entire life. This was the blueprint to running a kingdom, the most sacred treatise on statecraft, economics, strategy, governance and leadership. This was Chanakya's entire life in ink.

Chandragupta touched the holy text to his forehead and went and placed it with honour next to the idol of Lord Vishnu at his personal altar. He was visibly overwhelmed and at a loss of words. It was Chanakya who smiled and broke the silence.

> 'Oh king, the palace belongs to the regal. A teacher belongs to the classroom. I shall now return to my world of books and students. The torch is lit, the darkness is dispelled, good days are here. You must now carry on your journey and fulfil our mission. Some little Chandragupta might be playing with his friends in your kingdom right now, ensure he gets treated on merit, not caste, and ensure justice prevails.
>
> Although I am there to guide you whenever you need me, you really shall not need me as long as you follow the *Artha Shastra* to its sincere implementation.
>
> Yours and mine, our lives are measured but the legacy we leave behind is eternal. And when we meet the creator after death, we shall be asked only one question — were we true to our dharma every single day? May you find peace and moksha living your dharma. Maa Bharati shall light your way, my dear son and my beloved king!'

Before Chandragupta could make any attempts to stop him or say anything, Chanakya disappeared. He gifted his motherland the first truly nationalist identity in the form of the legendary Mauryan empire, which during its peak spread from Gandhar (Afghanistan) in the east to Myanmar in the west, and from Kashmir in the north to Godavari in the south, covering an area of five million kilometres.

Once in several eons walks a consciousness like Chanakya's on this planet. He had once put forth a pertinent question — you are proud of Mother India, but is Mother India proud of you? Time stands testimony to the answer.

GANDHAR
TAKSHASHILA
PAKISTAN
SINDHU (INDUS)
KASHI

KEY TAKEAWAYS

History has generously glorified descriptions of many great kings from time immemorial. History however speaks highly of only one **kingmaker** and that is Chanakya. Chanakya, in fact, overshadows the greatness of the kings he produces.

1. Mantra of Meritocracy

At a very tender age, his father is killed. He is ostracized by society. Instead of surrendering to fate like a coward, he decides to pursue higher education. He travels a thousand miles to the best university possible — the Takshashila. He has no money and no contacts. Based on his merit alone, he clears the interview and grabs himself a seat at the prestigious university. And he excels there, so much so that the university bends its rules and makes him a professor the very day he graduates. He is not a big fish in a small pond; he is the big fish in the biggest pond. His mantra is meritocracy. And even when he chooses his team, he only considers merit. Caste, creed, contacts have no relevance. He picks up an unknown boy literally from the streets of Patliputra and equips him with so merit that he becomes the emperor of India.

Let your merit be your mantra to success

Identify and reward merit in others

* * *

2. Being Unstoppable

Chanakya does not take 'no' for an answer.

He shall go to any extent to achieve his goal. He creates whatever he does not have. He does not have a worthy king, he makes one. He does not have an army, he creates one. He does not have money; he creates sources of funding. He needs unbeatable assassins, he creates them. Chanakya knows what he wants. And he keeps creating from scratch whatever he needs to get him to his goal. And that is how Chanakya, a lone teacher from a university, becomes the creator of the largest empire of India.

He does not change his goals based on his means.

A lot of times we settle for what we can get or we change our goals based on the means. And then we either regret it later or we convince ourselves that this is our destiny.

We tell ourselves 'why' we cannot achieve our goals instead of 'how' we can. Well, Chanakya makes his own destiny and he lives without regrets. He does not compromise. The world calls his goals unrealistic but he does not redefine his goals.

Don't tell me why you can't.
Tell me how you can.

* * *

3. Become Trainable

Those who obey learn to command.

An important lesson from Chandragupta Maurya:

Becoming someone trainable is a priceless skill. It takes immense amount of surrender and focus to undergo such tough training. It takes a special attitude to say, *'I am ready to go through the fire. Make me gold'*.

Becoming someone who can be trained is a definitive trait of a future leader.

Those who obey learn to command

* * *

4. Leading without Authority

There are three types of leaders:

a) Those who lead only when given authority/position (**Reactive Leader)**
b) Those who don't lead even after they are given authority/position (**Inactive Leader**)
c) Those who lead without any given authority/position (**Proactive Leader**)

Chanakya has no official position/title/authority. He is just a professor at a university. Yet, he leads the entire revolution against the Greeks and manages to conquer Magadha, the largest superpower in India at the time. He has no fancy office, no leadership overheads, no demands for credit and recognition, no business card. Chanakya reminds me of an old Sanskrit proverb:

नाभिषेको न संस्कार: सिंहस्य क्रियते वने

No one officially coronates the lion as the king of the jungle. No ceremony or rituals take place. Through his sheer might, the lion becomes the leader.

Such leaders are the most powerful ones and create a long-lasting impact. They lead from wherever they are.

They don't crib for lack of official positions. They take responsibility and make changes happen.

You can be a leader without authority/ position
Proactive Leader

* * *

5. Chanakya's Chatushtaya Upaayas for Strategic Influence

Chanakya has no room for emotions and yet he demonstrates a very high index of emotional intelligence. He understands the immense force emotions carry. And he uses this force in his favour and against his enemies. He also understands that emotions when backed by intellect are lethal — they can move heaven and earth. So, his underlying principle is:

Use your head to stir the right 'emotionollectual' (emotional + intellectual) response from others and victory is guaranteed!

He operates according to a powerful mix of his four principal Upaayas. The aim is to use emotional intelligence to strategically influence the other party/organization's behaviour:

The Four Upaayas are

1. Saam (peaceful persuasion)
2. Daam (prize/purchase)
3. Bhed (partition/polarize)
4. Dand (punish/penalize)

The Chatushtaya Upaayas

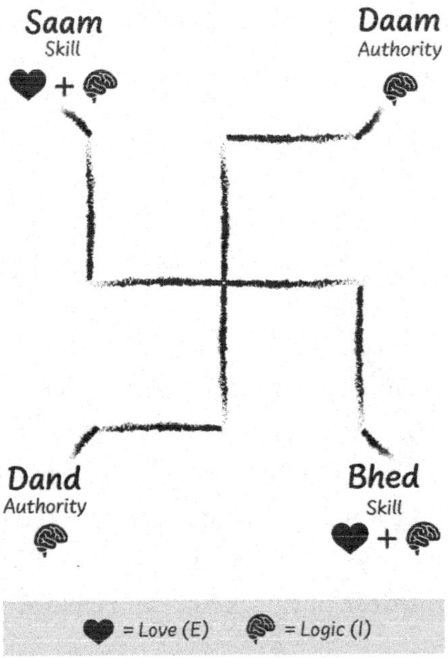

Saam: Peaceful Persuasion

This is where you try to persuade the other person/party by using feelings, peaceful diplomacy, and a careful mix of words. The formula here is 'love + logic'.

In this case, you use your head to kindle the emotional space and simultaneously an intellectual space in the other party. This is the perfect place to start any negotiation, no matter who is on the opposite side. This method helps you achieve what you want while protecting the relationship.

Strategy: peaceful persuasion

Positioning: other party is equal or higher to you

Orientation: people and skill based

Approach: love + logic

Role: counsellor/ well-wisher

Impact: emotion + intellect

This is when a boss tries to influence a team member to take up a new role, a team manager wants to convince another team manager to adjust their project deadlines, a country wants to build an alliance/friendship with another country, the seller wants to convince the buyer that their product/service is worth the price or a friend wants to make a buddy agree to the choice of holiday location. It's basically a **request** but backed with **reason.**

Daam: Price/Purchase

As the name suggests, this is when you try to influence the other party by offering a reward or an incentive. The reward/incentive may not be always monetary but it is definitely tangible and usually immediately granted (not some promise in the future). This is where you use your logic to invoke a strong feeling of greed in the other party. As the Godfather famously said, 'I shall make an offer he cannot refuse'.

Strategy: purchase

Positioning: other party is lower to you

Orientation: task and authority based

Approach: logic

Role: boss/manager

Impact: emotion (greed)

This is when the manager offers a salary hike/promotion to the employee for taking up the new role, politicians offer money/other benefits for votes, you offer to buy your friend lunch if he/she agrees to come along with you for the party/movie.

It's simple — if you do this, you get that.

Bhed: Partition/Polarize

This is a complicated and powerful strategy and must be used sparingly and skillfully.

'Bhed' means division, dissension, discord, partition, polarization or isolation. In this strategy, the influencer tries to weaken the other party by dividing their team, their ideologies and creating a bias, a sense of disharmony. You use your intellect to kindle strong emotions backed by powerful reasoning.

This is a high-risk high-reward strategy and must be used with skill and caution. The impact is long term.

Strategy: partition /polarize

Positioning: other party can be lower, equal or higher to you

Orientation: people and skill based

Approach: love + logic

Role: consultant or coach

Impact: emotion + intellect

Bhed can also mean that you divide your stakeholders into smaller groups, meet them separately to influence them and then achieve an overall consensus. To each group, you offer arguments and evoke emotions customized to them. You achieve consensus outside the boardroom.

Contrary to popular opinion, bhed does not mean finding out the secrets of the other party and blackmailing them.

Bhed can also mean convincing someone to act by invoking a particular sense of identity or purpose in them.

For example, terrorists who are not persuaded by peaceful talk (saam), monetary rewards (daam), threat of punishment (dand) can be influenced by bhed (inspiring by an extreme ideology to commit the act of terror). The same applies to soldiers, social workers, spiritual seekers or passionate entrepreneurs. They are made to feel that they are different, unique or special. Most of them don't operate from greed, fear or sweet talk. They operate from a strong sense of identity/commitment to a cause which is fuelled by bhed. The influencer needs to encourage or break down an ideology/a sense of identity for bhed to work.

Dand: Punish/Penalize

The last option is Dand.

As the name suggests, here you threaten the other party with possible punishments. The punishment can be of any nature but should be severe enough to obtain compliance from the other party. The golden rule here is — *threaten more, punish less*. But threaten only when you have a genuine power to punish or at least a 'perceived' power to punish. This means that the other party should feel that you indeed have the power to punish. The success of this method lies in a strong threat and not actual punishment. However, sometimes, a punishment might be required for setting the right precedent for future negotiations.

Strategy: punish

Positioning: other party is lower to you

Orientation: task and authority based

Approach: logic

Role: CEO/king/law enforcement officer/police

Impact: emotion (fear)

This is where the boss threatens of legal and future career consequences if their offer is denied by the employee, where heads of states issue warnings of forceful actions, where a business party threatens of possible negative impact on other business deals if this offer is not accepted, where you threaten emotional/other consequences to your friend for not agreeing to your suggestions. *This is simple — if you don't do this, then I shall do that or If you don't do this, I shall also not do that.*

In the famous example from Ramayan, Lord Ram requests (uses saam) the God of the Ocean to give way to him and his monkey army so that they can cross the ocean and go to Lanka. For three days, Lord Ram requests but the ocean does not budge. On the fourth day, Lord Ram invokes a celestial weapon that can dry up the entire ocean and instantly the Lord of the Ocean appears, apologizes and cooperates. This incident gives rise to the popular quote:

भय बिन होए ना प्रीती

(Without fear, there is no cooperation/friendship.)

Important

Now, it's interesting to ponder on how you would respond if you were on the receiving end of these Upaayas. Note that you are also free to use the Upaayas. If someone is playing a daam on you to make you agree to something which you don't want to do, you can play a saam in response or a mild bhed in response.

These four Upaayas may not be always in sequence, although it is recommended to always use saam first and dand last. Also, an influencer might need to use all in varying proportions to win over a single negotiation.

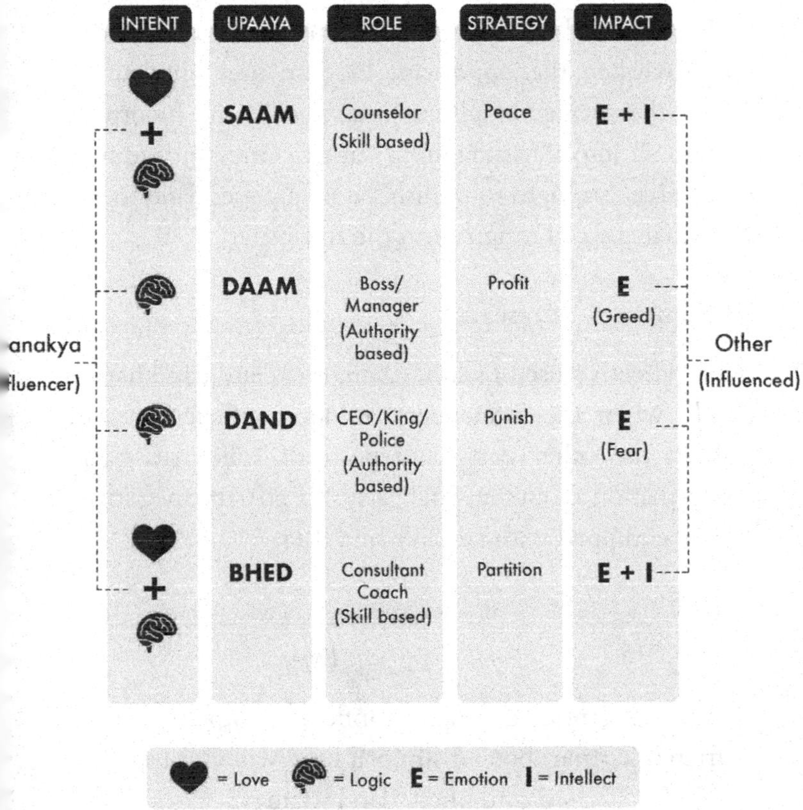

Chanakya Uses the Upaayas

He first attempts to explain this to Dhanananda using saam. No impact. Then, he decides to make Chandragupta the emperor and expunge Dhanananda. For this, he uses daam on several occasions with people who are greedy. He uses bhed to create disharmony in the enemy camp and weaken the opponent. He also uses bhed to win over the smaller kingdoms individually and incorporate them all into Chandragupta's army. Once he acquires a perceived strength to punish, he finally uses dand to force Dhanananda to resign from the throne.

Importance of research

The effective use of saam, daam, bhed and dand happens only when the influencer has done sufficient research about the other party and possesses solid data-backed information about the other party. So, go to the negotiation table equipped with research and data.

Manthan

Pause. Introspect. Express.

1. Next time you want to influence someone (your friend, partner, boss or junior), how will you use saam, daam, bhed, dand strategy?

2. Do you typically do enough research on the other person/party before you get into the negotiation/influencing zone?

3. Can you develop the skill of anticipating what the other person/party would respond with when you deploy different strategies? Do you have a counter response/offer ready?

4. The next time someone is trying to influence you, would you be able to read through their strategy and plan your response accordingly?

* * *

5. The Sthitapragya Model of Leadership

Balancing the Opposites

The world is full of dualities. We live in an ocean of opposing forces and creating a bridge over these troubled waters is the hallmark of a leader. Ancient civilizations saw the world as a manifestation of dual primary energies — the Shiva and the Shakti, the Yin and the Yang, the masculine and the feminine, the Purusha and the Prakriti.

Any leader today needs to strike the delicate balance between opposites and skillfully walk the razor's edge to success, both professionally and personally. Chanakya does it beautifully. He remains centred in the most challenging war of the opposites. He knows when to use the head and when to use the heart. He knows when to invoke the Shiva and when to invoke the Shakti. He does this effortlessly and hence creates sustainable growth. He loves order but is comfortable with chaos, he is a recluse (Shiva or Hara) internally but engages with all kinds of people externally (Vishnu or Hari), he sometimes embodies Lord Ram (maryada or rule-following) and sometimes Lord Krishna (leela or rule-breaking). He has a million shades to his complex personality.

- Every man has a little bit of a woman inside him. Every woman has a little bit of a man inside her. We need to create businesses and organizations that celebrate both qualities and strike the right balance. The right balance is in identifying and acknowledging uniqueness instead of forcing equality. In this model of leadership lies the empowerment of humanity.

The Sthithapragya leader

Centre-Forward

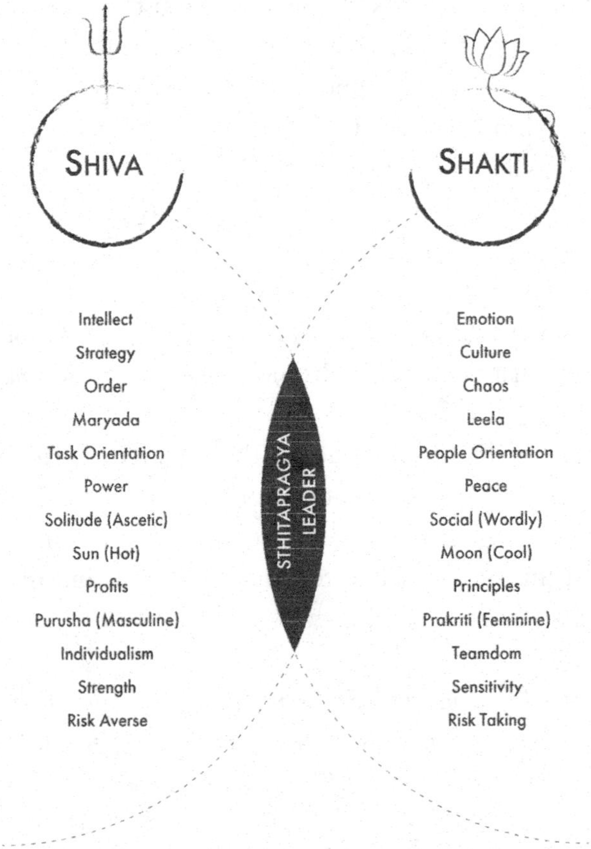

In the beginning of a relationship, career, business or a new role, as an individual contributor — life is simple. You generally have only one perspective to handle, one boss to please, one primary stakeholder. But as you grow and progress, and more so when you come into a leadership position, you realize the world has changed a lot. You now have many stakeholders and must accommodate diverse perspectives. At this point, the dilemma of choices is strong. There are opposing forces pulling you. Now you need to demonstrate the rare ability of managing the opposites and staying centred.

Chanakya remains centred and aware under all circumstances (**Sthithapragya**). *Only if you are centred, you can move forward!*

He never gets carried away. He is Captain Cool and yet takes hard decisions. His motto is — *keep calm and win the war!*

He might act on one of the Shiva or Shakti-like qualities in a particular situation as a deliberate move but always returns to his default state, centred and calm. That is his biggest secret to thinking clearly and making brilliant strategic decisions.

The ability to use both Shiva and Shakti qualities is ***skill****.*
Knowing which one to use when is ***intelligence.***
Coming back to the default centred state is ***wisdom.***

Chanakya or the wise leader also knows that ultimately, the totality is beyond duality and so at some point, one has to rise beyond the apparent duality and take refuge in the invisible totality.

Manthan

Pause. Introspect. Express.

Are you comfortable dealing with the opposites mentioned above?

Sthitapragya Leader

Questionnaire

Below is a questionnaire you can take to understand yourself more in light of the Sthitapragya discussion we had above. This questionnaire is made by the author and is representative purely of the authors views alone.

Please answer the questions below for yourself in an honest, unbiased way.

Never Sometimes Always

1. 2. 3. 4. 5.

Sr. No	Statement	Score
1	I think of long-term implications of my actions before I act.	
2	I take decisions based on emotions and how they will affect other people.	
3	I function best in a systematic, structured environment.	

Sr. No	Statement	Score
4	My higher focus is to get the task done.	
5	I am very comfortable with risks.	
6	I like to be honest and straightforward in my communication with people. I speak my mind directly.	
7	I like to work by myself; my own ideas and thoughts energize me.	
8	I believe rules should be broken and changed when needed.	
9	I believe in standardization and consistency so that there is predictability.	
10	I believe in clearly defined power and authority equations for best results.	
11	I think achievements are not dependent on my efforts alone; so I put my effort and then happily surrender to God.	
12	It is important for me to not hurt anyone's sentiments when I am communicating with them.	
13	I believe in open-ended and flexible power equations for best results.	
14	I feel customization and organic adaption helps me achieve best results.	
15	I believe conflicts should be left to time and they will ultimately resolve themselves.	
16	I believe in following the rules, no matter what the situation is.	

Sr. No	Statement	Score
17	I am most comfortable working with a group of people; interaction with them energizes me.	
18	I am at my best working in a free-flowing, fluid environment.	
19	My higher focus is to take care of people and their emotions.	
20	I take rational decisions based on logic and data.	
21	I believe in resolving conflict through direct confrontation and clear communication.	
22	I don't like taking risks.	
23	I believe I am responsible for achieving whatever I need with my efforts.	
24	I take care of immediate short-term implications of my actions before I act.	

How to score: mention the scores of the individual questions as marked below:

Shiva Score Questions:	Shakti Score Questions:
1:	2:
3:	8:
4:	11:
5:	12:
6:	13:
7:	14:
9:	15:
10:	17:
16:	18:
20:	19:
21:	22:
23:	24:

Total Shiva score: ____ (Add up all the points of the Shiva questions.)
Total Shakti score: ____ (Add up all the points of the Shakti questions.)

Plot your score

On x-axis, plot your total Shakti score and on y-axis, plot your total Shiva score.

Interpreting Your Score and Graph

The Quadrants

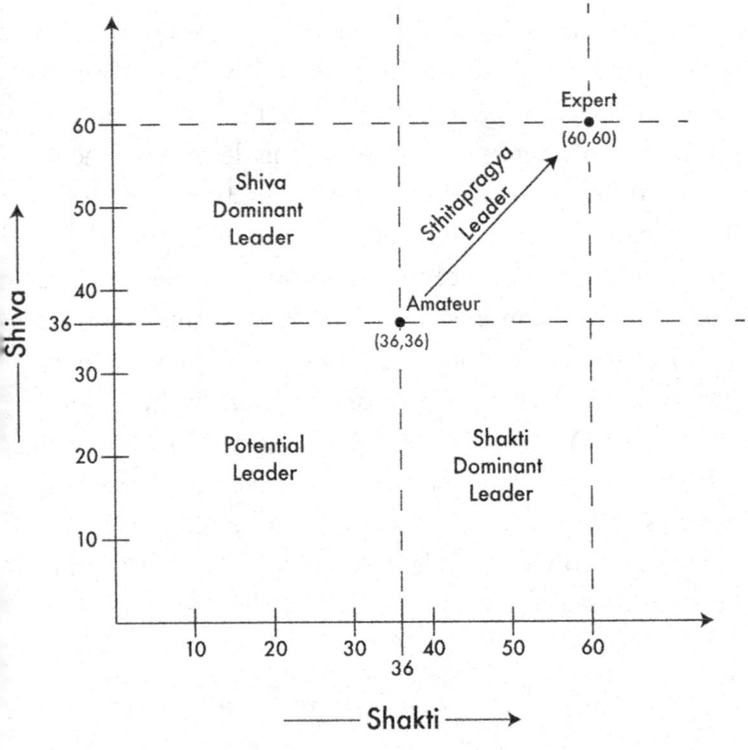

The Sthitapragya Leader Quadrant

If both your Shiva score and Shakti score are above 36, then you enter the 'Sthitapragya Leader' quadrant. Congratulations. It's an honour and a responsibility.

This means that you have high amounts of both Shiva and Shakti leadership qualities. This also means that you know when to use more of Shiva and when to use more of Shakti qualities.

If your score is say 37,37 then you have just entered the Sthitapragya Leader quadrant. You can look at yourself as an amateur Sthitapragya Leader. What you need to do is grow and develop this leadership more. Also you have to ensure you don't slip back when new challenges come your way. If you are in the middle of the quadrant, then you need to maintain your position and keep growing upwards. There is room for improvement.

If you are at the top of the quadrant, the responsibility on your shoulders is to train others and help them climb the ladder. You role is now that of a mentor, a coach. When you are at the peak, what will give you satisfaction and a sense of purpose is training others and sharing with the world how you made it to the top. This is the time for succession planning.

Leaders don't just create more followers; they create more *leaders*!

Shiva Leader Quadrant

For the sake of discussion of this theory, we consider the term 'Shiva' as not the universal Lord Shiva or the Shiva tattva as understood in spirituality but more so a representation of a set of qualities such as intellect, power, objectivity, masculinity, order, rule-following, risk averseness, task orientation. If you are in this quadrant, you lead based on dominant Shiva qualities and you need to now develop more of Shakti qualities.

Shakti Leader Quadrant

Shakti here does not denote the omnipotent, omniscient Devi but is a representation of a set of qualities such as emotion, femininity subjectivity, love, care, people orientation, ability to handle chaos etc. If you are in this quadrant, you lead based on dominant Shakti qualities and you need to now develop more of Shiva qualities.

Potential Leader Quadrant

If you are in the Potential Leader quadrant (both Shiva and Shakti scores are below 36), the good news is you have identified where you are and where you want to go, and that's a huge first step. Start moving with sincere conscious effort, your quadrant will change soon.

Saraansh

A summary of learnings from this chapter

1.
Mantra of Meritocracy

2.
Be Unstoppable

3.
Become Trainable

4.
Chatushtaya Upaayas for Strategic Influence:
(saam, daam, bhed, dand)

5.
Learn to lead without authority/position

6.
Don't change your goal based on your means

7.

Don't tell me why you can't.
Tell me how you can.

8.

Sthitapragya Leader (Centre-Forward)

9.

Balance the Opposites

10.

नाभिषेको न संस्कारःसिंहस्य क्रियते वने

(No one coronates the lion as king in the jungle.)

11.

| स्वदेशे पूज्यते राजा विद्वान सर्वत्र पूज्यते|

The king is worshipped only in his kingdom, but a wise scholar is worshipped everywhere.

5

Hanuman Uvacha

'Monkeys are very proud of their tails I hear . . . '

He took a deep breath in and inhaled the ocean once again. The ocean roared and invited him, rather challenged him. *How would he go to the other side?* But go he must, for this was not the time to be faint-hearted!

'Hanuman', called his friend Angad, 'Let's go Hanuman, Lord Ram awaits us in his chambers'. Gathered around the massive Natraja statue in the royal chambers, the members of the Vaanar Sena (monkey army) were sitting in deep contemplation. Who would be the one to fly across the ocean and convey the message of their beloved Lord Ram to his wife, Maa Sita? As Hanuman entered the room, all eyes turned to him. Deep inside, Hanuman knew this was his calling. He was born for this very day. And so, he smiled and let out in his thunderous voice their famous war cry *'Jai Shri Ram'* (Victory to Lord Ram).

Equipped with the strength of a thousand elephants, blessed by the God of the Wind, Vayu, and with the grace of Lord Ram, Hanuman did the impossible — he flew over 100 yojanas (approximately 1,300 km) of the ocean to set foot in Lanka, the land of pure gold, the abode of the demon king Raavan. His mission was as clear as the rays of sun on his gada (the mace) — to convey Lord Ram's message to Maa Sita, to meet Raavan and then fly back. Simple. Yet he had a strange intuition that he was going to have a very adventurous trip.

* * *

Many hours had passed since Hanuman landed at the Lankan shores. There was not one dull moment in these hours.

Presently, Hanuman stood shackled in chains inside the royal court, awaiting an audience with Raavan.

'Lo and behold, oh Rakshas Raj (king of demons), we have captured the vaanar (ape) who destroyed your beautiful Ashok Vatika (garden) and killed your son, the great Akshay Kumar', said the guards as they presented Hanuman in Raavan's royal court.

The royal palace of Lanka was unlike anything Hanuman had ever seen in his life. It was an architectural marvel created by the legendary architect, Vishwakarma. Seated on a shining throne of glittering diamonds, atop a flight of intricately carved stairs, sat the emperor of Lanka, the conqueror of the world, the mighty Raavan! On either side of his throne stood two massive lions made of spotless white stone and exactly opposite Raavan, at the other end of the court room, stood a humongous 30-feet high statue of Lord Shiva in the Ardhanareshwar (half male, half female God) form. That Raavan was an ardent Shiva devotee was common knowledge.

But why was Hanuman imprisoned?

Well, once he landed in Lanka, Hanuman immediately got to business. With a quick aerial survey, he located Sita Maa, who was held captive in the beautiful Ashok Vatika. Hanuman had anticipated that Sita Maa may not believe that he was indeed Lord Ram's messenger, and so he was carrying an irrefutable proof of authenticity — Lord Ram's finger ring. After meeting Sita Maa and giving her the much-needed assurance that Lord Ram, Laxman and the entire Vaanar Sena would soon come to rescue her, Hanuman unleashed himself to feast on the delicious fruits of the garden. When the guards attacked him, he swiftly erased them like he would a bunch of bananas. The complaint was escalated to Prince Akshay Kumar, one of Raavan's sons, who came to capture Hanuman but lost his life instead. Finally, Raavan's eldest son, the supremely powerful Indrajit had to come to take Hanuman captive and present him to Raavan for suitable punishment.

Raavan looked at Hanuman standing in the royal court, several chains bound around his body. Raavan's eyes burned with anger and the desire for revenge. He missed noticing the glow on Hanuman's face, the total lack of fear in his stance, the ocean of knowledge in his eyes and the power of the gods in his aura! In the Bhagvad Gita, Lord Krishna tells Arjuna, '*Anger clouds judgement and deludes the intellect, which ultimately destroys the man*'.

And the biggest misfortune for a leader is to live in a bubble of adulation, surrounded by ministers who praise the king unconditionally, pushing him down a dungeon of arrogance and complacency. And so, noticing that

King Raavan was craving revenge for his lost son, the brave Indrajit suggested that Hanuman's head be severed immediately, for no lesser penalty shall suffice the degree of his crime.

To this Hanuman smiled.

Said the king of Lanka, 'Who are you, monkey? On whose command have you destroyed the beautiful Ashok Vatika and killed my beloved son Akshay Kumar? Have you not heard with your monkey ears the tales of Raavan's glory, have you no fear of death that you dare to displease the Lankesh *(*The God of Lanka*)*'?

'Listen, oh great Raavan', said Hanuman in a calm, confident voice, 'With whose might and intention the universes are created and dissolved, with whose strength Brahma (the creator), Vishnu (the sustainer) and Shiva (the transformer) carry on their respective roles, with an iota of whose might the three worlds can be captured — know me to be his envoy. My name is Hanuman, and I am Vayu Putra (the son of the Lord of the Winds). I have surely heard your glory tales, especially the one where the great monkey king Bali carried you in his armpit for six months'.

Raavan was stunned by this introduction. He concealed his rising curiosity and concern in a smirk and brushed off Hanuman's comments.

Hanuman continued, 'As far as eating the fruits of the garden is concerned, I had flown over the ocean and was hungry. To nourish the body is deh-dharma (the duty of the body) and hence I ate the fruits. When your guards attacked me, in self-defence, I killed them and your son'.

'Oh, mighty king of the demons, pray listen to me further', continued Hanuman, now changing the tone of his voice and his stance.

'Prabhu (lord), your bravery and power are unmatched in the whole world, your wisdom equals that of a thousand pundits, you carry the scriptures on your tongue, you have pleased Lord Brahma and Lord Rudra to bestow many boons on you and bless you with incredible powers and weapons. You are the epitome of fearlessness, a master of war strategy and have conquered even the devtaas (gods). Your kingdom is the richest in the whole world and your subjects are happy and healthy.'

Raavan smiled.

'I pray to you with joined palms, my respectful lord, please don't let this kingdom and its people suffer just because of your deluded attraction to someone else's wife. It is but a mental fog that has clouded your vision, shrug it off and see the truth of dharma. Oh Dashanana (the ten-headed one), please think of your generations to come and your pious ancestor — Sage Pulastya, and please let Maa Sita respectfully go back to her husband, Sri Ram. Do not bring upon yourself and your lineage permanent destruction, which shall indeed happen if you choose to fight with Lord Ram. Even Kaala (the Lord of Time) and Yama (the Lord of Death) tremble in front of him, and even Brahma, Vishnu and Mahesh cannot defeat him in any form of combat, let alone an ordinary king like you.'

Raavan's smile disappeared.

Said the Lankesh in a thunder, 'Listen oh shatt (fool), you seem to have no awareness about my powers and secret boons and yet you speak like some great guru! It's amazing that even shallow species like apes come to my royal court and speak like pundits! There is nobody in this entire cosmos who can defeat or kill me, such is the unchallengeable boon I have received from Lord Rudra himself'.

Said Hanuman then, 'You did receive the boon from Lord Rudra but looks like you have forgotten the clauses of that special boon, ahankaari (the egoist) Raavan. I recommend you go and read up the contract again. In that boon, you have been exempted from getting killed by all species or life-forms except two — nar and vanar (human and ape). Right now, I am in the ape form and let me tell you, I hold the power to deliver you to death right this moment. But since I am here as a messenger of Lord Ram, I do not have the authorization to kill you. And remember that Lord Ram, an avatar of Narayan himself, is currently in the form of a human being and hence your boon shall not save you from him'.

Raavan's jaw dropped and fists tightened in anger at the realization of Hanuman's words.

How does this ape know all this?

'Lord Ram is compassion incarnate and shall surely forgive your grave crime of kidnapping Maa Sita if you go and surrender yourself and ask for pardon at his feet. It's not too late even now. In a moment of delusion, you took this irrational decision of abducting Maa Sita but now that you realize your mistake, take Sita Maa back to her rightful place with dignity, seek apology and save your clan.'

'Once again, oh Lankesh, I request you to avoid war and let peace prevail. Return Sita Maa and continue ruling this great nation. Else, be prepared to die! This is my final warning to you', roared Hanuman.

A deafening silence engulfed the royal court. No one moved an inch. No one had seen Raavan spoken to like this, let alone surrender to anyone. Indrajit was furious and wanted to kill Hanuman right that moment. Hanuman had insulted and threatened Raavan in his very court. This was unprecedented.

'You seem to be in a hurry to die, foolish monkey, and so be it. Kill him!' Raavan ordered the guards to severe Hanuman's head immediately.

'Wait!'

'Oh Rakshas Raj, my lord, may I say something with your kind permission'? said Vibheeshan, the younger half-brother of Raavan, and the only one in the Rakshas clan who was an ardent devotee of Lord Ram and on the side of dharma. Raavan had always disliked Vibheeshan and considered him a traitor and a coward. But since he was a legit minister in the court, he was allowed to voice his opinion.

'I see no advantage in killing this ape. To me, this monkey man seems like a mere messenger and killing the doot (messenger) is against raj-dharma (the law of the rulers) and neeti shastra (the law of order/justice). We must punish the monkey for sure but maybe administer a different kind of a punishment.' The council of ministers nodded and Raavan reluctantly agreed to this wise advice, much to the disappointment of Indrajit.

'All right then. Monkeys have a lot of pride and love for their tails. It's said that the tail is the ornament of the monkey. Set his tail on fire so he and his master understand the humiliation that shall come their way if they dare to challenge then Lankesh. This is my final order.' Raavan rose and the stormed out of the court.

What happened next would haunt Raavan and the entire Rakshas clan for generations to come. As per Raavan's command, the demon army surrounded Hanuman, covered his tail with a piece of cloth soaked in oil, and set his tail on fire. Much to the surprise of the demons, Hanuman cooperated fully for he already had a plan, and the demons were only making his task easier.

As soon as they set his tail ablaze, Hanuman thundered '*Jai Shri Ram*', and with one strong jerk of his hands, he broke the iron chains that shackled him. Before the

Lankan guards could even react, Hanuman leapt up and reached the top of the Lankan fort wall.

And then, the unimaginable unfolded.

Hanuman burnt down the entire city of Lanka. Fort walls, the city centre, the office complexes, everything. Even Raavan's own palace was not spared. The exquisitely beautiful and grand golden Lanka came down in ashes and rumble, along with Raavan's massive ego.

* * *

KEY TAKEAWAYS

1. The Art of Introduction

Did you notice how Hanuman introduces himself?

Hanuman lets Raavan speak first since it's his territory. As expected, Raavan asks Hanuman to introduce himself. This part is crucial.

How should Hanuman introduce himself?

Hanuman intelligently choses to first introduce his master and then himself. He chooses the highest praises possible for Lord Ram, establishing indirect credibility for his own self. It's like if you work for a top global company, the name and logo of the company on your business card is what gets you entry into closed doors, not your individual name. And a smart executive is aware of this. However, if the messenger appears too weak then the other party shall not take him seriously and so he must come across as fearless and brave too. Since Raavan threatens Hanuman in the opening remark, Hanuman uses humour to counter Raavan by making a mocking comment about Bali defeating Raavan in a battle.

And only in the end, Hanuman answers the mundane question about why he ate the fruits of the garden. Had Hanuman begun by explaining why he ate the fruits, his opening statements would not have carried the weight they did and would have made him defensive right at the start of the conversation.

A skilled communicator selects the sequence of his words carefully.

Manthan

Pause. Introspect. Express.

How do you introduce yourself? Do you have a nice introduction ready? This is one of the most-asked questions to us and yet we rarely have a good introduction ready for use.

(Do it now)

Write a five-line introduction of yourself.

Here are a few tips:

The ICCI Rule

Your introduction must be **Impressive.**
Your introduction needs to gain you **Credibility.**
Your introduction should be **Customized** to the audience.
Your introduction should be **Interesting.**

* * *

2. KYC: Know Your Competitor

Value of Research

The most interesting part of this conversation is where Raavan tells Hanuman of the boon he has received that makes him indestructible. To this, Hanuman responds by pointing specific clauses in the boon that do not exempt Raavan's death by both Hanuman (an ape) and Lord Ram (a human). Hanuman knows everything about Raavan. On the other hand, Raavan knows nothing about Hanuman and worse, is not asking the right questions either.

When we want to negotiate or influence, it is critical to have done your homework so thoroughly that you know the opponent better than the opponent knows himself/herself. You need to have access to information that can shatter the confidence of the opponent.

A quote by Desmond Totu captures this essence completely:

Don't raise your voice; improve your argument!

Specific information or statistics, or data-driven comments said in a poised and calm manner, can cause more devastation than screaming insults and threats. If you are on the receiving end of such an argument, know that either your opponent is smart and diligent, or there is a leak in your own tank that the opponent is exploiting. Raavan is blinded by his ego and arrogance, like the CEO of a multinational company with a major market share who is unwilling to acknowledge the competitor's power and intelligence.

Manthan

Pause. Introspect. Express.

Think of a person/entity you consider as your competition. Do you know everything you need to know about your competition? Where can you find out more?

* * *

Communication Skills

3. Climate Controlling a Conversation

A skilled communicator/negotiator knows the art of changing the feel and temperature of the conversation.

After the initial unpleasant opening, Hanuman begins his speech afresh by singing praises of Raavan's fame and bravery. Raavan smiles and this changes the air in the royal court. One aspect of communication is intellectual, and the other is emotional. Hanuman now touches a chord with emotion, and what better way than to praise the opponent. He throws Raavan off-guard by praising him, manages to get his emotional attention and surprises his loyal ministers too.

Tough conversations often create an air of bitterness and discomfort. It's a priceless skill to know how to diffuse the tension and change the environment to pick up the dialogue again instead of allowing it to go towards a deadlock. It's important to get the other party into a listening mode, and that happens when you do climate control.

* * *

4. The Club Sandwich Model

Layered Communication

Hanuman's communication is layered, or what we like to call the 'club sandwich model' of communication. The model basically requires the principal communicator to adopt different layers (techniques) — some positive and some negative.

One typically opens with a layer (say the top bread) of positive communication. This raises the spirits of the listener and creates a positive vibe. Then the patty/cheese/veggies form different layers as per need. And usually, the end is again a layer (bottom bread) of positivity to leave the receiver on an optimistic note. However, there is no set formula for this. If you think it necessary, you can even have the last layer as a threat or a suggestion.

The essence is that in tough conversations like this one, the communicator needs to have the skill to keep mixing an array of layers to portray a range of emotions, and use different permutations and combinations of praise, power, threat, challenge, request, satire and friendliness.

After praising Raavan to the seventh heavens (climate control), Hanuman switches gears and brings forth elements of power and threat into the conversation. You can give the opponent an illusion of a temporary advantage in the conversation but should know to pull back the reins in your control quickly. By suddenly changing his stance and the tone of his voice, addressing Raavan as 'ahankari' instead of 'prabhu' and 'Dashanana', Hanuman threatens Raavan to not mess with the almighty Lord Ram and prevent the collapse of his kingdom.

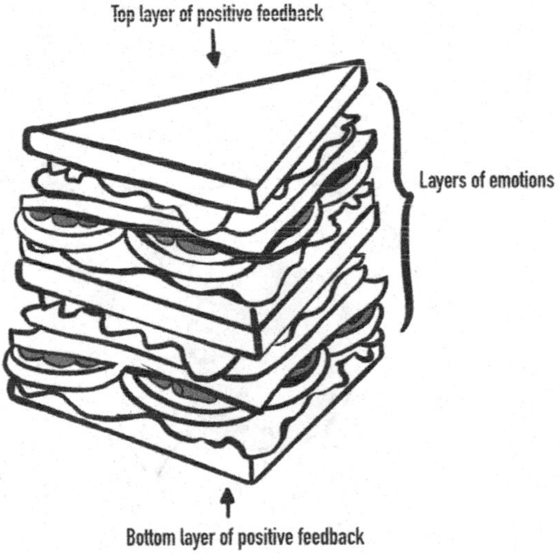

* * *

5. Negotiation Zone

We are negotiating all the time!

The next time you are getting ready for a negotiation meeting, whether it is formal or informal, whether it is with a business partner or your child, ensure you have thought through the following six questions:

1. Where do I stand right now?
2. What do I want?
3. What am I willing to give up?
4. Where does the other person/party stand right now?
5. What does the other person/party want?
6. What would he/she/they be willing to give up?

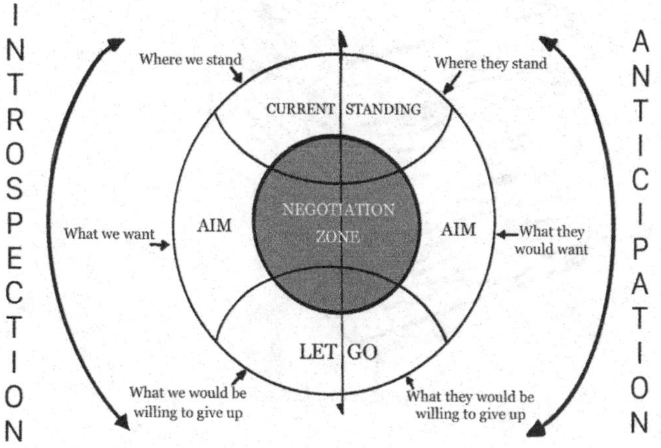

These six questions help you create what is known as the 'Negotiation Zone'. Initially, you would need to do this exercise consciously. After a few times, this method of thinking would become internalized, and you will do it automatically. Asking yourself these questions really brings clarity in your mind and helps you take the negotiation to the next level — call to action.

Note: Read Chanakya's Chatushtaya Upaayas for strategic influence in the Chanakya chapter of this book.

Manthan

Pause. Introspect. Express

Do you have an important negotiation conversation coming up soon? Sit down and write the answers to these six questions. Once done, observe how you feel more prepared and confident. Can you make these six questions a part of your thinking process?

6. Communication Styles

We all have difficult conversations/negotiations on a daily basis. Most people fall into one of the following communication styles:

1. **Aggressive** (I win, you lose)
2. **Submissive** (I lose, you win)
3. **Assertive** (I win, you win)
4. **Regressive** (I lose, you lose)

The most desired yet the rarest style is 'assertive'. Hanuman displays an assertive communication style. In assertive communication, you are polite but firm, you negotiate hard but remain logical and centred, you are clear on your boundaries and respect the other person/party, you know when to say 'no', you don't change *what* you say, but *how* you say it. In this style, you strive for a win-win situation by maximizing your own odds to get what you want. For assertive communication, we need emotional intelligence.

Being assertive does not guarantee success at the negotiation attempt. You are aiming for a win-win but the other party may or may not come from the same space.

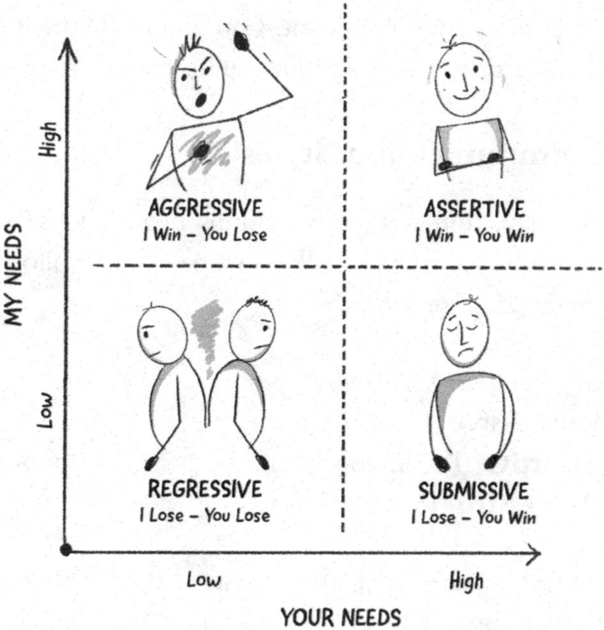

Manthan

Pause. Introspect. Express.

Who do I typically have tough conversations with?
My boss, business-partner, my teacher, my life partner,
my colleague?

How can I be more assertive in my communication
with them? How can I skillfully say 'no'
when I want to?

* * *

7. Emotional Intelligence

Emotional Intelligence (EI) is the game changer if you want to be successful in your professional and personal life. According to Daniel Goleman, EI consists of the following four domains:

1. Understanding your own emotions (introspection)
2. Managing your own emotions (self-management)
3. Understanding someone else's emotions (empathy)
4. Managing someone else's emotions (influence)

You will notice that Hanuman exhibits high levels of EI in the way he handles the conversation with Raavan (and Sita too, although we haven't covered that in this chapter). The more emotionally intelligent we become, the easier it will be to manoeuver difficult conversations and situations.

Note: In the other stories in this book, you will observe that all leaders indeed demonstrate high levels of emotional intelligence, be it Chanakya, Chhatrapati Shivaji Maharaj, Rani Abbakka or Kabir.

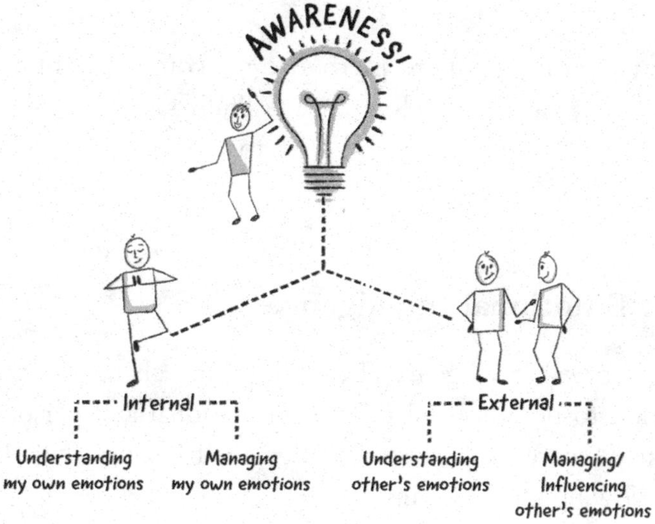

How to Increase Emotional Intelligence

I did my PhD on studying the impact of meditation on emotional intelligence and, in turn, the impact of emotional intelligence on leadership abilities and entrepreneurial abilities.

I found, and there are other studies which conclude similarly, that meditation and breathwork practices (we used the SKY — Sudarshan Kriya Yoga technique for our study) have a positive impact on EI and can significantly enhance EI. Thus, one of the easiest and most concrete ways to enhance EI is by adopting a practice of meditation.

So, a sure-shot way to increase EI is to

BREATHE & MEDITATE

Literally, taking a few deep breaths in moments when you are experiencing a storm of emotions can change the way you perceive the situation and deal with it. And regular meditation will not allow your mind to come to a tipping point of emotional imbalance.

Hanuman is *Pavan Putra* — the son of the wind. Hanuman represents the vital force of breath in us and points us to using this force to become emotionally resilient just like him.

DIY (Do It Yourself)

Every morning, before you kick-start your day and each night before you go to bed, take a few deep breaths and sit for ten minutes in a quiet space of introspection and meditation. Do this for at least ten days.
See what changes.

* * *

Saraansh

Summary of Learnings from this chapter

1.
The art of introduction
(The ICCI Rule)

2.
KYC (Know Your Competitor)

3.
Climate Controlling a Conversation

4.
The Sandwich Model

5.
The Negotiation Zone

6.
Assertive Communication Style (Win-Win)

7.
Don't raise your voice, improve your argument

8.
Emotional intelligence

9.
Ways to increase EI — breathe and meditate

6

The Narada Diaries

'Narayan Narayan'

His sweet voice accompanied by the strums of the veena (musical instrument) echoed in the forests. When he sang, the trees danced along and the birds joined the chorus. He was a festival on the move, a presence that this creation cherished. For him, every moment was a celebration and every breath an invocation of the Lord. Wherever he walked, the earth stood scented and the skies looked a deeper blue. Thousands of years ago, time had witnessed this splendid phenomenon called Narada, the one who was intoxicated in devotion to his creator, singing uninterrupted praises of the Lord almighty. Titled as Devarishi (the Divine Sage), he was one of a kind.

Narada Muni was a cosmos trotter, constantly travelling across the various lokas (realms) inhabited by their respective beings. He was the first 'Yellow Pages' of the world. He was a messenger and a messiah, a friend and a seer, a young monk with ancient wisdom. In him, the deepest knowledge of the Vedas blended effortlessly with the naughtiness of a child, the intelligence of all creation merged beautifully with the innocence of devotion. For him, the only reality was that nothing is real, and life is leela or the play of consciousness — so why should one take life so seriously?

The word 'Narada' itself is so beautiful. It is the spoke that joins the circumference to the centre. One who holds you to the centre is Narada. Often, love and devotion decentres you. It throws you off-balance, makes you emotionally and physically weak. Love and devotion are the greatest strengths of humankind, and yet without wisdom, the same love makes you vulnerable and weak. That is why people hurt themselves in love.

Narada is the one who holds you to the centre and yet makes you rise to the pinnacle of love and wisdom.

* * *

Story One

Enlightenment

One day, dressed in his trademark red dhoti and wearing a garland of fresh mogras (jasmine), with his famous veena in one hand and a khartal (wooden hand-clapper) in the other, he was travelling through the dense forests, fearless of the ferocious animals that lived in them. Suddenly, he saw something that made him halt in his tracks. Under a massive banyan tree sat an old sadhu covered in the holy ash and lost in a deep state of meditation. He looked as ancient as the tree, his locks almost touching the ground. Suddenly, Narada heard a voice.

'Pranam Devarishi! What brings you to this forgotten path today?'

His eyes were still closed. His lips did not seem to move. Narada smiled. Mystics always amused him. Politely, he said,

'Oh holy sadhu. Pranam. I am passing through the forest this day on my way to Vaikuntha, the abode of Lord Vishnu. Is there anything you would like to ask the Lord? I could take your message', offered Narada.

'Oh yes! When you meet the Lord, can you please ask Him how much longer I would need to wait for enlightenment? I have been meditating in this very spot for the last three decades.'

'Sure. I shall ask your question. I take your leave now. Narayan Narayan' (Narada's usual greeting and goodbye).

He had not gone too far when yet again he saw something that made him stop his journey. Once again, under a tree, sat a meditator lost in the bliss of internal joy. But this time, the yogi was but a very young boy. Narada was amazed to see the glow on the face of the boy and the stillness of his being. He could not hold himself from speaking:

'Dear friend, who are you, and at this age, why are you in the forest meditating?'

The young boy slowly opened his eyes. He instantly recognized the famous Narada Muni, respectfully bowed down and replied,

'Oh Devarishi, age is only to the body, the soul is but eternal. I find unparalleled joy here in the silence of the jungle and the company of the subtle'.

'Wonderful. By the way, I am on my way to meet the Lord. Is there something you would like to ask Him?' Narada made the same offer. The boy smiled and said, 'This existence cannot be captured in questions and answers, but only in wonder and silence. I am content and question-less.'

'That is so nice. But you know, I am anyway going to meet the Lord. Let me ask Him when you would get to realize the ultimate Brahman and become enlightened', poked Narada, just being himself.

'Sure, oh sage', said the boy.

'Very well then. I shall be back with the Lord's reply soon. Narayan Narayan', said Narada and disappeared.

Many months passed by. The monsoons had left the jungle denser, greener and cooler. Narada was now on his way back from Vaikuntha and as promised, came to meet his two meditating friends. He decided to meet the old sadhu first. As expected, the sadhu was still there at the exact same spot. Seeing Narada approach him, he jumped out of his asana (seat) and said,

'Did you meet the Lord? Did you ask Him my question'?

'I sure did. Are you ready to hear His answer'? asked Narada.

'Of course. Since the time you left, I have only been thinking about what His answer would be. I plead you, revered Narada Muni, pray tell me His answer immediately', said the sadhu in desperation.

'Well, the Lord said you shall get enlightened for sure.' A big smile spread across the sadhu's face. His eyes lit up. *But when?* He waited with his heart beating faster!

Narada continued,

'And it will take you as many lifetimes as the number of leaves on this tree under which you sit'.

The sadhu's jaw dropped and his eyes burned with rage and disappointment. He could not believe what he had just heard. He got up in a fit, threw his asana aside and yelled,

'This is so unfair! The Lord is merciless. There are hundreds if not thousands of leaves on this tree. Am I expected to wait forever to get a glimpse of the Lord? Where is the compassion He is supposed to show to his devotees? I have already spent my entire life meditating. Oh what a waste it has all been!' The sadhu walked away blabbering to himself.

Narada smiled and moved on to the young boy. As expected, the young boy sat at the same spot, with eyes closed and a gentle smile on his face. Narada waited for some time but the boy was still lost in his own space. Finally, Narada said,

'My dear one. I am here and I have the Lord's message for you'.

The young boy slowly opened his eyes and politely said,

'Pranam Devarishi. It's nice to see you again'.

'Would you like to know what the Lord said when I asked him about your enlightenment?'

'I bow down to thee oh sage, for you have just met my Lord and in you I see His reflection. Please tell me what the Lord said.'

'Well, the Lord told me to tell you that you will get enlightened for sure, but it will take you as many lifetimes as the number of leaves on this tree', said Narada.

What happened next took even Narada by surprise. He was not expecting this.

The young boy jumped out of his seat and started singing and dancing and praising the Lord. Bursting with joy he said,

'Oh my Lord is ever so compassionate! He is ready to reveal the highest to me! What have I done to deserve this'?

'But this tree has more than a thousand leaves maybe! This will take forever', poked Narada.

'I will happily wait oh sage. *My destination makes my journey worthwhile.* At least, one can count the number of leaves on this tree. It's a finite number. Longing for my beloved in itself is pure joy. And the assurance that I shall merge with my beloved one day is all a devotee needs', said the boy still continuing to dance.

'But you have been doing such hard tapasya at such a young age. Don't you think it's unfair for the Lord to make you wait so much?' continued Narada, testing the boy further.

'Unfair? Oh great Muni, you are an authority on devotion and love. In your famous Narada Bhakti Sutras, you mention "love is unconditional". There are thousands of trees in the forest. The Lord chose just one tree. There are thousands of devotees who want to realize the ultimate truth. The Lord chose me. There are thousands who long to hear from the Divine. The Lord chose to send me a message! How much the Lord loves me!'

'I will happily wait for an eternity to merge with my Lord.'

Narada bowed down to the little boy in the forest that day. The boy, oblivious to Narada's presence, was soaked in bliss and dancing away in unison with his spirit. Narada took the mud from under the tree and rubbed it on his forehead, for the soil where a true devotee sits is holy.

It is said the young boy got enlightened that very moment.

* * *

KEY TAKEAWAYS

Gratitude is the Attitude of Happiness

A little shift inside us, from complaint to gratitude, is all we need to be happy and to make others happy. Are we grateful for what we have received? We take so many things for granted. Are we grateful for our body, our eyes and ears, the fact that we can walk and talk, our family and friends? If we can make gratitude a habit, then we shall be able to smile even in the most testing times, knowing that *it could have been worse.*

Patience is a gift. It can change the quality of our lives. Patience comes when there is faith. Faith, that I shall get what is meant to come to me. Faith that there is a higher power that shall take care of me. When you have faith, it is easy to be patient. Legendary is the faith that can withstand a million chances of doubt! Faith, or Shraddha, is, in fact, considered a type of wealth as per our scriptures.

Gratitude and Patience

Practice till they become your nature

Remember

Gratitude is the Attitude of Happiness

Manthan

Pause. Introspect. Express.

Make a list of ten people/things/situations in your life that make you feel 'Wow, I am so lucky'. Not later, do it right away. Use this box to write them down.

Gratitude Box

Story Two

Ratnakar Meets Valmiki

Narayan Narayan Jai Govind Hare
Narayan Narayan Jai Gopal Hare.

Every step was in sync with every breath. Every breath was in sync with every word. Every word was echoing the Lord's name. Narada's song was eternal. It was for all seasons and all times, day or night.

Presently, it was night. Pitch dark in the deep jungle. The buzz of the insects and distant cries of the wolves served as a background score to his gentle hymn. The smell of the raatraani (night jasmine) enveloped his swampy path. He was walking alone, singing his song.

Suddenly, four men jumped out of the trees and blocked his way. Narada saw a faint silhouette of a man holding something like a stick on his right shoulder. Moments later, light emerged from a mashaal (flaming wooden torch) to show a tall, dark-skinned man with a thick handlebar moustache and a long sword resting on his shoulder. He had a broad muscular chest and battle scars all over his torso. He stood a few metres away while his men surrounded Narada from all sides.

'Choose to fight or surrender. I am Ratnakar, the king of this forest. I give my opponents a fair chance to fight before I kill them.'

'Greetings Ratnakar. I am Narada. I possess nothing worth your interest. If you care for this veena and my clothes, you may have them. I live freely. I have no fear of death. If killing me makes you happy, you may do so. Make up your mind and let me know. I will sit and take some rest, for I have been walking for many hours you know', said Narada and sat down comfortably, resting his back against a giant mango tree.

Ratnakar could not believe his eyes. This was the first time he had met a human being who did not care about life, who was casually smiling in the face of death, and showed no respect for his threats. He was accustomed to seeing frightened faces pleading for mercy. *Who was this man*, he wondered.

'You foolish Brahman, don't pretend to be so brave. I know inside your heart you are calling desperately to your Narayan to come and save you! This smiling face is a facade.'

'Ratnakar, my friend, I told you I have no fear. But you cannot identify fearlessness because you have not experienced it yourself. So, tell me honestly, who are you afraid of?'

'Ratnakar does not know fear.'

'C'mon now. Are you scared of the emperor and his soldiers?'

'Definitely not', said Ratnakar, getting frustrated now.

'Are you scared of the society and what people think of you?'

'No.'

'Are you afraid of God and your evil deeds?'

'There is no God and my deeds are not evil', screamed Ratnakar.

'Then why do you hide in the forest? Why do you live in the jungle and loot in the night? Why don't you roam around like a free man?'

Ratnakar froze. He had no answer. All he could feel was an intense wave of rage running through his veins. *Why was he always hiding?*

'I will answer for you', said Narada. 'You do paap (evil acts of de-merit) and you are afraid of the consequences of your paap! You know, some day you will pay for your sins.'

'I have heard a lot about you. Narada, the sage of the devatas! Narada, the wise one! Listen, Narada, paap and punya (merit and de-merit) are just perspectives. Their definitions change with time and the powerful decide the definition. I have not done any paap'! yelled Ratnakar.

'Are you sure your wife and children think the same? Do you feel they will stand by your side when the consequences of your karma unfold'? asked Narada.

'Of course! Whatever I do, I do for my family. All my karma is for their happiness, for their comfort. They are with me in my good and my bad actions', replied Ratnakar.

'All right then. Why don't you go and ask them once — will they partake of the sin that you are accumulating every day? I shall wait for you right here Ratnakar. Go and ask them', said Narada in his cool, composed manner.

Ratnakar was a little shaken, intrigued and confused. He decided this question was worth asking. He ordered his men to hold Narada hostage and dashed towards his home. When he reached his hut, he saw his wife cooking in the kitchen. He walked up to her and asked her straight, 'Will you partake in the sin of my bad karma'?

She was shocked and caught off-guard. She tried to skillfully dodge the unpleasant question but Ratnakar insisted. Finally, she took a deep breath and said,

'My dearest Ratnakar. You know I love you from the bottom of my heart. But the truth of life is that a man has to face the consequences of his karma alone, whether good or bad'. She walked away, not having the courage to look her husband in the eyes. Ratnakar turned to his father and his two children, but their faces and their body language gave away their answers loud and clear. Ratnakar fell to his knees in heartbreak. The world blurred in front of his eyes. He felt an unusual heaviness in his chest. Soft tears rolled down his face. For a long time, he sat alone in silence. Then, he gathered himself somehow and went back to Narada.

Narada saw Ratnakar and knew what must have happened. Ratnakar fell at Narada's feet weeping. Narada kept his hand gently on Ratnakar's head caressing him.

'I am alone Munivar (saint). You were right. I am accumulating all this sin for no reason.'

'Being alone in a crowd is a sign of wisdom. Being in a crowd when you are actually alone is ignorance. You are now awake, Ratnakar.'

'But I feel weak being alone.'

'Your mind is with you. And you mind is your best friend or your biggest enemy.'

'Guide me towards my purpose Munivar. Show me the path to my moksha.'

'Those who know the purpose will not tell and those who tell do not know! This is your journey. Your mind, intellect, memory and ego had created that world of paap. Now using the same faculties, you have to create your new reality. Possibilities are infinite. You just need to awaken your true potential within'.

'Chant the name of Ram and meditate upon Him', saying this, Narada blessed Ratnakar and continued his travels.

And thus began the journey of inner transformation, the journey from Ratnakar to Valmiki, the dacoit of yesteryears to the future author of the epic Ramayana. It is said that Ratnakar meditated for many years in the same spot where Narada had blessed him. His body was so still, that anthills (Valmik in Sanskrit) appeared around him, and hence he was called Valmiki. Sage Valmiki is famously known as the Adi Kavi (the first poet) and Ramayana is known as Adi Kaavyam (the first work of poetic brilliance).

* * *

KEY TAKEAWAYS

Purpose

Why are you doing what you are doing?

This is the single most important question you need to answer. What is the purpose behind your actions? Why do you want that promotion? Why do you want to lose weight? Why do you want that relationship? Why do you want to start your own business? Why do you want to serve people?

If the purpose, the **why** is clear, you will notice you will not need any external motivation. You will also not get frustrated easily and you will not quit.

The real purpose may also be hidden beneath a bunch of apparent purposes. Don't settle at the surface, dig deep. Keep asking 'why' till you get to the real reason.

Ask WHY I am doing whatever I am doing

Manthan

Pause. Introspect. Express.

Think of some of the most important aspects of your life, or areas you are struggling with. Ask WHY are you doing what you are doing in these areas. If needed, discuss with a friend/coach to get clarity on the why!

* * *

Story Three

The Illusion of Reality

It was a beautiful sunny day at the icy Mount Kailasha, the abode of Lord Shiva. Maa Parvati and Lord Shiva were discussing the matters of the subtle world while their two sons, Kartikeya and Ganesha played a wrestling match on the side. Just then, they heard the sweet words:

Narayan Narayan!

'Welcome Narada. Glad your travels have brought you to the mountains today', greeted Shiva.

'Pranam oh Lord and Devi', said Narada paying his obeisance. 'I have something which I wanted to give you personally.' Saying so, Narada pulled out a golden mango from his jute bag. Ganesha and Kartikeya dropped their game and rushed to see the mango.

'Narada, you have come all the way to Kailasha just to give me a mango'? asked Shiva, amused.

'My Lord, this is no ordinary mango. It's the fruit of knowledge. Whoever eats this shall get the boon of the ultimate knowledge and wisdom.' Shiva happily accepted the fruit and was about to break the fruit into two halves for the boys when Narada interrupted,

'But there is one condition, Mahadev (another title for Lord Shiva)'.

Shiva stopped and looked at Narada with a smile, 'I should have known. When Narada gives something, it has to come with some conditions and maybe some mischief as well. What is the condition?' asked Shiva.

'The fruit cannot be split. It has to be eaten by only one individual', said Narada.

'Oh dear, now how shall we decide whether Kartikeya or Ganesha will eat this fruit?' muttered Paravati.

'Narada, since you have created the confusion, you will have to come up with the solution', said Shiva, tossing the ball in Narada's court.

'Very well then, boys', said Narada with a mischievous smile. 'Whoever between the two of you is fastest in going around the world three times shall get the unique mango. Your time starts now!'

Narada had barely even finished his sentence when Kartikeya leapt on to his vehicle, the high-speed peacock and started his first circle around the world. Ganesha on the other hand was in no apparent rush. A worried Parvati asked him with motherly concern, 'Ganesha, my dear child, are you not going to compete with your brother? Don't you want the delicious mango'? She did not want Ganesha to be left behind. She knew Kartikeya was the more athletic one and wanted to encourage Ganesha to be a sport. With a calm face, Ganesha said, 'Wait a minute Maa. Let me think about this'.

At this point, Kartikeya zoomed past Kailasha finishing his first round. Teasing Ganesha he said, 'C'mon Gannu. At least try. I know I will win but I want the thrill of defeating a worthy opponent'. Kartikeya's peacock gave a mocking smile to Ganesha's vehicle, the mouse.

More time passed by. Ganesha sat lost in deep thought. Parvati's heart was beating faster. Narada and

Shiva were enjoying the contest. Suddenly Ganesha's face lit up and he jumped from his seat exclaiming, 'I got it! I am going to win'. Kartikeya swooshed past the second time. Ganesha waved at him with a broad smile, thus confusing everyone present, including the mouse!

Ganesha came to his parents and did a shashtang namaskar (full body prostration) to them. He then circled them three times. He had just about finished his third circumambulation when Kartikeya arrived after finishing his third circle around the world and enthusiastically announced, 'I won!'

'Sorry bhaiya (elder brother), but I have won', said Ganesha politely.

'Excuse me? How can you claim victory when you have not even moved from Kailasha, let alone go around the world? Everyone witnessed me going around the world three times, including you'! replied an agitated Kartikeya.

'I did go around the world! I went around my parents three times', clarified Ganesha.

'Yeah right! Well, the deal was to go around the world three times Ganesha, not around our parents'.

'My dear bhaiya, *my parents are my world*! They are the epicentre of my life, the cause of my very presence. In them and around them, my world exists. Else, it dissolves and disappears. *You went around your world. I went around mine*'.

Kartikeya was stunned. His anger melted away as he grasped the full power of Ganesha's thought and action.

He felt a surge of love and adulation for his little brother. He wanted to give him a tight hug but he decided to have some fun with Narada first. Winking at his father, he put on a furious face and spoke to Narada,

'Uncle Narada, this is unfair. I have won this race. You have to intervene and give me justice. Isn't it, father?'

'I agree. Narada, you have to declare who should get the fruit! I do not want any quarrel in Kailasha because of a mango'! said Shiva in a stern voice.

Narada felt the heat now. A cute mango-craving Ganesha, a concerned and displeased Parvati, a protective fatherly Shiva and an angry impatient Kartikeya stared at him. Narada strummed his veena, managed a big artificial smile and said,

'Oh, I suddenly remember Lord Vishnu must be waiting for me. I need to rush to his service immediately. I am sure you all will do justice to the winner. Anyway, it's just a mango and the two boys are storehouses of knowledge already. *Narayan Narayan*!' saying this, Narada turned and ran down the mountains never daring to look back. The four of them burst out laughing!

Ganesha devoured the mango instantly, throwing small chunks for his mouse, who felt relieved that he didn't have to carry Ganesha around the world three times. Kartikeya was happy he got a much-needed work out. Kailasha was cheerful and peaceful as always! Shiva closed his eyes and the world disappeared.

* * *

KEY TAKEAWAYS

Perception

Reality is Only Limited by Our Imagination

What is real and what is not? Who is right and who is wrong? Whose version of the truth is to be believed? Kartikeya went around his perceived world, his version of truth. Ganesha did the same. We all do the same. Every moment, we choose our reality. We create our reality.

In the story of Alexander trying to conquer the whole world with India as his final pursuit (reference: read the Chanakya story in this book), following is the conversation between Alexander and an ascetic Indian sadhu:

'What are you doing'? asked an impatient Alexander.

The sadhu slowly cracked opened his eyes and said, 'Well before you interrupted me, I was bathing in the bliss of infinity'.

'What are you doing'? asked the sadhu.

'I am on a mission to become the first man to rule the whole world', answered Alexander.

They both looked at each other. Each thought the other was insane.

Who is wise and who is a fool here? It's all a matter of perception.

Perception is shaped by our belief system. Belief system depends on our context — birth, culture, religion, nationality, parenting, education etc.

Consciousness – Conversations – Conduct

What we believe in, what is there in our consciousness starts flowing in our conversation, it shows in our bhasha (language). And whatever we speak about starts impacting our actions, our behaviour, our conduct. To change belief, to get the right thoughts in the consciousness — awareness is required.

Manthan

Pause. Introspect. Express.

Are we aware of our belief system and how it influences our behaviour? Do we agree and acknowledge that someone else's perception can be totally different in the same situation? Do we give room for differences to flourish? Are we aware of our own biases?

* * *

Narada Muni
The Unique Coach

Narada does not preach. *Narada only pokes.* He asks powerful questions and leaves you to work out the answers. He opens up possibilities and leaves you to stir up the latent potential. *He deliberately creates conflict so that you emerge stronger and wiser.* Contrary to the popular image of Narada, he does not indulge in unnecessary gossip or create problems for people for no reason. He is lighthearted and jovial but never off-centred.

Narada's job is to create confusion, which ultimately leads to clarity. Narada is a very non-intrusive coach. He always knows the answers but he never reveals them because he wants you to discover them, to enjoy the sense of achievement and satisfaction of finally reaching the right conclusions.

Manthan

Pause. Introspect. Express.

Do you have a Narada in your life — someone who pokes and nudges you to your highest potential? Can you play a mini Narada to someone else?

Saraansh

Summary of Learnings from this chapter

1.
Gratitude is the Attitude of Happiness.

2.
Practice patience till it becomes your nature.
Patience comes when there is faith.

3.
Legendary is the faith that can withstand a million chances of doubt.

4.
A sense of 'Purpose' is critical.
Ask WHY you are doing what you are doing.
Keep asking the 'why' till you get to the real reason.

5.
Our reality depends on our perception.

6.
Perception depends on our 'belief system'.

7.

Consciousness – Conversation – Conduct

8.

Conflict and Chaos can lead to clarity.

7

Adi Shankaracharya

'Tell me mother, may I now . . . ?'

It was a lazy summer afternoon. Little Shankara decided he needed another dip in the river and splashed his way into the waters of the Purna, while his mother nearby plucked flowers for the evening prayers. The serene village of Kalady (Kerala) stood motionless as the temple bells rang far off in the forest.

Suddenly, the silence of the afternoon was shattered by a sharp scream from the eight-year-old Shankara. From nowhere, a crocodile had appeared and caught Shankara by the leg, dragging him deeper into the river. Aryamba, his mother, rushed to the banks, helplessly watching her little son in the jaws of death.

'Amma, there is only one way for me to survive now', said Shankara, loud enough to reach his weeping mother's ears. 'Give me your permission to renounce this world and become a sanyasi (monk) and I am sure the crocodile shall release me.'

Aryamba's heart sank deeper in sorrow hearing her son's request. This was not the first time Shankara had expressed his desire to leave the world and take to the path of a renunciate. Having lost her husband already, she was strongly against the idea and dreaded to imagine her life without her only son. But in her heart, she knew

Shankara would go one day. Such was the prediction of the wise sages even before Shankara was born.

A billion thoughts crossed her mind in a split second. But this was not the time to think. The crocodile had her son by its teeth and if she waited any longer, she may not have a son at all, leave alone a hermit or a householder. Reluctantly, she gave her consent. Shankara immediately chanted 'Sanyasto ham' (I am now a sanyasi) three times and miraculously the crocodile released him that very moment.

As he made his way back to the banks unhurt, Aryamba hugged her son in a mixture of gratitude and sorrow, her smile shining through her tears. In the last few minutes, she had almost lost her son, regained him and lost him again. Shankara on the other hand was feeling doubly relieved, both of the crocodile and samsara (the world). The ancient scriptures prohibit a man from even renouncing the world without the permission of his mother. He finally had the necessary approval. However, he was pained to see his mother feeling abandoned and miserable.

'Shankara, you have to make one promise to me, as my last wish', said Aryamba.

'Yes mother, whatever you ask for. What do you want?'

'When the time comes for me to leave this body, promise me you shall be by my side and you shall do my last rites with your hands.'

'My dear mother, I promise. Although we both know that a sanyasi is not allowed to come back to his family and perform any rituals for the dying, I promise you I shall do your last rites. Just call out my name when you need me and I shall be there. By the holy waters of Purna, I promise.'

'I go now to the unknown to actually know my true self. Bless me Amma, that I may find my purpose. From now on, whoever feeds me is my mother, whoever teaches me is my father, my students my children, my breath my bride, my body my temple, gyana and mrityu (wisdom and death) my best friends, the earth my bed, the skies my roof and the divine my only support.'

Aryamba tearfully hugged her son one last time. Shankara took the mendicant's staff in his right hand and his kamandala (mendicant's water pot) in his left and waved goodbye to the first stage of his life. Probably for the first time in the history of the world, an eight-year-old was becoming a renunciate. Aryamba watched him walk away till his little figure disappeared into the hills. The fact that her son was the embodiment of the great Lord Shiva Himself did not make any difference to her. To her, he was and would remain her little Shankara.

* * *

And thus, the journey began. A journey that would be discussed for centuries to come. A journey that would inspire millions to walk the spiritual path. The journey that started with a search for an enlightened guru.

The search took him across the Deccan plateau all the way north to Omkareshwar, a city on the banks of the mighty Narmada. The hills that comprise the city resemble the figure of Om, as does the Narmada, while it skirts the city. It is here that Shankara heard of a realized master by the name of Govindapaada. It was believed that the sage lived inside a mysterious cave hidden in the forest and no one had seen him enter or leave it for decades. Intuitively, Shankara knew he had found his guru.

The cave had a very small, narrow entrance. Shankara stood outside the cave for many hours, not knowing what to do. He was determined to see his teacher, but Govindapaada was lost in deep samadhi and had no desire for any sight or interaction with the mortals.

How to get the guru to notice him? How to get darshan (sight) of the sage who would be his doorway to the infinite?

Shankara performed pradakshina (circumambulation) of the cave thrice, as a mark of respect to the sage, and then started singing to him. He sang the glory of the sage and praises to Dakshinamoorthy, the form of Shiva, as the first guru of creation. He praised the lineage that Govindapaada represented and humbly requested him to accept this little boy as his disciple.

Govindapaada slowly came out of his superconscious state and heard only the last part of Shankara's beautiful hymn, but whatever little he heard touched him. Curious to know more about the source of this childlike voice, he said:

'Who are you, my child?'

The question elicited a response from Shankara which would be written in golden ink on the pages of Indian history forever. He spontaneously composed a song using the negation or neti method as the basis of his answer. The grandeur of thought and depth of expression came together beautifully when Shankara sang:

न भूमिर्न तोयं न तेजो न वायुः
न खं नेन्द्रियं वा न तेषां समूहः ।
अनेकान्तिकत्वात् सुषुप्त्येकसिद्धः
तदेकोऽवशिष्टः शिवः केवलोऽहम् ॥

I am neither earth not water, neither fire nor air nor ether,
I am neither any sense organ nor their aggregate
(as they are all uncertain),
I am however in the experience of deep sleep,
I am the one, the absolute, the auspicious, the Shiva
consciousness.

न वर्णा न वर्णाश्रमाचारधर्मा
न मे धारणाध्यानयोगादयोऽपि ।
अनात्माश्रयाहंममाध्यासहानात्
तदेकोऽवशिष्टः शिवः केवलोऽहम् ॥

Neither the castes nor the rules of the castes nor
the stages of life,
Not even concentration, meditation, yoga etc.,
The mistaken sense of 'I' and 'mine', based on the non-self
are abandoned,

I am verily the absolute, the auspicious self.

न माता पिता वा न देवा न लोका
न वेदा न यज्ञा न तीर्थं ब्रुवन्ति ।
सुषुप्तौ निरस्तातिशून्यात्मकत्वात्
तदेकोऽवशिष्टः शिवः केवलोऽहम् ॥

I have neither a mother nor a father, nor the gods or specific realms/worlds. I am in neither the Vedas nor the Yagyas (rituals) not even pilgirm places, so say the saints. For in deep sleep, none of the above exist, it's a state devoid of any object of perception. The one that remains then, the residue, the absolute self, Shiva, I am.

'Oh revered saint, this is who I am', concluded Shankara.

There was a long silence at the other side of the cave. Govindapaada was still basking in the glory of Shankara's poem, smiling in his heart. They say the guru longs to find a disciple worthy of learning the highest. Govindapaada was convinced he had found one. He finally opened his eyes and said:

'My dear child. You have spoken the highest with such ease. I am pleased to accept you as a disciple and shall help you find the purpose for which your holy soul has taken a human shape.' Govindapaada slowly extended his feet outside the cave. Shankara touched his forehead to the guru's feet, chills running down his spine. Govindapaada then whispered the secret of Brahmagyaana, encapsulating the essence of all self-knowledge in the form of four mahavaakyas (great Vedic statements). To Shankara, this was both a new initiation and a rekindling of what he already knew in seed form.

Shankara stayed under the guidance of Govindapaada for the next few years during which he mastered the scriptures and the true essence of the Vedas. He was now nearly twelve years old. What would take people decades to even comprehend, Shankara easily mastered to perfection in a few months. When Govindapaada realized the time had come for Shankara to spread the Vedic knowledge across the land, he called upon him and said:

'Shankara, the time has come for you to fulfil your purpose. You should travel and preach this eternal wisdom to the people of this land. You may not be aware, but thousands are waiting for you.'

'Oh revered master, all I wish to do is remain dissolved in the supreme bliss of Brahman', said Shankara.

'No my dear child, you do not have that luxury yet. Your mission is to educate and enliven the scholar and the common man alike. The former suffers from ego and intellectual misinterpretations without practical experience, and the latter is precoccupied with rituals and superstition. You have to remove both these kinds of ignorance.'

Shankara listened intently to his guru's words.

Govindapaada continued, 'I wish you to write a commentary on Maharishi Vyasa's Brahma Sutras and proceed to the holy city of Kashi without delay. Hold debates and discussions with the scholars and invoke devotion in the masses. Once and for all, establish the supremacy of the Vedic knowledge in this ancient land of the rishis.'

From now on, the world shall know you as Shankaracharya.

This is both my blessing and my instruction.

Digvijayi bhava! (May you be victorious in all directions)

Having said this, the old sage closed his eyes forever and merged into the divine.

* * *

Kashi, on the banks of the holy Ganga, stood as the epicentre of education and as the glorious spiritual capital of India. Believed to be the oldest city of the world, Kashi was flooded with gurukuls and temples, the most prominent being the Kashi Vishwanath, the abode of Shiva Himself — the deity who presided over the city and was hence hailed as Kashikapuradinath (the lord of Kashi). A typical day in Kashi (now Varanasi) would see the ghaats of the Ganga inundated with several pundits discussing and debating passionately over the minutest intricacies of the scriptures, defending their preferred school of thought. In every lane and every house of this great city were learned men and women living their lives strictly as prescribed by the holy books. If Shankaracharya had to establish the supremacy of his principal philosophy — Advaita (non-duality), there was no place better to start than Kashi.

Stories of Shankaracharya's greatness and his grip over the written word had reached Kashi's pundits even before the twelve-year-old Acharya had set foot in the city. When he did arrive, he quickly gained the respect of the intellectuals and gathered a huge number of followers.

One crisp winter morning, after finishing his customary bath in the cold waters of the Ganga, the Acharya was walking towards the city to beg for alms with his disciples. As was his practice, the Acharya always walked right in the front, leading the group. Suddenly a man stood on the opposite side with four dogs on the leash, blocking the path of the Acharya. The man was dressed in rugged torn clothes; he was dark with pimpled skin and bloodshot eyes and emanating an unmissable foul smell. He was a keeper of the cremation grounds, considered a person of low caste in those times. The group was shocked and angry at this misbehaviour of this random man who ought to have moved aside and not dared to make eye contact with the monks.

Shankaracharya froze. Though angry, his disciples did not speak a word. The man stared straight at the Acharya, a mocking smile on this face. The Acharya raised his left hand and gestured at the man softly, saying, 'Move away. Move away'. The man, still looking deep into Acharya's eyes, responded in a loud confident voice,

> 'Learned scholar, you say "Move away". Pray tell me, who should move away? Should this body move away or should the spirit? If you address the body, then mine and yours are made of the same pancha-mahabhuta (the five elements — earth, water, fire, air and ether) and nourished by the same food. So why is your body purer than mine? If you address the spirit or the soul, it is by its very nature omnipresent and omniscient. So how can it move away? How can you move the wave away from the ocean?
>
> You go around teaching Advaita to the whole world. Then how come you identify yourself more with the body than the soul? Does it make any difference to the sun whether its rays are reflected in the holy waters of the Ganga or a muddy pond? It is amazing how the wisest of the wise fall prey to the maya of duality!'

Shankaracharya was stunned to hear these words. He instantly realized his error and immediately corrected himself. He joined his palms and said:

'You are indeed right. The same spirit shines through your body and mine. My friend, wisdom must have left my side momentarily and I fell victim to this social conditioning of the holy and lowly. To speak of Advaita is one thing but living it is another. I bow down to you, for he alone is my guru who sees the one divinity everywhere, in every human.'

And then, the Acharya did the unthinkable. He bent forward to touch the man's feet. The crowds who had gathered around were shocked, confused, impressed and moved. In one instance, the Acharya had demonstrated he was truly beyond the popular concepts of paap and punya (merit and demerit). When the Acharya looked up again, the man was gone. In his heart, the Acharya had a strong feeling that this random man had been none other than Lord Shiva Himself, who had come with the four Vedas disguised as the four canines, to remove the final residues of duality from the Acharya's consciousness.

The Acharya joyfully sang in his heart:

चिदानन्दरूपः शिवोऽहम् शिवोऽहम्
चिदानन्दरूपः शिवोऽहम् शिवोऽहम्

I am the form of chid (consciousness) and ananda (bliss). I am verily Shiva, the ultimate consciousness, the absolute.

* * *

Over the next few months, the Acharya poured himself completely into writing his commentary on the legendary Brahma Sutras. He also interpreted the Bhagvad Gita and the ten principal Upanishads, thus creating a treasure for the sincere student of the scriptures. His explanations were simple and based on direct experience and hence were the ultimate source of inspiration for beginners and the seasoned alike. He also held debates and discussions with the best known scholars in Kashi, and without exception defeated all those who stood to argue against the supremacy of his philosophy of the non-dual. He also left a marked impression on the masses and initiated hundreds into the order of the ascetics.

But his mission was far from over. In fact, it had just begun.

In those days, Indian society was torn apart by the conflicts between ancient Hinduism and newer faiths like Jainism and the more popular Buddhism. Hinduism itself was paralyzed by orthodox practices and the prevalent rigid caste system, which veiled the true teachings of the Vedas and reduced faith to mere ritualism. During Shankaracharya's time, the school of thought that reigned supreme was Purva Mimamsa, which proclaimed that the ritualistic interpretation of the Vedas or karma-kaand was the highest expression of the Sanatana Dharma (the eternal dharma). This was exactly the viewpoint that Shankaracharya wanted to dismantle and replace with the philosophy of Advaita, focusing on Uttara Mimamsa (the 'gyaana' or knowledge aspect of the Vedas).

The foremost proponent of the Purva Mimamsa school was a learned scholar by the name of Mandan Mishra who lived in the splendid city of Maheshmati (present day Bihar). If Shankaracharya had to permanently and authoritatively establish the dominance of his philosophy, then the only way was to defeat Mandan Mishra in a debate over the shaastras — a verbal combat called

Shaastraarth. And so to challenge Mandan Mishra, the Acharya embarked on a journey to Maheshmati.

Having walked to Maheshmati from Kashi, the Acharya and his disciples asked for exact directions to Mandan Mishra's house to a group of ladies drawing water from a well. What they heard amazed them. In a very matter-of-fact tone, one of the women said:

'Look for a house where at the gates, a bunch of caged parrots are passionately discussing topics like, "Do the Vedas need any external validation? Does God really exist? What happens to the soul once the body dies?" and so on.'

And that was exactly the scene outside Mandan Mishra's house. What a towering authority on shaastras this man would be, whose parrots sounded no less than learned pundits! The Acharya was thrilled now to have finally found a worthy opponent.

Standing outside the house, he called out loudly, '*Bhavati Bhikshaam Dehi*' (a Sanskrit phrase traditionally used by sanyasis to ask for alms).

Ubhaya Bharati, Mandan Mishra's wife, emerged with a pot of rice in her hand. She saw the young teenage boy with an unusual glow on the forehead and a serene smile on the face. As she walked up to the Acharya, he politely said:

'Oh Devi, I desire a different kind of alms from this house. I come here all the way from Kashi to debate with your learned husband.'

'Oh great ascetic, you are humble to not introduce yourself, but you are definitely the famous Shankaracharya, for who else can challenge my husband to a debate at this young age! Please accept food from my kitchen first and let me fulfil my dharma as a householder, and then I am sure my husband shall also be happy to debate with you.' With this, she invited the Acharya and his group inside the house. Mandan Mishra was a tall, thin man and must have been more than thrice the Acharya's age. He was supremely confident of his knowledge and accepted the challenge without any hesitation. It was decided that the debate would commence the next morning.

The room was abuzz with gossip and heated arguments amongst the followers on both sides the next morning. Hundreds of scholars and students had come in early to reserve priority seats for this exciting verbal dual. Bets on intellectual pride rather than money were being placed as Ubhaya Bharati's house staff rushed around making food arrangements for the guests. Food for thought as well as the body was to be available in plenty for everyone.

Mandan Mishra emerged first, accompanied by his wife, Ubhaya Bharati. Amidst loud cheers for the local hero, he bowed down to the statue of Maa Saraswati and took his seat. Shankaracharya arrived soon afterwards and was given a warm welcome too. It had been mutually decided beforehand that none other than Ubhaya Bharati shall be the judge for this debate. She welcomed the assembly and opened the debate by announcing the two most important rules of the debate:

'I shall place a garland of fresh flowers on both the contestants. He whose flowers begin to wither first shall lose the debate. And the loser shall consider the winner as his guru and shall adopt the philosophy of the victor. If the revered Shankaracharya loses, he shall become a householder and if my dear husband loses, he shall become a sanyasi!'

The crowd gasped in shock and disbelief at this announcement. Ubhaya Bharati was known to be an expert on the scriptures herself and a scholar of very high calibre. But today, she elevated herself to another level by the confidence and the smile with which she agreed to judge a contest that could take her husband and her whole life away from her! Invoking the Devtaas for their blessings, she declared the debate open.

Mandan Mishra spoke first.

'I accept the Vedas to be the ultimate truth. As per the Vedas and the guidelines of my revered guru, the great saint Jaimini, I believe that Vedas prescribe the rituals to be performed by the humans. The karma kaand (Purva Mimamsa) is the true message of the Vedas and should be given highest priority by us mortals. Our ultimate goal is to perform the Vedic rituals with utmost sincerity and devotion to attain the higher realms, the higher lokas.' A loud applause with unanimous cheers of '*Sadho, Sadho*' (bravo) rang in the assembly at this clear opening statement.

Now, it was the Acharya's turn.

'I also accept the Vedas to be the ultimate authority. Their main message, however, according to me, is that Brahman alone is real and the world a temporary illusion, which is the emphasis of the Gyaan Kaand (Uttara Mimamsa) of the Vedas. The individual soul, jivaatma, is identical and one with the universal soul, parmaatma. There are no two — just one, the all-pervading — the Advaita. The purpose of life is to realize the nature of the self through uninterrupted inquiry and meditation. The Vedas do prescribe rituals and recommend their adherence, which should be followed but performing rituals without understanding their hidden, superior motives and knowledge shall not carve the way to moksha and shall only result in endless cycles of birth and death.' There was a moment of deep silence in the room followed by thunderous applause.

And then, the debate began at full throttle. They went back and forth arguing and counter-arguing with passion, authenticity, depth and even sarcasm, but never disrespect or manipulated logic. The debate kept tilting in favour of both the contestants now and then, like an exciting wrestling game. Even the parrots at Mandan Mishra's front door were now getting exasperated with the never-ending debate. The verbal war went on for many days with only breaks taken for food, sleep and prayers. During the lunch break, Ubhaya Bharati would first offer alms to the Acharya as per the ascetic norms and then meals to her husband as per a householder's norms.

Ultimately, what was expected happened. One day, Ubhaya Bharati noticed that the flowers in her husband's garland had begun to whither. But before she could intervene with her verdict, Mandan Mishra stood up from his seat and with joined palms announced:

'Oh revered saint, I am now convinced that you speak the highest truth and your reasoning is irrefutable. I am happy to accept my defeat in this debate and request you to accept me as your disciple.'

The assembly showered flower petals on both the participants. With dignity, Shankaracharya welcomed Mandan Mishra into his commune and initiated him into sanyasa. As per the tradition, he was given a new name — Sureshwara. With the grace worthy of a devi, Ubhaya Bharati accepted that her husband was now a monk and this time, invited both Shankaracharya and Sureshwara to accept alms from her kitchen.

* * *

Having successfully influenced the classes and the masses in all parts of northern India, the Acharya now commenced his travels down south. While passing through a small town called Sri Bali (present day Udupi region in Karnataka), a couple came to seek the Acharya's help in the matters of their seven-year-old son, who looked handsome but behaved differently compared to other children. The boy would just sit the whole day doing nothing, saying nothing. If no one fed him, he wouldn't eat. He would not play or study. He had a perpetual blank look as if he were living dead. Sometimes, he would laugh all alone.

The father was obviously worried and helpless and asked the Acharya to intervene.

'Why won't you talk, my child? Who are you'? asked Shankaracharya in a compassionate voice. To everyone's surprise and the parents' disbelief, the child replied with a poem in polished Sanskrit:

'Oh great teacher, I am not the insentient being people think I am. I am the ultimate witness of all action and yet I am not involved. I remain untouched and ever pure. I am the Aatman, the basis of all existence.'

The Acharya smiled. His first meeting with his guru flashed in front of his eyes. Times and roles had changed. The essence of the question by the guru and the beauty of the answer by the disciple were the same. He said to the boy's father, 'I ask this boy of you as my student. He does not engage with your world anyway and is only a source of worry for you. Give him to me. He is special and has a purpose'. The parents, just like the Acharya's own mother, reluctantly agreed.

'The highest knowledge comes naturally and easily to you, just like an amalaka (gooseberry) sitting on the hasta (palm), easily visible and readily consumable. From today, you shall be known to the world as Hastamalaka.' Saying this, the Acharya initiated the boy into monkhood. He grasped the Vedic knowledge quickly and soon became established in Advaita completely. Shankaracharya now had three principle disciples — Padmapaada (who had already been with the Acharya before the others),

Sureshwara and Hastamalaka. Destiny had a fourth one in the waiting.

And he came one day like an unexpected rain shower, searching for the Acharya just the way little Shankara had searched for Govindapaada. His name was Giri. He was a young boy with a lean frame and childlike innocence in his eyes. He was in love with the Acharya from the very first sight and all he wanted to do was to serve his master. Unlike the other shishyas (disciples), Giri was not the intellectual kind and was not well versed with the shaastras. He did not desire knowledge or even liberation. His only aim was to bring comfort to his master, and in this regard, his commitment and single-minded focus was exemplary. He would know what his guru needed even before the Acharya could express it. They say when you don't want anything, you find liberation. When you don't even want liberation, you find divine love!

One day, the Acharya was ready to begin a discourse on a new topic and all the shishyas gathered around in excitement, eagerly looking forward to the freshly baked knowledge which was soon to flow. But the Acharya was delaying the commencement of the discourse. After patiently waiting a long while, Padmapaada couldn't resist any more and said:

'Oh revered master, are you looking for something?'

'Yes dear Padmapaada. I am waiting for Giri to join us.'

This came as a surprise to the entire assembly, for Giri was considered to be a dull boy incapable of understanding the scriptures.

'Oh Master, Giri anyway does not understand a word of the knowledge you share. Teaching him is like teaching a stone. Is it worth holding up the entire class for someone like Giri'? objected Padmapaada, thereby echoing the sentiment of almost all the disciples. Shankaracharya smiled and closed his eyes.

At that moment, Giri, unaware that he was late for the class, was lovingly washing Acharya's clothes at a nearby river, chanting his name with every breath. He suddenly felt a strange outpour of love from the guru and his entire being shook. His heartbeat quickened and he felt goosebumps all over his body. It was as if some divine energy took over him and the essence of all the scriptures dawned to his intellect in one moment of eternal awareness. His legs automatically started moving towards the Acharya, with tears flowing down his cheeks. In this state of utter devotion and gratitude, he started singing spontaneously. The assembly saw him walking joyfully towards them and could now hear his song. A wave of shock and shame took over the entire class.

Giri, lost in his blissful state, was singing of the deepest Vedic knowledge in erudite Sanskrit and that too in a very complex musical metre. He came and fell at the Acharya's feet, still crying in gratitude for the unconditional love his master had bestowed on him.

The Acharya looked at the class and said, 'Faith can make a piece of stone worthy of worship. It can make a mute talk and a cripple climb mountains'. The biggest lesson was quietly learned by each disciple that evening.

The metre in which Giri sang his impromptu poem was called 'Trotaka'. From that day, Giri became Trotakacharya and later, the fourth eminent disciple of Adi Shankaracharya.

* * *

One day as the Acharya was lost in deep meditation in the early hours of the morning, he saw a flash of his mother calling out to him. He knew that the time had come for her to leave her body. He remembered the promise he had made to her. It was time to go back once again to where it had all started. It was time for one last visit to Kalady.

As he walked into his ancestral house, a wave of childhood memories flooded his mind. The house was mostly dark, with only one small diya by the bedside, fighting the wind all alone. There she lay, a weak old woman longing to see her son one last time. The Acharya walked into the dim room and prostrated before his mother. She opened her eyes slowly and took some time to adjust to the image of a sadhu in her room. And then she broke into tears.

'Shankara! You have come!' She hugged her little Shankara like she used to.

'Amma I am here. It's time for you to rest now. Is there anything I can do to bring comfort to you?'

'My dear son, I hear from people that you have now become a great saint. I feel overwhelmed when I hear stories of your greatness. What more can a mother ask for? But if you do want to comfort me, pray bestow on me words of Vedic wisdom that shall liberate my soul and help me peacefully leave this body.'

Feeling compassion and love for his mother, the Acharya began to instruct his mother into the highest knowledge of the Brahman. But he soon realized that his simple mother was unable to grasp the complex theories of non-duality. He then sang praises of Lord Shiva, hearing which the escorts of Shiva presented themselves to carry Aryamba to the divine abode of Shiva. But Shiva's emissaries looked scary to Aryamba and she got frightened. The Acharya then invoked the Maha Vishnu. The beautiful emissaries of Narayana, feeling pleased with the hymns of devotion, emerged with the divine vehicle and carried Aryamba's soul to Vaikuntha, the abode of Vishnu.

The Acharya rose and called upon his neighbours and relatives to help with the last rites of his mother. To his surprise, everyone outright refused to help him. His own near and dear ones scorned at him reminding him that he was a sanyasi and had no business performing the last rites for his dead mother. The Acharya, unperturbed as always, collected the wood himself and set up the funeral pyre all alone. He performed the last rites and kept his promise.

He sat there watching agni (fire) engulf the mortal coil, a reminder of the impermanence of the gross body.

* * *

The four of them walked in quick steps towards the Acharya's kutir wondering why they had been summoned urgently. The Acharya sat like a statue, eyes partially open, as if balancing delicately the mundane and the abstract. They sat in a semi-circle at the Acharya's feet admiring their beloved master. He gradually opened his eyes and said in his sweet voice:

'Knowledge must flow and spread like water. The Parampara (lineage/tradition) and the Vedas must be protected. I have decided — we shall establish four mathas (centres of learning) along the four directions and you shall each lead one, thus ensuring the essence of the Vedas spreads in all the four directions across Bharat.'

They smiled and sighed at the same time. They felt honoured to be part of the Acharya's great plan to re-establish dharma and saddened at the idea of separation from their master. But none of them said a word. The Acharya's instruction was their command. No one asked for more details about this plan. They were definitely not in any rush to bid farewell to their master. The Acharya did not reveal more. But the seed for India's religious renaissance was planted that day.

The travels resumed. The Acharya never stayed in one place for too long. He was constantly on the move and yet his mind was ever still. During one such journey, the group was passing through the beautiful town of Sringeri (Karnataka) named after the famous sage Rishyashringa. The mid-day sun was at its peak, unleashing fire on earth. The Acharya, walking in the front as always, suddenly halted. He could not believe what he saw. Slightly off the path in the bushes, a king cobra had spread its hood over a frog in labour to protect it from the brutal hot rays of the sun! The Acharya kept admiring the sight and thought to himself, 'This is truly the land of compassion where even beasts overcome their basic instincts of violence. Surely this place carries the vibrations of the Mother Divine'. That very moment, he decided that this would be one of their mathas where Maa Saraswati shall bless the human race with her knowledge and compassion. (Today, the Sringeri math dedicated to Maa Sharada stands there).

The Acharya now turned eastward and travelled through Kalinga (Puri) at the shores of the Bay of Bengal and then to the opposite end of Dwaraka (Gujarat) on the western corner of India. He then walked up the heartland to the north reaching the foothills of the Himalayas at Kedarnath. The Acharya loved the cold mountains and the silence they offered. He wore his thin loin cloth in the sub-zero temperatures and took dips in the semi-frozen Ganga with ease, defying all logical bodily limitations. After spending many months in Badrinath and Kedarnath, the Acharya moved further north up to Kashmir, which was given the title of 'paradise on earth' due to its unmatched beauty. He knew he had one final debate he needed to win. And that would be in Kashmir.

Hidden in the lofty snow peaks of the Himalayas in Kashmir lay the sacred temple of Maa Saraswati, popularly known as the Sharada Peeth (the Royal Seat of Learning). In the sanctum sanctorum of this temple, made of pure marble and studded with diamonds, was the 'Throne of Omniscience'. The temple had four doors in four different directions. Only a person who commanded total authority in all branches of knowledge was allowed to enter the temple and sit on the throne. Till date, no one had successfully entered the temple from the south door. This was exactly what the Acharya intended to do.

But it was not that simple. The scholar claiming the throne had to go through a series of tests put forth by experts in each field of knowledge. With every test won, the claimant would enter a small door that would then lead to the next door, the next test. The Acharya was questioned by the leaders of various paths like the Sankhyas, the Mimamsas, Jainism, Buddhism, the Shaktas, the Kapalikas and many more. The Acharya answered them all in a calm demeanour and with absolute authority. The doors kept opening till the Acharya reached the final door. He opened the door and proceeded towards the throne. As he was about to ascend the first step, a melodious voice rang in the skies saying, 'My dear child, the learned ascetic, you are not only the most knowledgeable but also the most pure. May you succeed in your mission of re-establishing the Vedic era'.

The Acharya bowed down, recognizing this to be the voice of Maa Sharada herself. With humility, he graced the throne and received the supreme honour. Expressing his gratitude to the mother divine, he composed the 'Soundarya-lahiri' or 'Waves of Beauty' in honour of the Devi.

* * *

The Acharya was now thirty-two. When he was born, the sages had clearly predicted his life on the planet would be of merely sixteen years. But realizing the significance of his purpose, it is believed that he was granted another sixteen years of life. He knew the end was near and he couldn't wait to merge into the Brahman forever. In the last few years, he had been so disinterested in his physical body that it was now showing signs of decay and disease. The group was presently camped near Kedarnath. He summoned his four disciples for the last time. He said:

आकाशात् पतितं तोयं यथागच्छति सागरम्

(Every drop of rain, no matter where it falls on the earth, ultimately merges into the ocean.)

'My work is now complete on this planet. I have nothing more to do with this body. We have travelled, eaten and learnt together. Now, it's time for you to carry the mission forward without me.

Establish the four mathas in four corners of this great land — Shringeri in the south, Puri in the east, Dwaraka in the west and Jyothirmatha Badrikashram in north. I suggest Sureshwara, Padmapaada, Hastamalaka and Trotakacharya lead these respectively.

Remember, not everyone is meant to be a sanyasi. The knowledge of the Vedas is to uplift the entire humanity while they continue following the prescribed karma. We must function within the body and within the society and yet be firmly aware of its illusory nature. Kindle a spirit of truthful inquiry in every man, woman and child, and let that spirit be the basis of this spiritual revolution.'

He paused. He gazed into the evening skies and gently asked, 'Would any of you like to say or ask anything'?

The four men in front of the Acharya sat dazed and shocked, motionless, tears gushing down their cheeks. Intellectually they were Vedantis (Vedanta followers) but emotionally they were his children. Shankaracharya looked at them and smilingly said,

'Does the knower of Brahman grieve over this body made up of the five elements? It is true that I shall leave this body, but where will I really go? I was with you, in you, and will always remain. Only the illusion of this body shall be rested.' He paused again, looking up the sky deeply as if communicating with the other worlds. It seemed like he was having two parallel conversations.

'Really there is nothing more left for this body to do', he almost whispered this time. 'Oh great Lord Shiva, revered Rishi Vyaasa and my dear Guru Govindapaada, I hope I did justice to your instructions and blessings.' He remained silent for a long time. He then closed his eyes softly and chanted the Shaanti Paath:

ॐ पूर्णमदः पूर्णमिदं पूर्णात्पुर्णमुदच्यतेपूर्णश्य पूर्णमादाय पूर्णमेवावशिष्यते
ॐ शान्तिः शान्तिः शान्तिः

That is whole/complete. This is whole/complete. From the whole, the whole is born. When the whole is taken away from the whole, the whole remains.
Aum. Peace. Peace. Peace.

They never saw their Acharya again.

* * *

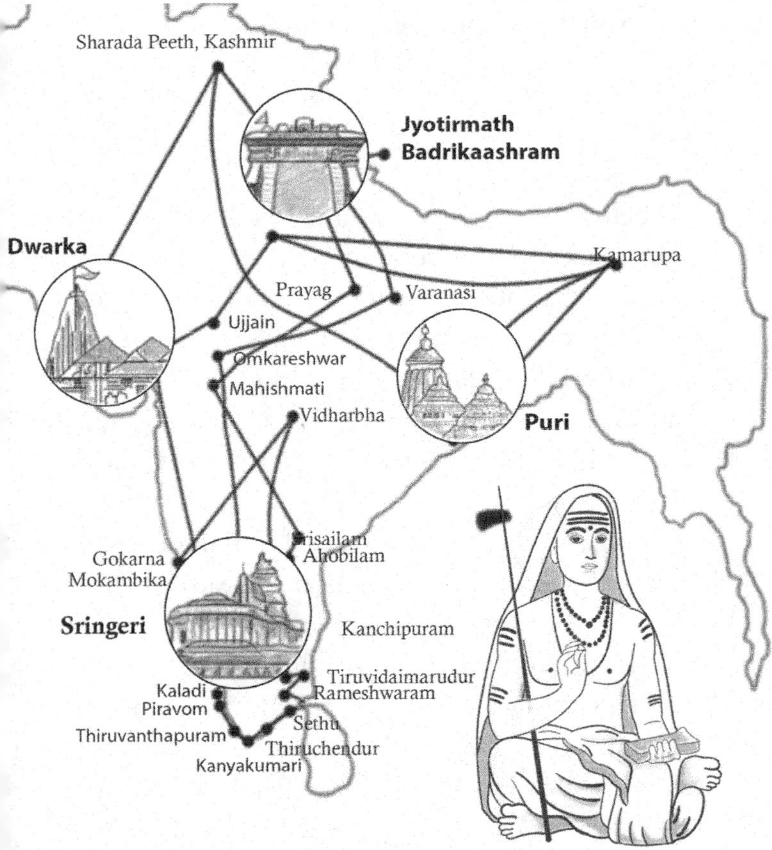
Sharada Peeth, Kashmir
Jyotirmath
Badrikaashram
Dwarka
Kamarupa
Prayag
Varanasi
Ujjain
Omkareshwar
Mahishmati
Vidharbha
Puri
Ahobilam
Gokarna
Mokambika
Sringeri
Kanchipuram
Tiruvidaimarudur
Rameshwaram
Kaladi
Piravom
Sethu
Thiruvanthapuram
Thiruchendur
Kanyakumari

KEY TAKEAWAYS

1. The Spiritual Conquest of India

Great men conquer lands and kingdoms. Legends conquer minds and hearts.

Much before our country was a politically consolidated nation, Shankara successfully implemented the first ever spiritual national integration of Bharat/India. He travelled from Kerala to Kashmir (around 3,300 kms), and Puri to Dwaraka (around 2,200 kms), covering the length and breadth of this massive country. He did it on foot, and he did it at least twice! All this, within a short life span of thirty-two years.

He united the diversified and often quarrelling Hindu sects into one common thread of Vedic knowledge. As we know, Hinduism was broken, divided and suffered from internal conflict. Shankaracharya unified all schools of thought respectfully and brought them under one banner of Sanatana Dharma, pretty much how Sardar Vallabhbhai Patel brought the different states of India under one nation. In fact, he re-established Sanatana Dharma to its full glory across India. Apart from establishing the four mathas in the four corners of India, he connected the dots on the spiritual map of India with twelve jyotirlinga*s* (special Shiva shrines) and the eighteen shakti-peethas (special

Devi shrines), thus giving every Hindu the aspirational goal of teerth yaatra (holy pilgrimage) before leaving their bodies.

Unify the Divided.
Connect the Dots.

Manthan

Pause. Introspect. Express.

Do I have the skill it takes to bring conflicting or diverse individuals/teams together by dialogue? What do I need to do to develop/improve this skill?

2. Integrate. Don't Eliminate

Shankaracharya battles Mandan Mishra, his biggest opponent or competitor. After a fierce struggle for dominance, the Acharya wins. What does he do next? He takes Mandan Mishra into his fold and inspires and trains him to become his principal disciple who champions his cause further. *The competitor becomes a collaborator.* It's a classic case of a merger and acquisition done right. He spends quality time with Mandan Mishra to ensure the new partner is completely convinced and loyal to the new philosophy. Hence, integrate and not eliminate the competition.

Note: The competitor must be worthy of integration.

Integrate. Don't Eliminate

Manthan

Pause. Introspect. Express.

- Are you aware of your competition? Do you know your competition inside out? Shankaracharya knows everything about Purva Mimamsa in detail (just like Hanuman knew everything about Raavan). For businesses today, *competition intelligence* is a key metric to be invested in.

- Do you hate your competition? Do you avoid or ignore them? Shankaracharya has no hatred or even dislike for Mandan Mishra. In fact, he respects him.

- Are you focusing too much on your competition? While it's important to know your competition well, focusing on them too much can impact your mind and your business. Always focus on your business, values and your value to the customer.

3. A Civilization of Dialogue

Every debate was a battle. And they were fought with honour and grace. It is remarkable to note that the Indian civilization was one of dialogue and debate. The wise took to discussions to resolve the most complicated and delicate matters and the one defeated gracefully accepted and further, even adopted the ideology of the victor. There was never any violence or forced conversions. The culture of dialogue also demonstrates that people had a priceless skill in plenty — *the ability to listen.* The mindless screaming and harassment that take place today in the name of debate is pitiable. It would be beautiful to see high-quality debates and discussions come back in schools and corporates, and of course, in the government.

The golden mantra of meaningful debate (mostly credited to Desmond Tutu):

Don't raise your voice. Improve your argument.

How does one improve the argument?

1. Read/research. The more you know, the finer will be your line of thought.
2. Come from a space of contribution and not competition.
3. Be humble.

4. Accommodate the Opposites

Adi Shankaracharya is the best example history can offer of a man who displayed the perfect combination of intellect and emotion. His intellectual loftiness and emotional devotion were developed through first-hand experiences and not just bookish theories and concepts.

Shankaracharya established the practice of Advaita, believing in the formless, nirgun (without attributes) all-pervading Brahman and at the same time celebrated and worshipped the sagunishvara (that with a form and attributes) and wrote several hymns in praise of Shiva, Vishnu and Devi. Pilgrimage to temples and establishing more pilgrim sites was central to his work.

Shankara once found a very old man feverishly trying to learn the rules of Sanskrit grammar even though he was towards the end of his life. The Acharya then spontaneously composed his evergreen hymn, '*Bhaja Govindam*' where he advises the old man — 'Chant the name of the Lord, oh foolish old man, for when the time comes to leave the body, the rules of grammar will not save you, only the grace of the Lord will'!

Note: *Also refer to the 'Sthitapragya Leader' in the learning section of the Chanakya story for more on accommodating opposites as a leadership attribute.*

Accommodate the Opposites

5. The Art of Spiritual Leadership

Adi Shankaracharya is not just a monk who lives in caves and writes deep commentaries on the Bhahma Sutras and the Upanishads that are beyond the grasp of the common man. He realizes the importance of being with the masses and the need of a structure to protect and propagate the message of the Vedas. *He is a visionary ahead of his time.* He establishes the four mathas in the four corners of India, thus ensuring the seed he has planted blossoms into many gardens in the coming centuries. He knows India is too vast and linguistically diverse to have just one centralized headquarters so he covers the expanse with four centres. He sets up clear guidelines for the functioning and the administration of the mathas. These centres function as pilgrimage sites and locus points for spreading social awareness. The mathas offer free food to all the visitors (some even till date), take responsibility for educating the under-privileged and run many other social welfare schemes. His exemplary leadership is evident in the simple fact that the mathas are continuing with his lineage even to this day, more than a thousand years after the Acharya left his body. The best funded and the mightiest of institutions collapse within a decade of the founder leaving. Here is a humble devotion based system, which has stood the test of time. His faith in his own training to his students and his readiness to delegate are the hallmarks of his leadership style.

His leadership style is based on spiritual values and yet he succeeds in creating sustainable growth and a flourishing ecosystem.

6. TEDex

Jagad Guru Adi Shankaracharya, at thirty-two, was probably the most mature human being alive on the planet at that time. He was at the peak of his fame and success and the world had accepted him as the unparalleled authority on philosophy. At that juncture, being the dispassionate monk that he was, he decided it was time to pack up and leave. The world has seen too many top leaders refusing to retire gracefully and waiting till they are forced to step down. When you feel the purpose is served and your role is complete, that's the time to draw the curtains, pass the baton and move on. The formula seems to be:

TEDex
Train. Empower. Delegate. Exit.

Manthan

Pause. Introspect. Express.

- If you are the leader, are you consciously creating new leaders? Are you actively investing your time and energy in succession planning?
- If you feel you have the potential but you are not getting the training necessary to become a future leader, can you do something about it?

7. Age Is Just a Number

Shankara was all but twelve when he started holding debates, travelling and teaching the highest knowledge. Swami Vivekananda was thirty when he delivered his famous lecture in Chicago. Chhatrapati Shivaji Maharaj was sixteen when he conquered his first fort. Chandragupta Maurya was around twenty-one when he ascended the throne of Magadha.

On the other hand, A.C. Bhaktivedanta Swami Prabhupaada was seventy-one when he started the ISCKON movement. Recently, we saw Pravin Tambe, who started playing cricket professionally at forty-one.

Next time anyone tells you that you are too young or too old to do something, give them a big smile and move on.

8. Minimalism

Much before the concept of minimalism took off in the west in the last decade, Shankaracharya and many other saints of India lived by this very code: **simple living, high thinking**.

Minimalism means decluttering our lives, keeping only that which is needed and which truly gives us freedom and happiness. It means not falling prey to the diseases of accumulation and showing off. It's the opposite of the mindless consumerism that we see around us in this century.

Minimalism does not mean not buying or owning stuff. It simply means you own that which you truly enjoy and that which adds value and comfort to your life — physically, emotionally, spiritually. It means you have thought through in detail about what you want to buy, own and keep. It also means you are aware of how much importance you attach to the things you own. It means saying 'no' to stuff you don't need, even if it's for free or super cheap.

Minimalism is Freedom
Declutter your life

Manthan
Pause. Introspect. Express.

Right now, what do you have in your life that is taking up space, time and energy and is not adding any value? What can you do away with? Check your wardrobe, your house, your life — keep what you like and need and do away with the rest.

9. Adi Shankaracharya's Works

Revered Acharya wrote a massive body of literature, which is difficult to read and appreciate in a single lifetime. Below is a very partial list of some of his shorter forms of writing (Ashtakams — an eight-stanza poem) and Stotrams (hymns) that I have personally enjoyed and benefitted from:

Ashtakams:

1. Niravan Ashtakam or Atma Ashtakam
2. Kala Bhairav Ashtakam
3. Linga Ashtakam
4. Krishna Ashtakam
5. Achutya Ashtakam
6. Bhavani Ashtakam
7. Guru Ashtakam

Stotrams and Hymns:

1. Bhaja Govindam
2. Annapoora Stotram
3. Guru Paduka Stotram
4. Brahma Gnanavali Mala
5. Saundarya Lahiri
6. Das Shloki

Saaransh

A summary of your learnings from this chapter

1.
Unify the divided. Connect the dots.

2.
Integrate. Don't eliminate.

3.
Don't raise your voice. Improve your argument.

4.
Create a culture of dialogue.

5.
Accommodate the opposites.

6.
TEDex
Train. Empower. Delegate. Exit.

7.
Age is just a number.

8.
Minimalism is freedom. Declutter your life.

8

Srinivasa Ramanujan

'The Devi speaks to me . . .'

'When you divide any number by itself, the answer is always one', declared the old maths teacher of the neighbourhood paathshaala (school), as he dusted the chalk off his palms. Seven-year-old Ramanujan raised his hand to ask a question.

'Sir, when you divide zero by zero, is the answer still one?'

The teacher was surprised. Children in his class typically copied the results and learnt the formula by heart. They didn't ask questions, definitely not imaginative ones. In an instructive tone he asked,

'Have you finished reading through the textbook already'?

'Yes sir. This and those of two grades higher also', replied a partially scared Ramanujan.

'How did you even get the advanced books'? asked the teacher.

'Oh, I borrowed them from the students of the senior grades. There is nothing you can't get in return for two cups of strong filter coffee', he chuckled.

The teacher smiled and said, 'Well, the answer to your question is not defined. Maybe it is infinity. Maybe it's not. It's a mystery'.

'Oh, in that case, I shall find it and define it too', said Ramanujan with innocent confidence.

Just then the school bell rang, declaring the end of the day. The subdued, quiet children transformed into roaring free beasts and stormed out of the classroom. Ramanujan stayed back alone, scribbling away on his slate.

* * *

He was now in his personal chambers, his getaway island of peace and serenity, nestled in the forgotten back alley of the grand Sarangapani temple. His eyes took some time to adjust to the darkness. Away from the noise and the bright sunlight of the main temple area, dimly lit by small oil diyas spread in disciplined rows and columns, lay Ramanujan's secret garden of infinity. Years of Vedic fires lit by ardent priests had blackened the stone walls of the temple and given the place a divine subtle energy that could be felt by the sensitive souls.

This is where Srinivasa Ramanujan had his personal audience with the Devi, Goddess Namagiri, his guide in all matters of life. He sat with his eyes closed and chanted verses from the Devi Mahatmyam, letting his mind dissolve into deep relaxation. Having invoked the mother divine, he then opened his eyes and unleashed endless formulae and equations, scribbling his chalk away onto the stone slabs of the temple floor. Hours passed by, though it felt like a few moments to him. Finally, overcome by extreme pangs of hunger, he headed home.

Having taken a quick dip in the holy Cauvery, the Ganges of the south, he finished his Sandhya-Vandanam (evening prayers) and was now sitting on the floor with a huge banana leaf, ready for dinner. Out came boiled red rice, which Ramanujan made into a small hillock, creating a dent in the centre for some ghee (clarified butter). Then came his favourite hot and spicy rasam, which was poured on top of the rice. Before starting to eat, like a dutiful Hindu Brahmin, he took a few drops of water in his right palm and sprinkled it clockwise around the banana leaf once. Then he took a morsel of food and kept it outside the leaf. Saying the mantras taught to him since childhood, honouring the food on the plate with gratitude, he devoured the rasam rice. This was followed by a helping of rice again, this time with yogurt and mango pickle.

As soon as he finished dinner, he promptly went back to his first and only love — mathematics. The relatively cooler and quieter nights would offer his mind beautiful insights into the world of numbers.

* * *

'Unfortunately', said the head master of Ramanujan's high school to the assembly, 'he has only managed a 100 on 100 in the exam'. Everyone was perplexed. The head master continued,

'If left to the selection committee of maths teachers, they would have given him more than the highest possible marks! Students, I am happy to share that Srinivas Ramanujan has topped the whole state of Tamil Nadu in the maths exams and has been awarded a scholarship for his college degree'. Although he was slightly heavy, his friends lifted Ramanujan on their shoulders and paraded him around in joy. Given the obsession Indians have with exams, marks and scholarships, he was a local prodigy, almost a mini-celebrity in his town. Trouble though, was about to begin.

He came across the book that was about to change his life. Through a random accident, someone gave him Carr's *Synopsis of Elementary Results in Pure Mathematics*. The book was a collection of around 5,000 theorems, starting from the basics and proceeding to advanced theorems, which Ramanujan had no exposure to at all. The uniqueness of this book was that it did not explain the proofs behind the theorems. It just stated them, as a matter of fact. Ramanujan was triggered and his mind was on fire. He took it as a personal challenge to derive each one of those theorems on his own, unsupported by the knowledge of higher mathematics or any other aid. Armed with his black slate, pieces of chalk and his elbow, which he used to erase the chalk repeatedly, he took a long lone walk to becoming a mathematical genius. In the next two years, on his own, Ramanujan proved the most advanced theorems, a feat that would leave future mathematicians in awe of his raw genius. In proving one formula, he discovered many others and finally started compiling them in a rough notebook. But in the process, he flunked all his subjects except mathematics and lost his scholarship.

He attempted to clear his graduation thrice and failed each time. He was declared unfit for a college degree. He was alone on the streets of Madras, broke and beaten down. He desperately needed a job to keep himself going and so he started teaching maths to high-school children. Shockingly enough, he failed as a maths tutor too. He realized he might be brilliant at maths, but teaching was a different ball game altogether.

His mother, seeing her son losing confidence and hope, decided there was only one way for him to bounce back in life — marriage! She got him married off to a thirteen-year-old girl from a nearby village. Her name was Janaki.

Janaki did bring in Lady Luck with her. Ramanujan finally got a job as a clerk at the Madras Port Office, a post way beneath his intellectual abilities. The only good thing about this job was he was encouraged by his supervisor, a certain Mr. Narayan Iyer, to pursue higher mathematics. For the first time, Ramanujan met someone who identified potential in his work and guided him forward. A mathematician of sorts himself, Narayan Iyer realized that Ramanujan's work was special and demanded global recognition. He nudged Ramanujan to try his luck and write to British mathematicians sharing his ideas. Ramanujan wrote to several established mathematicians but only received polite rejections.

As his final attempt, he wrote to the legendary Prof. G. H. Hardy of Cambridge, London.

* * *

It was a beautiful English morning. Prof. Hardy sat alone in his study overlooking the lush green Cambridge campus, the sun beaming through the huge glass windows, lighting up his plush teakwood desk, which was laden with books, loose sheets of paper, and a cup of hot Earl Grey tea waiting to be sipped. Prof. Hardy was a mathematical sensation all over Britain, a member of the august Royal Society and one of the most respected professors at the prestigious Trinity College, Cambridge.

Suddenly, he heard a sharp double knock on his door. The room was now graced with the presence of Prof. Littlewood, a short, stout fellow with blue eyes and thick, blonde hair. He was quite a contrast to Hardy, who was tall, thin and exquisitely handsome.

Littlewood was himself a distinguished mathematician and commanded an expertise that was hard to find, even by Trinity standards.

'I receive unusual letters all the time but this one wins hands down! It's from a poor Indian clerk who claims he can solve the infinite series', said Hardy, tossing an envelope to Littlewood. Littlewood read the letter aloud:

Dear Sir,

I beg to introduce myself to you as a clerk in the Port Trust Office, Madras with an annual salary of only twenty pounds. I have had no university education but have gone through the ordinary school course. I am twenty-three years old now, striking a new path in mathematics with a special investigation in divergent series and the results I get are termed by local mathematicians as 'startling'.

I would request you to go through the enclosed papers containing my work. I would like to get my theorems published. Being inexperienced, I would highly value any advice from you. Requesting to be excused for the trouble I give you.

I remain,
Yours truly,
S. Ramanujan.

Enclosed were nine pages of intense mathematics with indigenous research and bold claims, all written in neat schoolboy handwriting. Hardy and Littlewood read the nine pages multiple times, each time their eyebrows rising higher. Several hours of uninterrupted evaluation later,

'Hardy, you don't believe in God, right'? asked Littlewood.

'That's damn right. I only believe in science', replied Hardy.

'Well, if this guy is genuine, you may soon need to search for some explanation of higher powers', teased Littlewood. Hardy was lost in deep thought.

'He must be genuine. No one can have the imagination to invent this kind of stuff.'

He opened his official letter pad and started writing a response. He decided he wanted to see this clerk and soon.

* * *

'Just cut it'! said Ramanujan to his wife, Janaki. He closed his eyes and clenched his fists tight, his face contracting in pain. Janaki whispered *'Aum Namo Narayanaye'* (Salutations to Lord Narayana) and praying for forgiveness, moved the scissor through, cutting his kudumi (tuft of hair) in one strike. His mother almost fainted.

It was not just his tuft that Ramanujan had cut; with his decision to cross the forbidden seas, Ramanujan had cut ties with his Bharatiya (Indian) roots, with his friends and relatives, and with tradition. But in a vivid dream the previous night, Devi Namagiri had appeared before him and given her approval for the travels, and that's all that mattered. Hardy had taken immense troubles to convince Cambridge authorities to invite Ramanujan to England for mathematical research. He finally had a chance to pursue pure mathematics, that too at the global stage. He was not going to let this opportunity pass. He was going to England.

In the next few weeks, he learnt how to wear western clothes and eat with a fork and knife. He packed his life into one suitcase, a difficult task for someone who had never even travelled outside Tamil Nadu, let alone the country. With a heavy heart, he bid farewell to his mother and wife and entered the second-class cabin of the S. S. Nevasa, his ship to Britain. As the steamer drifted off the port of Madras, he wondered when he would see his family again.

The sea route took him through Sri Lanka, sailing up to the Red Sea, along the Spanish coast and finally through the English Channel. His second class cabin grew unbearably hot during the journey through the Red Sea, while the rich folks enjoyed the cooler cabins marked 'Post Outward-Starboard Homeward' (origin of the word 'posh') enjoyed the cool breeze. Ramanujan didn't mind though, he was heat-trained by Madras. Fortunately, he managed to get his pre-booked vegetarian meals and did not experience sea sickness. After forty days and 6,000 miles on the waters, on 14 April 1913, S. S. Nevasa arrived at the mouth of the Thames and finally docked at the London Harbour.

London was a city of five million people, about ten times the size of Madras. If Madras was the capital of south India, London was the capital of the world! Ramanujan stepped on the Queen's soil, all alone. With his mediocre English, he managed to take a horse-drawn carriage straight to Trinity College, Cambridge.

* * *

'Welcome to Cambridge', said Hardy with a huge smile, as Ramanujan entered his office.

'Thank you, sir. It's an honour', replied Ramanujan, confused whether he should do a namaste or shake hands. He ended up doing neither. They checked each other out. After two years of friendship through letters, they were now face-to-face.

He looks much younger than I imagined! was the common unsaid thought in their heads.

Littlewood joined them soon, looking much older and shorter than the two. For the lack of matters to discuss and suffering from the social awkwardness that scientists sometimes face, they decided to jump straight into mathematics.

'We went through the theorems and results you shared, and we are very impressed, to say the least. In due course of time, we hope they will be published', said Hardy.

'That is my hope and prayer', remarked Ramanujan.

'I am sure it will happen Mr. Ramanujan', said Hardy. 'By the way, am I pronouncing your name right?'

'Perfectly, sir. Well I am very excited to share more results that I have discovered. The letter only contained a small sample of my work. Here is a notebook with more details', said Ramanujan, as he pulled out a sketchy, rugged notebook with pages over pages of handwritten formulae and equations. Hardy and Littlewood were noticeably taken aback and slowly took the notebook, glancing through the pages. The looks on the faces of the two Englishmen was priceless!

Hardy requested his office staff to take Ramanujan to his room and help him settle in. He had come to Hardy's office straight from the port. As soon as Ramanujan left the room, Hardy and Littlewood buried themselves in the two notebooks.

They could not believe what they were witnessing. Slowly, page by page, as they studied Ramanujan's notebooks, reality dawned on them. They were staring at a collection of breathtakingly new and extraordinarily original research, which could change the future of mathematics forever.

'I have never seen anything like this before. I can only compare him with Euler or Jacobi'! announced Hardy, still buried into the notebooks. Littlewood nodded in agreement.

Euler and Jacobi! Really?

Leonhard Euler and Karl Jacobi were towering figures in the history of mathematics, celebrated as some of the most profound and productive mathematicians. And Hardy was comparing them with this mysterious Indian clerk with no formal background in mathematics. *What did Hardy see in those notebooks?*

The notebooks contained thousands of theorems, corollaries and examples, most without any proof or explanation. These two humble notebooks would frustrate and dazzle generations of future mathematicians for the sheer density of mathematical riches they contained.

It was a sense of enigma and awe with which Littlewood and Hardy left the room. They knew their lives would never be the same again, especially so for Hardy. His head was bursting with the possibilities that lay ahead of them and the revolution they could bring into the world of mathematics.

There was one problem though. There were no proofs or explanations for Ramanujan's claims! No journal would publish them. No mathematician would believe them.

* * *

He touched them, ran his hand through their softness, smelled their thick odour and just kept looking at them in deep admiration. He finally had the one luxury he had craved for his entire life. Pristine, shiny, white sheets of high-quality paper! An entire ream sat on his study desk in his studio apartment. After romancing them for a few minutes, Ramanujan quickly showered and unpacked. The first thing he did then was establish a small altar and place with all his devotion the little bronze idol of Devi Namagiri that he had carried from India. This marked a new beginning.

He started his new life in England, but it was not easy. The knives and forks felt like invasions in his mouth, his feet which had been unconstrained for so many years were harshly pinched by uncomfortable tight shoes, the coat and the trousers were suffocating and ill-fitting. The man who could untie the mysteries of complex equations found it very challenging to get the tie knotted right. His little head shake which easily communicated a 'yes' in India was interpreted as a 'no' by the British. Ramanujan knew the English language but did not know the English people. And even his language was heavily accented, which was embarrassing to him. He caught the looks on their faces staring at him when he walked by. If a group of people were laughing around him, he invariably thought they must be laughing at him.

The biggest issue, however, was food. He soon realized the college kitchen served almost no vegetarian food, and so the man who had never stepped inside the kitchen his entire life had to depend on his own horrible cooking. But the ingredients required to cook even a basic Indian meal for himself were unavailable. Ramanujan was perpetually hungry and survived somehow on milk and fruits, although they tasted alien to him. He had no friends and sometimes just longed for a pleasant conversation without the fear of being judged for his skin colour or religion. The culture shock was too jarring for him and he never fully adapted. And so he did the one thing he should not have done — he withdrew in isolation.

But he easily forgot all this when he walked into Hardy's office every day and dove deeper in numbers than the depths of Cauvery, and when he walked into the Wren Library, which was home to greats like Newton's *Principia Mathematica*, the bible for scientists. He imagined his notebooks kept there one day; a dream worth chasing. In the stone churches, medieval chapels, lush green gardens and cobbled pathways of Cambridge, Ramanujan found the perfect ambience for intellectual leisure. He was at home away from home.

* * *

'I need the bloody proofs!'

Hardy had raised his voice to Ramanujan for the first time. He was exasperated. He had been trying for months to get Ramanujan to understand and adopt the methods of operation in the western world of science.

Ramanujan sat there stunned. He felt anger, frustration and helplessness. Suddenly, he was reminded he was in a foreign land, alone and thousands of miles away from home and family. His heart sunk further. He heard Hardy's voice again, softer this time.

'Ramanujan, how do you know all these theorems and results?'

Hardy finally asked the one question he was craving to ask Ramanujan since the time he had seen the first letter. Without any hesitation or ambiguity, in a calm and clear voice, Ramanujan replied,

'The Devi speaks to me'.

There was a heavy silence in the room. Hardy was so shocked that he kept staring at Ramanujan for an uncomfortably long time. Hardy was an atheist, and a staunch one at that. He struggled with the idea of divine intervention in his world of pure mathematics. Ramanujan went on to explain how Devi Namagiri gave him visions on mathematics, sometimes in his dreams, sometimes when he just sat with the intention to tap into the unknown.

'You would probably be more comfortable with the word "intuition". I call it faith. An equation has no meaning for me unless it expresses a thought of God!'

Ramanujan left. Hardy stood there, staring blankly out of the window, into the open skies. He suddenly remembered something he had seen scribbled away in a corner in one of Ramanujan's notebooks, a note that made no sense to him at all. He fanatically searched for that page. Finally, he found the inconspicuous note that read:

The primordial and the several:

$$2^n - 1$$

Ramanujan had hurriedly written further to explain the above mathematical quantity, stating:

when n = 0, the expression denotes shunya (zero), the primordial, nothingness or everythingness;

when n = 1, the expression denotes one or unity, the one supreme God or the non-dual self;

when n = 2, the expression denotes three, or the holy trinity of Brahma, Vishnu and Mahesh or the three Gunas of Sattva, Rajas and Tamas and other connotations of the digit three as per Hindu scriptures;

when n = 3, the expression denotes seven, or the Sapta Rishis (the Seven Sages) or the Sapta Dhaatus (seven bodily tissues as per Ayurveda), so on and so forth.

Hardy kept staring at this side note in disbelief. Ramanujan wasn't being silly, superstitious, unnecessarily abstract or ridiculously religious when he claimed: *'An equation has no meaning for me unless it expresses a thought of God'*.

* * *

It was a cold November night. Winter was beginning to set in. Hardy was by the fireside at his home, with his pipe lit up and a book in his hands when a knock on the door startled him.

Who could it be, this late in the night?

He opened the door to find Ramanujan. Dressed in his south Indian loincloth underneath his English coat and his feet in Indian sandals, he was a pretty amusing sight. For all his mathematical eccentricity, Ramanujan was quite a likeable character. He was mostly cheerful and quick with a joke or two. The most striking aspect of his personality was undoubtedly his sparkling eyes. Ramanujan noticed the subtle shock on Hardy's face and said, 'I just feel so comfortable in this attire. I do better maths that way'. Hardy smiled.

'I hope I didn't disturb you. I know it's a little late in the night', continued Ramanujan.

'Not at all. I was just enjoying a light read. Do you usually stay up late at night'? asked Hardy, gesturing Ramanujan to take a seat.

'Yes I do. The night fascinates me. What the human eyes miss in the day, the night reveals openly. You can see the infinity of the stars and the skies only in the night. The day is like zero, the absolute reality, while the night is like infinity, the subjective reality of endless possibilities.'

'And what did the night reveal to you'? asked Hardy, amazed by the ease with which Ramanujan stitched together mathematics, mysticism and metaphysics.

'Well, I was working on partitions when the numbers took the form of a voice and spoke to me. What they said shook me.' Hardy was listening attentively. Ramanujan continued,

'Look at you humans with bloated egos, so proud of your little brains. How much do you really know about us? How much do you really understand the world you inhabit'?

'Not much, but I am trying. You need to help me,' I said.

'Ask with devotion and act with sincerity and the universe shall reveal its deepest secrets to you. But keep it not for your own glory or satisfaction; share it with mankind for the benefit of the entire human race.'

Ramanujan paused, looked straight into Hardy's eyes, and pulled from within his coat a bundle of sheets. Putting them in Hardy's hands, he said, 'Here are your proofs. I now understand why my theorems need to be shared in a way that the world understands and ultimately uses them. I shall work on more. By the instruction of the kingdom of numbers, I promise I shall do whatever you ask me to, in your way'.

Hardy was stunned, moved, overwhelmed, joyful and guilty all at once. Not a single word came out of his mouth.

'I must go back now and maybe get some sleep. Who knows the Devi might share a vision in my dream for a new theorem, without a proof', chuckled Ramanujan. Hardy burst into laughter as he waved the crazy Indian mathematician goodbye. What an unusual team they made!

Over the next few months, Ramanujan did keep his promise. He diligently supplied elaborate proofs to his conjectures, he learnt the nuances of mathematics the western way from Hardy, he even attended lectures on traditional mathematics along with other students. When he realized that one of his claims was actually wrong, he humbly accepted it. 'Proof and rigour' — he was absorbing the gospel according to Hardy. The genius had been tamed and trained. Hardy kept his promise too. Together, they published beautiful papers in top journals, shaking and waking up mathematicians across the world to their fresh methods and results. Soon, Cambridge made an exception to their norms and decided to give Ramanujan a BA (Bachelor of Arts) degree, based on one of his research papers. Finally, he was a graduate. He was very quickly climbing the stairway to success and fame. It was his dream coming true!

* * *

But then, the first cannon sounded.

On 4 August 1914, Britain declared war against Germany, thus officially entering the First World War.

The imperial and extravagant Cambridge campus turned into a ghost town overnight. Makeshift hospitals sprung up treating wounded soldiers. Littlewood was gone. Research funding was gone. Most of the students were gone. But most disastrously, all the vegetables and fruits were gone! Ramanujan, guilty of letting go of his traditional Indian lifestyle to suit the west, had pledged to at least never pollute his palate. He had struggled with food ever since he came to England but now he was at his worst, surviving only on boiled rice, lemon and salt. The more extreme the situation became, the more inflexible he was. The same eccentricity and stubbornness that made him an intellectual giant was now making him starve himself.

To make matters worse, he was destroyed by the brutal English chill. The Madras boy was freezing in his little room with no heating arrangements. Had he asked for help, he could have got the heating in his room fixed. But he was too shy to ask. He went on for nights without sleeping, for days without eating and of course with no one to speak to. He lost tremendous amounts of weight and hope. Trinity rejected his application for a fellowship. The hardest blow to his life, much graver than food and climate conditions, was the fact that from the time he had left India, he had not received a single letter from Janaki. He was convinced she had forgotten him and moved on. He missed the simple life he had back home — hot rasam rice, the stone slabs of the temple and the love of his family. Ramanujan had become a malnourished, depressed emotional wreck.

In such a situation, one day, he coughed blood and somehow admitted himself to a hospital. He was diagnosed with advanced tuberculosis. This was the beginning of the darkest phase of his life.

When Hardy reached the hospital, he saw a version of Ramanujan that shook and saddened him. He silently sat beside Ramanujan a long time, feeling guilty for not having taken good care of his friend. Ramanujan slowly opened his eyes and managed to give half a smile. He took out a small note from his pocket and gave it to Hardy. The note had a formula in Ramanujan's handwriting which Hardy immediately recognized. And then Ramanujan said something Hardy would never forget.

'We are within 0.04 per cent error. As N tends to infinity, the error tends to zero. We have cracked the unsolvable partitions. We shall call it the Circle Method'.

Hardy skipped a heartbeat. He realized the power of that moment. He realized what a monumental breakthrough this was. He realized they were knocking on the doors of mathematical immortality. And before Hardy's mind could be pulled back into the realm of logic, Ramanujan, anticipating Hardy's words, took a few sheets from the table next to his bed and gave them to Hardy, saying:

'Here are the proofs. You might have to deal with a complaint against me for spending too much time in the bathroom every day. You see, that's the only place, which is somehow warm and quiet, and so I would work in the bathroom. The doctor thinks I take long baths against his advice', smiled Ramanujan.

A half-dead, starving tuberculosis patient is working from the bathroom to prove the partition formula! Hardy let that sink in for a few moments. Then propelled by the urgency to get this published, he got up to leave.

'I shall visit you again soon. On my way here, I took a taxi with a rather dull number plate. I thought it was a bad omen. Looks like I was wrong', said Hardy as he put on his hat.

'Oh really? What number was it?' asked Ramanujan.

'1729', said Hardy. He noticed how instantly Ramanujan's head tilted upwards and his left hand began to gesture in air, as if writing something. Within five seconds, Ramanujan said, 'That's a very interesting number Hardy, not a dull one at all. You see, 1729 happens to be the smallest number expressible as a sum of two cubes in two different ways'. Hardy stared at Ramanujan in utter disbelief.

How does he do this? How?

Hardy gave a broad smile to Ramanujan, took his hat off in a gesture of respect, and dashed off.

* * *

'I, Srinivasa Ramanujan Iyengar, elected Fellow of the Royal Society, pledge to abide by the laws and norms of the oldest scientific institution in the world.'

As he took his oath, becoming the first Indian to enter the Royal Society of mathematics, the audience consisting of the world's most eminent scientists tapped their knuckles on the tables — the signature salute of welcome to the new member. Soon afterwards, he became the first Indian and the first brown man ever to become a fellow at Trinity College, Cambridge. These were the highest honours a mathematician could aspire for. On foreign soil, he had made himself and his country very, very proud. Four years and several publications and prizes later, physically weak but mentally rejuvenated, Ramanujan decided to go home for a visit. The war was over and sea routes were safe for travel again.

'Write to me every week', said Hardy at the harbour. 'And come back to us in a year. We have only begun to scratch the tip of the iceberg.'

'I shall', said Ramanujan. 'Thank you for everything. You have indeed been my true friend'. They hugged, for the first time in four years.

Would Janaki come to receive me? Does she still love me?

Ramanujan's thoughts were drowned by the loud noise of the steamer drifting off. He resigned his mind to the waves. The matters of heart were, alas, beyond equations or formulae.

* * *

He decided he was going to overeat even before he had started. Ramanujan unleashed himself on the authentic south Indian food in front of him. Finally, the four-year-long wait was over. Apart from Devi Namagiri dictating equations, the only other visions he had in his dreams were of dosas and idlis!

Janaki did come. They were finally together again. A lot of misunderstandings were cleared. Janaki still loved him! Ramanujan was happy and dreamt of a life devoted to mathematics and with Janaki by his side. There was one problem though — his health was deteriorating at a rapid pace every day.

All the traditional and modern treatments were administered but nothing was helping. It just kept getting worse. He coughed blood often and was restricted to his bed completely. A competent astrologer himself, Ramanujan decided to check his charts. The findings were clear, he knew his time was limited. He had two options in front of him — to either take complete rest and attempt to steal a year or more of life or plunge at full throttle in his work and finish as much as he could. He chose the latter. He buried himself into mathematics deeper and harder.

On his deathbed, Ramanujan was at the pinnacle of his creative imagination and intellectual superiority. It was as if the approaching death had ignited a final flurry of ideas that were impossible during normal times. He scribbled his results on sheets of paper and put them in Janaki's custody, asking her to send them to Hardy. He wrote to Hardy informing him of his latest discoveries in mock theta functions.

In the early hours of 26 April 1920, Ramanujan merged into infinity. He was all but thirty-two years young.

* * *

'It is difficult for me to explain what I owe to Ramanujan'. Hardy was addressing the crowd that had gathered to pay their final condolences to Ramanujan in London.

> 'He had one gift which no one could deny — a profound and invincible originality that has been a constant source of suggestion to me. Littlewood once told me, 'Every positive integer is one of Ramanujan's personal friends'! I believe this is true, and friends share secrets with each other. For him, every equation had

> a personality, every number was a friend, and every formula had a form. His forays into the labyrinths of numbers were his way of experiencing beauty of the mother divine.
>
> He probably would have been a better mathematician if he was more trained in his youth. But then he would be lesser of a Ramanujan and more of a European professor. The loss would have been more than the gain.
>
> And sometimes when I sit alone and ponder over my life, or when I am forced to listen to pompous people, I think to myself, "Well, I have done something you would never be able to. I have collaborated with the genius of Ramanujan . . . on something like equal terms".'

Ramanujan was way ahead of his times. It was as if he had travelled millions of miles ahead in the field of mathematics and was patiently waiting there for others to catch up. He left a treasure trove for future mathematicians, who for centuries to come, would take giant leaps off his shoulders.

Ramanujan did not die. Ramanujans don't die.

This was the legacy of a self-trained mathematician who stumbled upon infinity.

* * *

An entire century after he left us, Ramanujan's work still remains absolutely relevant and continues to inspire modern-day mathematicians. It is mindboggling to note that his theorems are now influencing avenues of study that did not even exist when he was alive, such as computer engineering, black holes, string theory, Google Maps and even the cure for cancer. It was as if Ramanujan had described in detail alien inhabitants of a distant planet two generations before we even knew the planet existed. His equations are being snatched from history and applied to modern science. After 100 years of progress with the help of machines, mathematicians are now able to prove the conjectures he had made intuitively back then.

The Lost Notebook

Some of Ramanujan's most path-breaking work was done by him on his deathbed. These sheets were bundled hastily into a notebook, which was unfortunately lost in the dust of time. But destiny would not allow his work to be constrained to obscurity. In the most unlikely manner, befitting a suspense thriller novel, this notebook was discovered in 1976, a good fifty-six years after his death, tucked away into the basement of the Wren Library at Cambridge! Its discovery, one American mathematician said, was comparable to finding the tenth symphony of Beethoven. This new manuscript of Ramanujan fuelled a fresh flow of energy towards proving his theorems all over again.

* * *

KEY TAKEAWAYS

1. Passion Will Demand Sacrifice

Fortunate are those who find their passion, their calling in life and spend their life doing what they love. Even more fortunate are those who can make their passion their profession. But once you do find your passion, you have to pursue it with all your might. And remember — passion will demand sacrifice!

Ramanujan found no price too high for pursuing his goal. He was determined to succeed and sacrifice everything in the attempt — ready to even die if need be, a martyr for mathematics. Kabir once said, 'I can throw away this body and I can die trying to achieve union with God'. That is the kind of commitment one needs to achieve greatness.

He went door-to-door to show his notebooks to people. He did not give up when Indian and British mathematicians rejected him. He kept trying. He sacrificed his comfort, his new married life, his traditional Indian values. He was declared an outcast by his community — he didn't mind. His illness kept growing worse, but he did not let that come in the way. He struggled culturally, emotionally and physically in England, but he did not turn back. He was not distracted by success or failure. His only focus was his work. But while you pursue your passion, be sensitive to people around you, take care of your friends and family. Passion is not about becoming rich and famous. It's about living every moment, enjoying yourself thoroughly in action.

Passion will demand sacrifice.

2. Secret of Satisfaction

A lot of people are rich yet dissatisfied. Money can be acquired without passion, but satisfaction will come only when you love what you do, every single day. The only way to find satisfaction in work is by making your passion your profession. At least try to do so.

Secret of Satisfaction:
Make your passion your profession!

Manthan

Pause. Introspect. Express.

Are you really passionate about something? What sacrifices are you willing to make for your passion? Have you figured out a way to monetize your passion?

3. Geniuses Need Guidance

How to deal with geniuses or near-geniuses in your team? How to work with people smarter than you? How to lead them? How to manage star performers in your team/group?

Believe it or not, geniuses most often need guidance. Without Hardy, Ramanujan would have probably never become the legend he became. Hardy was himself a brilliant mathematician, but maybe not a genius. If you need to tame a genius, you need to be pretty good yourself. You need to be above a certain threshold in your calibre.

Geniuses need exceptions to the rule. If you are managing a star performer, know that they will need differential treatment and a fresh approach to get them to stay and perform. History is full of examples of geniuses who failed and are forgotten because they did not get the right guidance.

4. The Seen, Unseen and Semi-Seen Hands

No one is brilliant enough to make it to the top alone!

Whether it is Ramanujan, Homi Bhabha, Gandhi, Shivaji Maharaj, Rani Laxmibai or Chanakya; whether it is Edison, Stephen Hawking, Madam Curie, Elvis Presley or Sachin Tendulkar, no one makes it to the top all alone. There are hundreds of people who play a small or a big role in getting the genius to where they belong. Only talent does not take you to the top or make you stay there.

Ramanujan gets a scholarship, is born in an upper-caste family and hence has the privilege to access a community of other influencers who help him in his early days. Someone gifts him Carr's book, a friend pays for his surgery in Madras when he has no money, someone offers their house and food, Narayan Iyer encourages him to write to western mathematicians, Hardy actually sponsors his trip to Cambridge and lobbies hard to get him a BA and then a fellowship at the Royal Society, a lost notebook is discovered fifty-six years after his death and the story goes on and on. A series of complex unexplainable events unfold to manifest the ultimate reality of Ramanujan.

Whether or not you are at the top right now, there are many seen, unseen and semi-seen hands which have pushed you to get you where you are. Recognize them, acknowledge them and appreciate them.

Also, appreciate your own little role in pushing someone else to the top. Play that little role perfectly and rejoice in others' success. Remember the golden rule — *either you win or make someone else win; both are priceless.*

Be grateful for the seen, unseen and semi-seen hands.

Manthan

Pause. Introspect. Express.

Recall how many people have helped you reach where you are. Write their names down. Think of how you can express your gratitude towards them. When will you do it? Can you do it right now, or after you finish reading this chapter, or sometime today? Don't postpone it.

5. Believe in Yourself

Srinivasa Ramanujan has unshakeable belief in his theorems, his roots and his Devi. Whether he is a teenage boy in Madras or a Fellow of the Royal Society at Cambridge, he does not doubt his abilities or the grace of the divine. He is unapologetically an Indian Hindu mathematician, and he holds tight to his belief system. He is comfortable in his skin and identity. He is neither impressed nor disappointed with the west. Back in his day, India was ruled by the British. For an Indian in England to stand his ground and prove he is superior to the white man was revolutionary. *It was as if Ramanujan was fighting an intellectual freedom struggle against England in his own way.*

Of course, this belief was grounded in awareness and humility. He had in fact many moments of self-doubt and depression. But he won them over. There is a thin line between self-belief and arrogance. That thin line is sensitivity.

Self–belief is a Superpower!

6. Science and Spirituality

How do you explain the intuition of Ramanujan? Can you separate his mathematical genius from his spiritual faith in the Devi? What about Aryabhata, Bodhayana and Bhaskaracharya? How did they discover all they did thousands of years ago without telescopes, computers and calculators? India was the birthplace of mathematics and astronomy. Our ancient mathematicians created the decimal system and advanced algebra and geometry, when the Europeans were struggling with basic numbers. Our scriptures mention the value of pi, sine and cosine series, trigonometry, the speed of light, the concept of gravity, and the list is endless.

It is interesting to note that our ancient scientists were spiritual (remember they were mostly rishis) and practised meditation, which yielded higher intuitive powers. Science and spirituality always went hand in hand in India.

Great science needs intuition.
Spirituality is the key to unlock intuition.

7. Practice

The ten-thousand-hour principle

You may be good or great at a skill. You may be a genius. *You still* need to practice. In fact, it is observed that geniuses don't just work hard or harder than most others. They work much harder than most others. They spend every waking minute striving towards their passion.

So how much practice do you need?

One piece of research by Malcom Gladwell says that you need 10,000 hours of practice to start hitting excellence in your skill. This generic rule can be applied to Ramanujan, the Beatles, Bill Gates, Sachin Tendulkar, Lata Mangeshkar and to all other masters of their art.

Note: Practice does not guarantee success. It guarantees constant improvement, it guarantees pace and precision in your skill and that enhances your chances of success drastically. There is absolutely no shortcut to practice.

There is a three-step formula to excellence.

Step 1: Practice
Step 2: Practice
Step 3: Practice

Manthan

Pause. Introspect. Express.

Do you have a routine of serious practice? Are you consistent with your practice? How can you take your practice to the next level?

8. Mind over Matter

Multiple times in his life, and especially on his death bed, Ramanujan demonstrated repeatedly that it is mind over matter. Gurudev Sri Sri Ravi Shankar says, 'A strong mind can carry a weak body, but a weak mind cannot even carry a strong body'!

Mind management

How can you strengthen your mind? One sure-shot way is learning how to meditate and tapping into the deeper realms of the mind. The Bhagvad Gita says, 'Your best friend or your biggest enemy is your own mind'. And nothing gives access to the secret formulae and equations of the mind like meditation does.

9. True Education

What is true education? What is our education system lacking? Why did India fail to identify and glorify Ramanujan?

He was rendered unfit for college education and declared a failure. Why did Indian colleges not make the exceptions that Trinity made to accept and adopt him? His life begs us to ask: how many Ramanujans dwell in India today, undiscovered and unrecognized, forever lost?

Back to school

What are the five things that you think the Indian education system must teach children today?

Here is my list of five things I wish I was taught in school in a fun way:

1. Yoga and meditation
2. Financial literacy
3. Creative thinking
4. Entrepreneurship skills
5. Emotional and mental fitness

One special mention of another missing attribute: **seva**

(I elaborate on these skills more in my YouTube video called 'Back to School: 5 things I wish I was taught in school')

What are your top five?
Please write below.
Please see how you can get children to learn these skills either in school or outside.

1.

2.

3.

4.

5.

The Scientific Heritage of India

- The Right-Angle Triangle theorem attributed to Pythagoras was discovered by Bodhayana in 800 BCE (200 years before Pythagoras was born) and is mentioned in his *Sulaba Sutras.*
- Indians calculated the value of pi correctly upto thirty-one decimal places thousands of years ago.
- It was Aryabhata who first proposed that the earth is round, that it rotates around its axis and revolves around the sun. He did this in 500 AD, roughly a thousand years before Copernicus. Galileo was

sentenced to life imprisonment in 'modern' Europe as recently as the sixteenth century for proposing the same theory. Even without calculators or telescopes, Aryabhata calculated the length of a day, and these values are accurate according to modern science.

- The concept of the 'atom' was elaborated by the physicist Kanada in 600 BC. Europe did not acknowledge atoms till a few hundred years ago.
- The Fibonacci Series (0,1,1,2,3,5,8,13,21 . . .) is originally an Indian invention. Indian mathematicians Hemchandra and Gopala wrote this long before the Italian mathematician Fibonacci.
- Sushruta is considered the 'Father of Surgery' and describes various surgical operations including plastic surgery in his book, the *Sushruta Samhita* written way back in the sixth century.

This is just a small, partial list of mindblowing advances ancient Indians made in the field of mathematics and in all branches of science. In fact, the very fundamental basis of mathematics, the 'zero', the decimal system, was introduced by Indians. The sad part is that most Indians don't know about their rich scientific heritage and due credit is not given to the original heroes. Our education system does not teach us our true history. We don't even see movies or modern books on our academic heroes. In Ramanujan's case also, the best and the only motion picture on his life called *The Man Who Knew Infinity* was made by the west. Thankfully, we've recently seen

OTT series, like *Rocket Boys*. The country with the oldest tradition of science, that probably produces the largest number science graduates, hardly knows its own scientific heritage.

Saraansh

A summary of your learnings from this chapter

1.
Passion will demand sacrifice

2.
Secret of Satisfaction
Make your passion your profession

3.
Geniuses need guidance

4.
Be grateful for the seen, unseen and semi-seen hands
(No one is brilliant enough to make it to the top all alone)

5.
Either you win or you make someone else win — both are priceless!

6.
Self-belief is a Superpower!

7.
Practice

The 10,000-hour rule

The three-step formula to excellence: Practice, Practice and Practice

8.
Science and spirituality are two sides of the same coin

9.
Mind over matter

10.
Meditation is the code to access the mind

11.
True Education
(We need to take responsibility to give true education to our children)

12.
India is the birthplace of science and civilization. Let's feel proud about our scientific heritage.

9

Rani Abbakka

'Ahimsa paramo dharama,
dharam himsa tadevacha'

It was a sight to behold. Tucked away deep into the farms, covered by tall grass shoots all around, lay the secret akhaada (wrestling pit) no one knew about. The mud in the pit was mixed with ghee, milk, water and some herbs. At a makeshift altar on the side stood a small red idol of Lord Hanuman, the epitome of power and eternal source of inspiration for all wrestlers. Dressed in their traditional kushti garb, body dripping with oil and sweat, the two wrestlers were ready for malla yudha (wrestling combat). They took some mud from the pit and sprinkled it on each other as a gesture of goodwill. Bowing in obeisance towards Lord Hanuman, they both shouted '*Jai Bajrang Bali*' (victory to Lord Hanuman) and took their stance. With bodies leaning forward and their hands interlocked, they dug their heels a little into the mud for better grip.

He looked at his opponent. Short, dark-skinned. Tight, chiseled muscles and broad shoulders supporting an athletic body. Laser-sharp focus in the eyes and confidence on the face, kalava (holy thread) on the right wrist and long hair tied into a loose ponytail. The only thought in his head was:

Can she really fight?

Within a few minutes, he had his answer. Although an experienced wrestler and a bull of a man himself, he was no match for her speed and technique.

She faked an advance on the left but swirled to the right and got behind him. She tightened the lock around his neck, squeezing the breath out of his lungs. In a flash, she turned and pinned him to the ground, sitting over his chest. She was about to make her final move to seal her win when intuitively she raised her right hand behind her back and blocked the lathi (a heavy bamboo rod). Her surprise attacker had made no sounds at all, but she was seasoned and gifted. She rose up instantly holding the man on the ground under her left leg while she fought her new opponent with both her hands. Within seconds, she had one opponent by the throat and the other under her feet. Princess Abbakka Chowta looked like an enraged Maa Durga that moment.

Suddenly, she paused. She took a deep breath and let go of the two men. Catching her racing heartbeat, she walked to the left side of the pit. Lying on the ground were three swords. She picked one herself and flung the other two to her partners. For the next hour, they practiced swordcraft and free hand combat, switching occasionally to martial arts.

'*Sarve Dhanushaha*' (to your bow) echoed the words in the air. Abbakka knew this instruction only too well. This was her favourite part. Within a flash, she was off the pit and on her horse, which had been standing on the side all along. She now wore her quiver full of arrows on the back and held a special bow in her left hand. The bow was constructed out of soft bamboo wood, which gave it a unique short size and elasticity at the ends. On the back edge of the bow, engraved with silver ash stood the words:

'धर्मो रक्षति रक्षितः'

(Dharma protects those who protect it.)

An obstacle path was set for the princess. Even with stationary and moving targets and a counter-attack by other archers, she nailed the test. She got off the running horse swiftly and checked everyone to ensure no one was hurt in the training. She then took off her bow and quiver and settled down in a perfect padmasana (lotus pose), eyes closed in meditation. The training for the day had come to an end.

After some time, Princess Abbaka opened her eyes softly. In the meantime, one of the guards had shimmied up a tall palm tree and was raining down coconuts on the ground with loud thuds. Soon, the princess had savoured three coconuts with a smile. She did not forget her partners and even the helpers and ensured everyone got sweet coconut water to quench their thirst.

She dismissed the staff and decided to take a walk back to the palace. As she walked alone along the shore, she had no idea that she was being watched carefully all this while. Her dear and loving uncle, the great Tirumala Raya III, the honorary king of Ullal, had been secretly observing her training for the past two days. He needed the answer to a very important question — *Is she ready?*

As Abbakka went to bed that night, the only thought lingering in her mind was:

'Why do I train so hard? What battle am I preparing for?'

As Tirumala Raya went to bed that night, the only thought lingering in his mind was:

It's time now. Ullal needs her destiny, her queen.

* * *

The first rays of the morning sun lit up the grandeur of the thousand-pillar temple, making it look even more majestic. Ullal woke up to celebration and festivities. It was a special day. The day they had been waiting for. Today, they would get their queen, their ruler, their mother.

She sat at the centre of the Savira Khambada Basadi (thousand-pillar Jain temple). The temple was dedicated to the Digambar Jain Bunt community, the lineage of the Chowta dynasty. In the garbhagraha (sanctum sanctorum), stood a magnificent statue of Lord Chandraprabhu, the eighth Tirthankar of Jainism. Abbakka's ancestors had moved to Ullal from Gujarat in the fourteenth century and followed the matrilineal tradition. Following the age-old protocol, Tirumala Raya III anointed his niece, Abbakka, the first queen of Tulu Land with their capital in Moodibidri. Known as Jain Dakshin Kashi (Kashi of the south), Moodibidri was the cultural hub of Jainism in the south, with hundreds of Jain temples and centres of scholarship.

The puja concluded and after getting the crown blessed by the Lord, the head priest placed it on Abbakka Chowta. The citizens of Ullal burst into a thunder of cheers and slogans! And in that moment, the princess became the queen. Time does not prepare you for moments like these. Leaders rise to the occasion with grace and never look back. This was the defining moment in the life of the young leader.

Tirumala Raya had one more task to accomplish, which he did almost immediately after Abbakka's coronation. He arranged for her marriage with Lakshmappa Bangaraja, the king of Mangalore, which was situated very close to Ullal and had emerged as one of the biggest centres of coastal trade. The new couple had a happy married life and was blessed with a daughter. In accordance with the Aliyasantana (matrilineal) tradition, Abbakka continued to live in Ullal and rule her kingdom, visiting her husband at regular intervals. Her daughter lived with her — the future heir to the throne.

Everything was happy and hearty on the peaceful and prosperous western coast of south India.

But then, the first cannon was fired.

An ambitious king from a land far far away had set his evil eyes on the world's golden sparrow, Bharat. The Portuguese had arrived in Calicut, taken over Goa and now wanted Mangalore. Easily threatened and scared, Bangaraja agreed to all the conditions imposed by the Portuguese over sea trade and became a puppet king. But Abbakka refused to bow down to the firangis. In a heated argument between Abbakka and Bangaraja, she chose her country over her marriage. Returning her wedding jewellery to her husband (tantamount to a modern-day divorce), Abbakka continued ruling over Ullal independently, while the kingdom of Mangalore shook hands with the Portuguese.

* * *

The two men walked into the royal meeting chambers of the queen of Ullal. Both tall, slim and clean shaven, they wore thick red coats till their knees, white shirts with oversized collars and tight white pants. Their headgear was a curvy black fur hat which allowed their beige locks to fall out over their ears. They looked stiff and uncomfortable although they carried a cordial half-smile on their faces. Abdul, Ullal's commander-in-chief, welcomed the guests and signalled them to have a seat. On Abbakka's orders, today he was dressed in a long white Arab thawb. Abdul looked at the two men and wondered why they had dressed in such heavy attire that was utterly unsuitable for the Indian tropical weather. *Stupid, white-skinned firangis*, he thought.

Rani Abbakka sat on her grand throne at the centre of the large room overlooking the gorgeous shoreline of the

Arabian Sea. A pentagonal pond lay between the exquisite visitor chairs and the queen. She looked as majestic as the ocean. Draped in a crimson red nine-yard silk saree, she wore a golden kamarbandh around her waist, embedded with the choicest precious stones. On her forehead between the eyebrows, she wore a large circular tilak (forehead mark) with the outer circle of red kumkum (vermilion powder) and an inner one of yellow chandan (sandalwood). A massive fifteen-foot bronze statue of Lord Mahavira made for an impressive background to her throne. Unlike other formal meetings, today she deliberately chose to carry a large dagger in a shiny silver scabbard hanging from her waist. It was a tacit message for her visitors.

Although small, Ullal was a prosperous kingdom because of its strategic location on the Indian coastline, which made it an immensely profitable export centre for pepper and fabric. This is exactly why the Portuguese wanted control over Ullal. And hence, this meeting.

'Greetings, Your Highness', said the younger of the two men, deliberately choosing to skip the customary salute to a king or a queen in India.

'Admiral Dom Álvaro da Silveira and I come today in the holy name of Christ, on behalf of His Highness Manuel I, the great king of Portugal, to discuss a business proposal for you.'

'Greetings, young man. Welcome Admiral', responded Abbakka in a neutral tone without a smile.

The Admiral cleared his throat, looked at the queen and said:

'Your Highness, as you know the Càsa da India is now in charge of the sea routes between India and Africa and controls the ports of Goa, Daman, Diu, Bombaim, Calicut, Kochi and Mangalore. As per the Portuguese Sea Route Treatise, all trade and tourist ships traversing the high seas are obligated to pay cartaz (Portuguese sea tax) to maintain their license to trade in spices, clothes or any other cargo items and enjoy the protection of the powerful Portuguese naval force.

We would like to include your little kingdom in our preferred list of approved harbours to allow you to continue your trade uninterrupted.'

Abbakka smiled.

'And . . .'?, she prodded, knowing what was yet to come. She was well-aware of what her estranged husband, King Bangaraja of Mangalore, had signed up for with the Portuguese.

'And we require you to banish all the Muslim traders you deal with directly. Going forward, you shall go through our gatekeepers for trade with any Arab or African kingdoms or merchants', said the Admiral, avoiding eye contact with Abdul.

Abbakka looked away into the ocean as if she had sailed away with the winds. From the corner of her eye, she saw her young daughter who was sitting in one end of the room observing the conversation. After a long gaze, she turned to face Admiral Silveira and spoke in a calm, confident voice. 'Gentlemen, a long, long time ago, a great consciousness arose on the planet and was recognized as a true leader of the masses. I have been inspired by something he said once and I quote:

"You, my brothers and sisters, were called to be free. But do not use misuse your freedom, serve one another humbly in love. For the entire law is fulfilled in keeping this one command: love your neighbour as yourself."'

'Do you know who said these powerful compassionate words, Admiral'? asked Abbakka.

He shook his head.

'You, officer?'

He shook his head too.

'Jesus Christ. He is known as 'Yeshu' in Bharat', said Abbakka.

The two men stared at Abbakka, shocked and stirred.

Her face had changed now. The serenity and coolness of the ocean that her eyes reflected was now a storm and had the force of a tsunami. She leaned forward, looked piercingly into Silveira's eyes and said:

> You come as traders. But then you invade us.
> You threaten us but you call it a business proposal.
> You come in the name of Christ but then you crucify us.
> You offer us slavery, that too as a favour.
>
> This air you breathe in my country, this earth you walk on, this is my mother. This soil is the sandalwood

> I proudly wear on my forehead. How dare you insult her?
>
> We live life by a code, Admiral. It's the code of honour, of dharma, of mutual respect; words you know nothing about. We trade in spices, not freedom.
>
> Leave now, Admiral. Leave with your lousy threat. Your so-called business proposal is rejected. Ullal shall not pay you a single coin as tax. Ullal shall also not only respect but grow its trade with our Arab, Persian and African friends. And I promise you, if your men try to interfere in our affairs, I shall personally haunt every waking and sleeping moment of your life.
>
> Go and tell your impotent king — Ullal is not for sale. Not till this daughter of Bharat has a sword in her hand!
>
> Dismissed!

Abbakka rose and walked away, signalling with her eyes for her daughter to join her.

'So, what did you learn, young woman'? asked Abbakka in a playful sweet voice as she mounted the royal elephant. From a furious ruler and a passionate patriot to an elegant queen and a loving mother, she had the rare ability to switch between a gamut of emotions quickly and effortlessly.

The teenage royalty thought for a moment and then replied,

अहिंसा परमो धर्मः, धर्म हिंसा तथैव च

(Non-violence is the highest dharma. So too is violence to protect dharma.)

'Spoken like a true Jain Chowta princess! Ahimsa is our strength, not our weakness. Hail Lord Mahavira'! said the queen with pride and a broad smile.

Abdul stood there, arms folded on his chest, looking straight at the two firangis. For a moment, he thought this was a good chance. *Why don't I just kill these two losers here? What a delight it would be.* But this would be against doot-nyaya (rules for behaviour with messengers). The two men had been so shocked that they just kept sitting on their chairs. The Admiral finally got up and stormed out of the royal chambers in anger.

'She is just a woman. What can she do'! muttered Silveira as he boarded his horse cart. 'I will make her beg for her life. And then I shall destroy both her army and her personal honour', swore the Admiral.

* * *

It was an amavasya, the moonless night. A cool breeze from the Arabian Sea was blowing, silently adding to the rhythmic music of the waves. The tall palm trees swayed gently to the music, their leaves brushing against the wind.

She stood motionless at the watchtower of her harbour fort, staring into the depths of nothingness over the horizon. And then she saw them, slowly emerging out of the shadows. There must have been at least thirty or forty of them. Dancing over the high tides, they were swiftly closing in like a herd of drunken elephants marching on. Rising high and fluttering forcefully was a flag with eight castles on red stripes, a white centre-square with a prominent blue cross. The Portuguese navy was here.

The ships were rallied in the typical semicircular naval formation, the largest ones at the rear, each carrying eight or ten heavy long-range cannons meant to destroy the enemy fort's walls and if needed, the enemy ships. The Portuguese navy boasted of the most advanced ships equipped with high-tech cannons. Each ship carried a mountain of gun powder and ammunition needed to load and fire the cannons quickly. A team of one hundred oarsmen rowed constantly, sitting in the basement of the vessels. The oarsmen had their hands chained to the oars and were whipped on their bare backs if they slowed down the rowing. The ship also carried a platoon of 100 to 200 soldiers, some with swords and others with bows and arrows to engage the enemy in close- and medium-range combat. Long ropes hung from the tall sails to enable the crew to swing to the enemy ship if it was close enough. Admiral Silveira was on a ship strategically placed in the centre of the formation.

The information she had received was bang on. She was proud of her spy network. She had invested a lot of time and resources in creating a powerful web of loyal Tulu fishermen who travelled in small canoes up and down the coast towards Mangalore and Goa in the pretext of catching local seafood delicacies but were mainly tasked to keep a check on the latest developments of the Portuguese and the Arabs.

She saw the ships again. She had spent her entire life in and around the sea. She knew the enemy would be here in less than a ghatika (ancient Indian unit of time with a modern-day equivalent of twenty-four minutes).

'Let them come. We are ready.'

But the enemy must not know we are ready — that's a fundamental principle of war!

She quickly raised her bow and nocked on to the bowstring her special arrow — the dhandhwani teer (the whistling arrow). As a teen archer, this was a fun trick-arrow she would use to play pranks on the visitors at the royal palace. Today, this would be a useful tool in war.

She said a prayer to Maa Durga and quietly released her fingers from the string. The arrow propelled upwards in the sky making a unique whistling sound like a distant bird singing its song. The Portuguese, now within the line of sight, would not have even noticed the sound. But the Mogaveeras and the Billavas were only too familiar with it. This was their signal. Camouflaged on the top of the tall palms across the wide shoreline to beat the binoculars of the Portuguese captain, this was the sound they had been waiting to hear for the past six hours. Finally, they heard it — the silent whisper of war.

She then quickly climbed up the tallest tower on the edge of the fort to get a panoramic view of the ocean and the ships in front of her. She picked up her bow and touched it lightly to her forehead. Without turning, she extended her right arm behind her and opened her palm. A burning agnivaan was handed to her. The light from the flaming arrowhead revealed the engraved red symbol in the centre of her bow — the swaastika.

She closed her eyes and slowly chanted an ancient prayer:

ॐ महाज्वालाय विद्महे
अग्नि मध्याय धीमहि
तन्नो: अग्नि प्रचोदयात

(Oh great holy flame, let me meditate on thee. Oh, reverred Agni, the God of Fire, give me higher intelligence and power and illuminate my mind.)

Within the next few seconds, almost like a synchronized dance, she adjusted her stance, placed her left foot on the stone wall for better balance, relaxed her shoulders, and turned sideways with the bow in her left hand as her right hand stretched backwards holding the back head of the burning arrow. She raised her bow upwards adjusting the angle to aim for the right trajectory path and took one last long look at her target. She took a breath in. She released the agnivaan.

It shot across the dark sky like a shooting star. Admiral Silveira looked up to notice the flash of light moving in the sky. His eyes first showed surprise, which quickly turned into horror. As he realized the arrow was going to miss his ship by a huge distance, instead of relief, he experienced shivers down his entire body. He knew where the arrow was heading. Hc prayed hard. There are no atheists on a battleship.

'By Jesus… if that arrow hits the…'

Boom!

The agnivaan landed right at the centre-deck of the last ship in the Portuguese fleet, exactly where the gunpowder station was located. The ship exploded instantly into a million pieces, killing almost everyone on board and destroying the vessel with an ear-shattering noise.

What happened next was beyond the wildest imagination of the Portuguese navy. Hundreds of lit agnivaans filled the dark sky like fancy fireworks. The agnivaan was a weapon that was difficult to create and even more difficult to use. The essential part of the arrow was its iron head, which was carefully forged into four little branches to make an iron basket where the inflammable material was stored tightly packed. This ensured the flaming arrow remained lit when shot in the air. The material contained a concoction of sulphur, dead wood, camphor substrate and a mix of highly incendiary herbs. The archers had to wear special gloves to safeguard their palms and wrists. In the hands of a trained firestarter archer, the agnivaan could rain down death and destruction from the skies in unfathomable ways.

The whistling arrow shot earlier by Abbakka was the cue for the special forces hiding on the top of the tall palm trees. The Mogaveeras were trained to shoot long distance. They used special bows that were long and heavy and allowed the arrow to travel far. The Billavas on the other hand were specialists in short- to mid-range archery where accuracy was key, and used shorter bows bent from the edges and lighter arrows. The Mogaveeras and Billavas were fishermen who were trained by the queen to become excellent archers. The Mogaaveeras targeted the farthest of the Portuguese ships setting them aflame. Exactly at the same time, the Billavas targeted the frontal and the side rows of the fleet, damaging them and causing panic. To give themselves different shooting angles, the men swung from the top of one palm tree to another effortlessly. They had spent their entire childhood mastering this art. They were as agile as monkeys on those trees.

Shooting a burning arrow was a very complicated skill that required precision, speed and courage. If shot even a few seconds late, the arrow could burn the archer. If gone astray, the arrow could cause a wild jungle fire or a casualty on one's own side. If mishandled before nocking it on the string, the arrow could burn the very palm tree the archer was on, causing the archer to fall several feet down to a possible death. Abbakka's men were masters of this madness.

Since the caravels farthest from the harbour were on fire, the Portuguese fleet was now trapped inside an outer ring of burning ships. There was nowhere to run or hide. All the sophisticated cannons lay wasted.

And before the Portuguese recovered from the shock and could figure out a comeback strategy, Abbakka launched a full-fledged attack with her smaller and faster boats charging towards the enemy fleet. Within no time, the game was over. A few Portuguese ships were somehow retreating quickly and would get away soon if not chased. Abdul was about to give orders to his men to attack the fleeing ships when Abbakka stopped him. 'Let them go. Let the horrified eyewitnesses carry the bad news to their masters.'

Her message was clear:

'Come to us as guests and we shall open our hearts for you.

Come as traders and we shall make you rich.

But come as the enemy, and we shall deliver you to death.'

The waters of the Arabian Sea turned red that night. The Portuguese had paid in blood for their misadventure, walking straight into a well-planned but rather ambitious ambush by the queen of Ullal. Fortunately, it had worked in her favour. Luck generally favours the brave. Loud celebrations broke in the Ullal camp with drumbeats and victory slogans ringing all over the beach.

ಭೂಮಿಯಲ್ಲಿ ಅವರೊಂದಿಗೆ ಹೋರಾಡಿ,
ಸಮುದ್ರದಲ್ಲಿ ಅವರೊಂದಿಗೆ ಹೋರಾಡಿ,
ಉಳ್ಳಾಲ ಭೂಮಿಗೆ ಜಯವಾಗಲಿ.

Fight them on land
Fight them on sea
Victory to Ullal!

'Cannons can't always win you wars. Sometimes, you need camphor', chuckled the queen as she walked back to her fort. The flag of Ullal was flying high over the fort, untainted.

* * *

She raised her hand up in a full swing and brought the nariyal (coconut) crashing down on the floor. It split into two, water splashing around. The crowd burst into a claps and cheers.

It was a special day, the inaugural day of the Friends of the Seas, an international conference of sailors, sea merchants, ancillary business owners, investors and diplomats from across the world, hosted by Rani Abbakka at her beautiful harbour fort. Presently, they were all gathered on the front deck of Ullal's brand-new ship which was named by Ullal's princess as 'Varuna'. Varuna is the ancient Indian God of the ocean, most revered and feared among the coastal communities.

The ship was a true piece of art, constructed as per the Yuktikalpataru, the world's first treatise on the art of shipbuilding, ship repairing, navigation and naval warfare. In the centre of the deck was a huge display model of the Matsya Yantra, honouring the famous compass that ancient Indian sailors had been using for many centuries. Shining in the sun at the top of the ship's upper deck was an image of Lord Varuna, seated on his makara (crocodile), blessing everyone. Engraved under his image, in gold, stood the motto of Ullal's navy:

शं नो वरुण:

(May Varuna, the Lord of the ocean, be auspicious to us.)

Student groups from various gurukuls had put up exhibition booths around the side decks where they were explaining to the visitors the intricacies of building various types of ships, the usage of specific wood and metal, the construction of hulls, anchors and sails. The most crowded booth however was that of the Jal Aushadhi Vidya (the science of maritime medicine) where ayurvedic doctors were explaining how to overcome mild infections to serious diseases during and post-sea travel. Tender coconut water and piping hot sannas (regional rice cake delicacy) to be eaten with rasam, ghee and coconut chutney were being served to the guests.

Rani Abbakka was now in the conference room at the lower deck of the ship with a select few dignitaries. She knew conferences like these were opportunities to build stronger allies and gauge the international sentiment about an emerging common global threat — the Portuguese. Seated around her were the ambassadors of the Samuttiri of Kohzikode (the king of Calicut), the Nizam Shahi Sultan of Ahmadnagar and the Venkattappanayaka of Bidnur, the two brothers from Yemen who were the richest Arab merchants, an Egyptian who owned the largest fleet of ships in Africa, a Persian who was the head of the labour union and a few other representatives of various business enterprises and diplomats from near and far-off kingdoms along with their teams of translators. Mangalore had not been invited.

The queen did not need translators for herself. She spoke fluent Tulu, Kannada, Malayalam, Tamil, Persian and Arabic. She could read and understand Sanskrit and Prakrit. She was already taking lessons in Dutch.

Also present were Abdul, the commander-in-chief of Ullal's armed forces, Chenappa Mogaveera, Ullal's naval commander and two of Abbakka's most trusted spies.

Abbakka was the only woman in the room.

She was also the most powerful person in the room.

She opened the floor for a discussion after setting the context. A loud voice in a thick Malayali accent was heard first:

'It all began with that wretched Vasco da Gama begging our Indian traders to show him a route to the Indian west coast. And in return of our friendship, he burnt our ships and sacked Kozhikode (Calicut) and the white men took control. They killed the Muslims, the

Hindus and even the Syrian Jews. All in the name of business. Then they won Goa and soon Kochi, Daman, Diu, Dadra and Nagar Haveli and Bombaim', growled the ambassador of Kohzikode.

'And far away from your shores, the Portuguese conquered Mozambique on the coast of Africa, Aden at the Horn of Africa, Hormuz in Persia. In the far east, they now control Ceylon, Macau in China, Nagasaki in Japan and Malacca in south-east Asia', added the Persian labour lord.

'Hmm. So, they are basically creating choke points across the sea silk route. They surround the important cargo harbours and then force their draconic cartaz to allow the ships to pass', said Abbakka, horrified at what she had realized.

'Till now, the Indian Ocean and the Arabian Sea had been blessed with free and fair trade. These barbarians have forced us to fight every single day. They first create sea terrorists who are on their payroll and then they come as 'protectors' and save us from their own pirates! How low can these dogs stoop!' blasted the Egyptian fleet-owner. All eyebrows were raised at this revelation. Even the Arabs did not know this. Suddenly a lot of recent events began to make sense.

'They tax everything. Pepper, cotton, rice, ginger, betel, herbs, steel and even slaves', said the Arab merchant. 'Our profits have sunk by 70 per cent while theirs have tripled!'

'Revered queen, we also cannot forget the fanatic religious narrative the Portuguese feed to their forces. One of the low-ranked officers after getting drunk revealed to me the orders of their king from Portugal, which said, "The golden bird of India is plagued with the worship of the Devil. We must bring them to the holy feet of Christ and save them by washing their sins with their blood"', said one of the spies who had just returned from Goa.

The room fell silent for some time, each lost in thoughts of their past, present and the uncertainty of their future. Each wanted to protect their family and their country. But none had a plan or a passion that drove them to do anything different.

Rani Abbakka broke the silence.

> 'The Portuguese have found in India a supremely rich country that lives by the principle of Vasudhaiva Kutumbakam (the world is my family) and hence openly welcomes and trusts people from all backgrounds. Sadly, it does not know how to defend itself and worse, is diseased by infighting amongst its narrow-minded rulers; an ideal situation for the invaders.
>
> I don't have a solution for the whole nation. But I swear in front of this assembly that I shall not bow down to the Portuguese. Ullal shall remain independent and our trade with you fine gentlemen shall not be impacted by the cartaz. This I promise.'

There was a collective gasp from the men in the room. They kept looking at the queen in awe. She had a fierceness that was both scary and inspiring.

And she did keep her promise. For the next few years, the Ullal ships continued to trade directly with the Arabs and the Africans without paying the cartaz. The Ullal captains knew the sea routes better than the Portuguese and had also mastered guerilla warfare on the sea. When attacked by bigger Portuguese ships, they would hit and run or take the lesser-known river routes to one of the smaller islands and hide. Thanks to Rani Abbakka's excellent diplomatic relations with all the kingdoms around the Arabian Sea and Indian Ocean, Ullal's ships always got help secretly from all corners.

She had now become famous across Arabia, Persia, Africa and even Europe as this lone, enigmatic, brave queen of a tiny kingdom in south India challenging the might of the massive Portuguese naval empire. Her stories made for exciting conversations amongst the sailors and traders, kings and soldiers, and the larger masses. This was a time when Shehenshah Akbar, who ruled most of India and was considered an undefeatable emperor, was paying the cartaz so the Mughal ships carrying Haj pilgrims could sail from Surat to Jeddah. This was the time when the powerful kings of Persia, whose kingdoms stretched from Afghanistan to Turkey, were quietly paying the cartaz for trading on the waters.

At a time like this, when the mighty powers across the world had surrendered to the barbaric oppression by the Portuguese, one small candle kept fighting the storm. And that was beautiful.

* * *

The first rays of the morning sun had just dipped the temple's dhwaja (flag) in a golden hue. The powerful chants were reverberating intensely in the courtyard of the Someshwara temple and ringing across the entire city. The temple trust had invited all the citizens of Ullal with the queen being the chief guest. It was the first Monday of the Shraavan Maas, a special time to praise Lord Rudra/ Mahadev, the God of gods.

ॐ नमो भगवते रुद्राय।

(My salutations to Lord Rudra.)

ॐ नमस्ते रुद्र मन्यव उतोतइषवेनमः।

(My salutations to your benevolent anger and your arrows which destroy the evil.)

The priests continued the chanting from Sri Rudram. Rani Abbakka along with her daughter and members of the royal family sat with eyes closed, immersed in the bliss of the mantras. Suddenly Abbakka's deep meditation was broken by the sound of Abdul whispering in her ears, 'Revered Queen, there is an emergency'. Abbakka slowly opened her eyes. 'Firangis have attacked us. They have sieged the city and broken into the palace. They have even taken control of the fort. You must leave immediately. They are looking everywhere for you. Your life is in danger.'

Abbakka took a deep breath in. She processed what she had just heard and then gave a series of instructions calmly but swiftly. She left with her daughter and bodyguards, with Abdul in the lead. The villages were evacuated, and the secret routes sealed. The havan (fire ceremony) continued.

'I know a safe place where we can hide for now. The firangis will never look for you there', said Abdul.

'And where's that?' asked Abbakka.

'The old durgah (Muslim shrine) at the foothills', replied Abdul. Abbakka nodded.

'Send the messages out to the chieftains. Assemble as many of our forces as you can before sunset', instructed Abbakka. Abdul knew his queen had done the calculations and made up her mind.

They sat there, huddled inside a small room at the basement of the unused durgah. Boys and girls, men and women. Hindus, Muslims and Jains. Sons and daughters of Ullal. Sons and daughters of Abbakka. Their eyes red with anger and humiliation, hearts beating fast, waiting for their queen to order them to charge against the enemy and die for their motherland.

She turned to look at the group of women at the corner. Dressed in black, they wore their sacred thread around their wrists with a tattoo of the shatkona (the six-pointed star, an ancient Hindu symbol) in the centre of their palms. Fire in their eyes and weapons on their person, they looked thirsty for Portuguese blood. They were the veeranganas (female bravehearts), the special all-women task force Abbakka had created.

She clearly remembered that day. It was about one year ago. She was watching over her daughter's sword fighting practice at the training arena when this group of young women had approached her and said, 'Oh revered queen, we belong to the villages and not the palace. Yet we love our motherland as much as you do, as much as the princess does. The blood in our veins is beginning to doubt our love for our country. When you can and she can (pointing to the princess), why can't we pick up a weapon and fight for our people?'

Abbakka was touched to her soul's core. A tiny teardrop had trickled down her cheek. She had hugged them and said, 'So be it. Let Durga shine forth in each one of you'. And, thus, had begun the creation of veeranganas, the women's wing of Ullal's armed forces. Today, the time had come to show their skill and valour in the battlefield.

Abbakka looked at her little army once again. They were heavily outnumbered. But they had a cause to fight for. They were fighting for survival and respect. The enemy, only for a port. And this was their winning edge. She rose and addressed her people:

'The Himalayas are the head, and we are the feet of this glorious motherland we call Bharat. And we at Ullal have the honour of washing our mother's feet with the cool waters of the sea and the blood of our bodies. I won't let my mother's feet get dirty by the firangi's touch. Tonight, only their spirits will leave our land, not their bodies!' There was an intense emotive silence in the room.

'Who we are today is based on the choices our ancestors made. And our next generations will depend on the choice we make tonight. Hundreds or maybe thousands of years from today, there will be sons and daughters of this land who will question our spirits, and why we succumbed to the invaders like weaklings. Why didn't we rather die protecting our dignity? What will we answer them?'

'We will fight.
We sink or swim together.
We bleed and breed together.
Tonight, we create history together.
Har Har Mahadev!
Jai Ullal Bhoomi!'

And the entire atmosphere reverberated with hair-raising chants invoking the love for their motherland. Abbakka was going to attack.

* * *

General Peixoto's army had created their camp in the mushy clearing close to the jungle, with the distant beach on one side and the dense forest on the other three. It was the third prahar of the night. As per the queen's orders, the Mappilah seamen had left behind large barrels of local liquor in the camp with the request that their lives be spared. They had also planted the theory in Peixoto's mind that the queen had fled to her capital Moodibidri a few miles north after seeing no hope in recovering the palace and the fort. The air inside the Portuguese camp was that of a relaxed victory.

Yet the Portuguese were a seasoned professional military force. General Peixoto was one of the most fierce and feared generals and had a history of winning difficult battles. The camp was a rectangular formation with four main gates, which were guarded heavily by armed sentinels. The centre of the camp was Piexoto's luxury canopy, surrounded by the tents of the senior officers and then concentric circular rings of barracks for the soldiers. The cavalry men kept their horses tied right outside their tents. At the outer ring of the camp stood forty sentinels covered in armour, each carrying a tall spear and a sword. Two parties of ten watchguards constantly took rounds around the periphery of the camp, checking on the sentinels. Huge mashaals (flamed torches) lit up the camp pretty well.

A short distance away in the jungle, unknown to the Portuguese guards, a group of twenty women were crawling slowly towards the camp. They were covered in black from head to toe. Black clothes, black face masks and black paint on their skin. Nothing was seen of them except their white eyeballs. Tied to their waists on one side was a bamboo flute-like stick and a tiny pouch and on the other a sharp curved dagger. The dagger was more for the animals than the enemy. They moved cautiously without making the tiniest sound. Each was a few feet apart to be able to cover the sight of the entire outer periphery of the camp. When they reached close enough to see the sentinels clearly but were yet not too close, they halted, lying flat on their stomachs. Gracefully they raised their upper bodies, resting their body weight on their elbows, almost into a bhujangasana (yogic cobra pose). The leader of the pack let out their trademark owl hoot cry, done to perfection.

The ladies quickly took out their bamboo flutes and placed them to their lips. They took a deep breath in and aimed the flute at the sentinels standing alert at their posts. They blew hard into the flutes. A miniature thin dart flew out from each tube with tremendous force and whooshed towards the sentinels. The tip of the dart, coated with highly toxic cobra venom and poison from wild berries, touched the first sentinel at the throat, creating an unnoticeably small puncture in the skin. The sentinel, assuming it to be an insect bite, gently scratched the spot on his throat. The next moment he experienced a spasm in his throat and white froth emerged from his mouth.

He dropped dead without a sound.

The bamboo flute was actually a blowgun, and the assassins carried a pouch of deadly poisonous darts. When blown right, the almost invisible darts could travel at very high velocity and knock the strongest human dead within a few seconds. They called their morbid attack form 'death by breath'.

The sentinels fell almost like a wave collapsing against the shore. Unfortunately, a couple of shots missed their targets and the enemy realized they were being attacked. One of the sentinels pulled the rope tied to the alarm bells and as they rang out, the Portuguese jumped to their weapons immediately. But it was already too late.

Around the same dense section of the jungle where the women lay on the ground, sitting on top of the trees were Abbakka's archers. The Portuguese appeared with their swords and spears only to see hundreds of arrows raining at them from the sky, each marking their death warrants. And just as the Portuguese cavalry had mounted their horses and were ready to counter-attack, they heard loud thumping sounds from the other side of the jungle. Soon, they heard the dreaded war cry,

'Fight them on land,
Fight them on sea
Jai Ullal Bhoomi!'

Abbakka, swinging blood-thirsty swords with both hands, charged into the Portuguese camp with about a hundred horsemen. The Portuguese were trapped between a non-stop shower of arrows from an invisible team of archers on the treetops and an aggressive cavalry attack. As Abbakka mounted piles of corpses on both sides of her horse, she yelled fiercely, 'Show no mercy! Kill them all!'. She signalled Abdul to give her cover as she rode at full speed towards Peixoto's canopy. The Portuguese general faced her head-on, proving to be a worthy opponent. But Abbakka was fighting as if possessed by Maa Kali's rage. With a clean sweep of her sword, she beheaded the Portuguese chief, blood splashing all over her otherwise beautiful face. She picked up the severed head by the tip of her sword and stared into the unblinking eyes of the dead man.

You have been avenged Mother, she said in her heart.

She turned around to notice some of the enemy men reaching to their ships trying to escape. She turned her horse and commanded to her forces,

'Chase them! Erase them'!

'Kill them all!'

Her forces obeyed their queen.

It was a massacre.

From that day, Abbakka earned the title 'Abhaya Rani' (the queen who knows no fear).

* * *

Over the next few years, Rani Abbakka buried herself in the task of growing Ullal's treasury reserves and military strength. She knew she was on the firangi's radar. The stories of Peixoto's death had travelled wide and far. With glory comes jealousy and with victory comes more battles. She built many irrigation canals and dams, got all the forts repaired and acquired better combat equipment for her army and navy. For her cavalry, she imported Arabic war horses, bought at a premium price. She ensured that while being constantly battle-ready, the citizens lived a happy and peaceful life. Education and justice were always her priorities. Since daylight had to be used wisely for urgent matters, she started a night court where she would personally administer justice in critical cases till late in the night, ensuring the judiciary was not burdened with a pile of pending cases.

A hallmark of Abbakka's administration and armed forces was the fact that it consisted of all the diverse communities that existed on her land — there were the Tulu speaking Bunts, Hindus and Jains like Abbakka herself. There were the Konkani speaking Konkanasth Brahmans, the Billava and Mogaveera fishermen who spoke Kannada. Amongst the Muslims were the Beary community who were traders and the Mappilahs who were Malayalam-speaking seamen. There was also a thriving community of traders — Arabs, Persians, Syrians, Egyptians and Africans.

Ullal felt like one tiny happy peaceful place that was a shining example of unity in diversity. But the Portuguese didn't like that.

* * *

It arrived late in the night. The parcel was confidential and precious. It was immediately presented to the commander-in-chief of the Portuguese forces. He opened it and a huge smile ran across his face. He immediately called for a meeting with his core leaders.

'To victory!' they raised their glasses and clinked them. They decided they would attack in the wee hours of the morning two days later. After an in-depth analysis, the contents of the parcel were secured in the commander's desk. On the bottom of the parcel cover lay the royal insignia of the Bangaraja Kingdom, the rulers of Mangalore. The parcel contained all the secrets of Ullal's armed forces — treasury, hidden sea and land routes, details of all its allies and a list of Ullal's corrupt officers who were up for sale. Abbakka's estranged husband and his nephew had cheated on the queen. It was tragic but true.

Everything the Portuguese were not supposed to know was now known to them. The war had already been won before it even began.

The Portuguese choked Abbakka's food supply and reinforcement lines. They launched a surprise attack both on land (using the secret jungle routes now known to them) and by sea. Although Ullal's allies, the Sultanate of Abdulnagar and the Zamorine of Calicut extended the promised support and fought bravely alongside with Abbakka, they didn't stand a chance in front of the technically advanced cannons of the Portuguese. In less than half a day's battle, the Portuguese emerged victorious.

Abbakka fought like a lioness on the battlefield. With every wound the enemy inflicted on her body, her strength and passion rose further. It took several men shamelessly attacking her from all sides, disregarding all code of war conduct, to finally bring Abbakka down. And then she fell, like a true hero. Her death shook even her killers.

There she lay, her sword still in her right hand, fingers curled around the hilt. She was cut deep in several places and the wounds were bleeding her slowly to death. Yet she had a strange air of peace and victory on her face.

There she lay, the Abhaya Rani, the lone woman who had the audacity to repeatedly defeat the single largest naval power in the whole world. Her last moments were here. She held her daughter's hands and whispered,

'Tell the people of Ullal that I am sorry. But tell them I sincerely fought till the last breath in my lungs, till the last drop of blood in my veins. If you ever tell them my story, let them know I died respectfully like a veerangana should. Tell them I did not let my mother down. And my daughter shall continue the war for independence and dignity. We shall remain free'! And then she merged with the divine like the waves merge back into the ocean.

What was this woman made of?
What a giant, knocking on the doors of immortality!

Salutations to the land where Abbakkas are born.

* * *

KEY TAKEAWAYS

1. Aikla Chalo Re (Walk Alone)

'Jodi tor daak shune keu na aashe
Taube aikla chalo re'

~ Rabindranath Tagore

When no one answers your call, walk alone!

The whole world decided to bow their heads to the Portuguese invaders. Some didn't have the courage, and some didn't have the will to stand up against the oppressors. They saw their temples being razed to the ground and innocents being killed, but they didn't protest.

And then rose one woman, Abbakka.

One woman with one tiny little kingdom. And she decided to walk alone on the path of the anti-Portuguese struggle. She walked alone with only her faith and her principles. Later, some joined her cause and chose to come out of their shackles and walk with her. But she started alone. And she would have continued even if no one else had joined her.

That's called courage. That's called character. That is the stuff leaders should be made of. It takes guts to stand out. It calls for sacrifice. The sheer audacity of the idea — to challenge a global superpower, and then to defeat them again and again. The sheer love for the motherland. Beyond poems of patriotism and songs of freedom, *devotion in action* is what defined Abbakka.

2. *Sanghachadvam* (Walk Together)

And although the leader does not shy away from walking alone, the leader knows how to nurture those who choose to walk with them. Abbakka displays the rarest quality for a leader of the masses — the ability to connect with people and make them walk with you. They say, 'If you want to go fast, walk alone. But if you want to go far, walk together'. *Abbakka did both, walk fast and walk far.*

Much like the India of the twenty-first century, the factors dividing her subjects were more than the ones uniting them. She managed to connect them instead of allowing divisions and infighting. How did she inspire Hindus, Jains and Muslims to stand together and fight? How did she get the fishermen and the seamen to become soldiers and spies? How did she train village women to become deadly assassins and warriors? How did she get foreign powers to offer her secret support against the looming danger of the Portuguese? How did she win the faith of the Arabs and the Africans to continue trading with her without the cartaz?

It's the soft power of the true leader. *The charm, the intelligence, the vision and the courage all rolled up into one abstract quality called* ***heroism.***

Abbakka, like a true hero, beautifully blends the dichotomy of walking alone and walking together. *As a leader, internally, one walks alone.* When you are the boss, the queen, the influencer, you deal with your doubts and fears alone. It can get very lonely at the top. You don't share all your thoughts with your team. But when you are with your juniors, subjects, shareholders and children, you share hope and wisdom and keep their spirits high. You evoke faith and loyalty and establish a strong connection with them.

Being in a crowd when you are actually alone is ignorance. Feeling oneness with a crowd is enlightenment.

Aikla Chalo Re
(walk alone)

Sanghachadvam
(walk together)

Manthan

Pause. Introspect. Express.

Can you walk alone when no one is with you? How can you get this ability?
Can you get people to walk with you? Do you have the skill to take them along?

3. The 360-Degree Leader

Lead from the front, middle and the back.

She shoots the first agnivaan and does it perfectly, giving her team a winning start. She leads the raid into the Portuguese camp and herself beheads the general. And she dies fighting on the battlefield with pride. She chairs a successful business meeting on the ship and establishes strong foreign diplomatic relationships. She sits late into the night and dispenses justice. She grows her military, education, infrastructure and trade network. She also trains her daughter for future leadership while playing the loving mother to her. She accepts all religions and communities in her army and as subjects. She does it all — the reflection of Devi in a human form.

She is not an armchair ruler, giving sermons from the high palaces. She is hands-on, standing shoulder-to-shoulder with her people. That's the flavour and culture of leadership today more than ever before — *practical, empirical and realistic.*

Women orient themselves to be great task balancers. When nurtured and determined, they can be heroes on all fronts. They have to balance multiple roles skillfully. The notion of balancing the home and office is just a gross oversimplification of the problem. The expectations from women are way higher than those of men and their challenges are way more complex. All leaders have challenges, but some challenges are unique to women.

It was this way thousands of years ago and it is this way now. Abbakka comes forth as a shining example of a truly holistic leader.

Become a 360-degree leader
Lead from the front, middle and the back.

4. Charitra Trishula

The Personality Trident

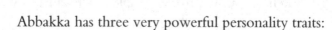

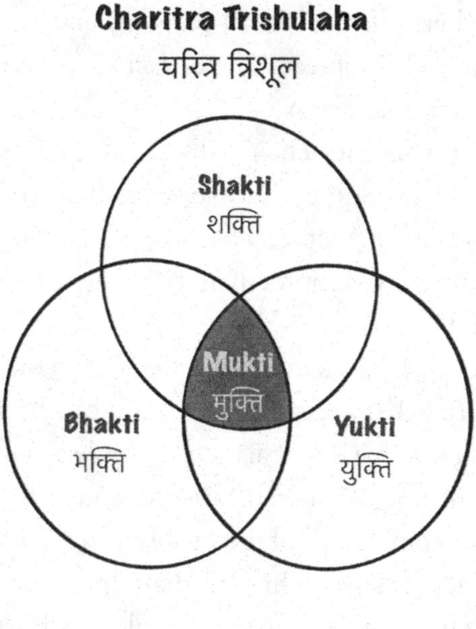

Abbakka has three very powerful personality traits:

Shakti (power)
Yukti (creativity/skill)
Bhakti (devotion)

Abbakka is powerful and she knows how and when to use her power. Known as 'Abhaya Rani' — the fearless queen, she has the private power to deal with her personal life crisis and professional power to rule as a queen. And she knows that power alone cannot solve problems. Sometimes skill and creativity (yukti) are more important than force and power.

The source of her power and creativity, apart from her confidence in her abilities and character, is also her surrender to the supreme power, her bhakti (devotion). She is a devout Jain. Her bhakti gives her the faith to pull through in tough times. Bhakti keeps you going even when situations seem hopeless. It keeps you humble and human.

Mukti

According to the ancient Indian scriptures, the purpose of human birth is to attain freedom or mukti. Although the goal is same for everyone, the paths can be many. The purpose of the journey of life is to find your path and to walk it with 100 per cent sincerity, so that it may lead you towards your mukti. This is called *swadharma* — the way of life that an individual uniquely chooses. For Abbakka, her karma was always aligned towards her purpose, and it led her towards her mukti.

Charitra Trishula
Shakti (power)
Bhakti (devotion)
Yukti (skill)

↓

Mukti (Liberation)

Manthan

Pause. Introspect. Express.

Do I have these three qualities — shakti, yukti and bhakti?
Do I tend to use one more than the other two or am I able to strike the right balance between the three?
Have I thought of what the path to my mukti is?
What is my swadharma?

5. No Sympathy Card

She is a single mother at a very young age. She has a tiny kingdom with a tiny army compared to her opponent. She herself has no experience of leadership or war. She has many diverse communities as her subjects and her husband has decided to become her enemy.

And yet, Abbakka never plays the victim. She never complains.

There are two ways to live life:

1. You get influenced by the environment/situation.
2. You influence the environment/situation.

Leaders don't allow the environment or situations to become more powerful than themselves. They don't complain about things they can't change. They accept the situational challenges and win despite the constraints.

Leaders influence their environment

6. Ahimsa (Non-violence)

What is ahimsa (non-violence)?

As per our scriptures, ahimsa exists at three levels — in thought, in words and in action.

What qualifies as 'himsa' and what qualifies as 'ahimsa'? That depends on the intention behind the action and not just the action. For example, when a thief uses a knife to cut someone's stomach, it is an act of violence, but when the same knife is used for the same act by a surgeon, it's an act of non-violence. A hostile acquisition of a company can be an act of 'corporate himsa' but firing an employee for an unethical action may be ahimsa. Himsa may also be done by harsh words or harsh thoughts.

Abbakka firmly believed in the Jain ideology of ahimsa but her ahimsa was not her weakness, it was her strength. Only the brave and the mighty can practice non-violence. That is why the great saint Vardhamana came to be known as Mahavira (the bravest one) although he never battled anyone physically.

Manthan

Pause. Introspect. Express.

Do I do himsa in thoughts, words or actions?

* * *

Reflective Exercise

It's interesting to know who we are and where we come from. In this busy life, we rarely take the time to find out more about our family's origins. Let's find out:

Know Your Roots

Who were your ancestors? Which region of India/world do you come from?

What was the primary profession of your ancestors? Are you from a matriarchal or patriarchal community? Is there any reason for this? What were the major events that shaped your ancestors' profession and geographical choices?

Fun Exercise

How many generations back can you personally trace your direct family tree?

Fill this in:

Father's or mother's name and year/place of birth:

Grandfather's or grandmother's name and year/place of birth:

Great grandfather's or grandmother's name and year/place of birth:

Great great grandfather's or grandmother's name and year/place of birth:

Great great great grandfather's or grandmother's name and year/place of birth:

Can you go further back?

* * *

Did you know?

- Vasco da Gama did not really 'discover' the sea route to India. He simply followed an Indian sailor's ship from the Cape of Good Hope to India. Indians were using that sea route for hundreds of years before Vasco da Gama was even born.

- The original name of Goa was Gomantaka and finds mention in the Mahabharata.
- Elephants have matriarchal communities.
- The words 'navy' and 'navigation' are derived from the Sanskrit words 'nau' and 'navgatih'.
- Tomatoes were brought to India by the Portuguese. It's amazing to think that what is now a core ingredient in most Indian curries was never used prior to the Portuguese coming to India.

Saraansh

A summary of your learnings from this chapter

1.
Aikla chalo re (walk alone)

2.
Sanghachadvam (walk together)

3.
Be a 360-degree leader.
(Lead from the front, middle and back)

4.
Leaders influence their environment.

5.
The Charitra Trishula
(Shakti, Bhakti, Yukti) → Mukti

6.
No sympathy cards

7.
Ahimsa should be your strength, not your weakness.

bibliography

Bhishma Vadh

Books

- Goendka, Jaydayal, ed., *Sankshipt Mahabharat* (Volumes 1 and 2, Hindi). Gita Press, 2017.
- Goendka, Jaydayal, ed., *Srimad Bhagavadgita* (Sanskrit Text with Hindi and English Translation). Gita Press, 2019.

YouTube

- Pen Bhakti. 'भरत राजा की कहानी, शांतनु-गंगा विवाह'. Mahabharat Stories. B. R. Chopra. EP–01. YouTube. 2 September 2019. (This can be accessed at https://www.youtube.com/watch?v=HnXkv_ozPQw&t=208s)

Jai Bhavani

Books

- Desai, Ranjit. *Shivaji, The Great Maratha*. Harper Collins, 2017.

- Khilnani, Sunil. *Incarnations: A History of India in 50 Lives*. Penguin Random House India, 2017.
- Maxwell, John C. *Teamwork Makes The Dream Work*. J Countryman, 2002.
- Tzu, Sun. *The Art of War*. Jaico Publishing House, 2010.

Online Resources/ Websites

- Gokhale, Aneesh. 'Chhatrapati Shivaji vs Afzal Khan: Pratapgadh 1659'. *Indiafacts*. January 2020. (Available at https://indiafacts.org/chhatrapati-shivaji-vs-afzal-khan-pratapgad1659/).

YouTube

- ABP News. "Bharatvarsh: Episode 10: Chhatrapati Shivaji—The bravest Maratha ever". Youtube. October 22, 2016. (This can be accessed at https://www.youtube.com/watch?v=zxokFpgxh9U).
- Marathyanchi Charitrgatha. "पर्व२| प्रतापगडाचेयुद्ध | Shivaji Maharaj and Afzal khan | Pratapgadacharansangram | Afzal khan". YouTube. May 9, 2019. (This can be accessed at https://www.youtube.com/watch?v=XgnCXb81kTM).
- Prasar Bharati Archives. 'Bharat Ek Khoj | Episode-37 | Shivaji, Part I'. YouTube. June 24, 2020. (This can be accessed at https://www.youtube.com/watch?v=o0MriNWtgZc)

Kabir Vaani

Books and Academic Papers

- Lorenzen N, David. *Kabir Legends and Ananta-Das's Kabir Parachai*. State University of New York Press, 1991.
- Sahani, Bhishma. *Kabira Khada Bazaar Mein* (Hindi). Rajkamal Prakashan Private Ltd., 2010.
- Verma, Vinod. *Pilgrimage Upside-Down: Kabir Ulatbansi Pilgrim*. International Journal of Religious Tourism and Pligrimage.

Theatre/Play

- *Kabir*. Directed by Shekhar Sen.

YouTube

- ABP News. 'Bharatvarsh: Episode 6: Watch the inspiring story of undeterred poet of 15th century, Saint Kabir'. YouTube. 26 September 2016. (This can be accessed at https://www.youtube.com/watch?v=0T64PBUTNGI).
- Ajab Shahar – Kabir Project. 'Chalo Hamara Des: Journeys with Kabir & Friends (English)'. YouTube. 10 December 2015. (This can be accessed at https://www.youtube.com/watch?v=waOosA3Rf1g).
- Ajab Shahar – Kabir Project. 'Had Anhad: Journeys with Ram & Kabir'. YouTube. 7 November 2015. (This can be accessed at https://www.youtube.com/watch?v=Dr83axn1IbM).

- Ajab Shahar – Kabir Project. 'Kabira Khada Bazaar Mein: Journeys with Sacred & Secular Kabir (English)'. YouTube. 14 November 2015. (This can be accessed at https://www.youtube.com/watch?v=s9hMVeTaUw8).
- Prabjitpanesar. 'Vikram Hazra in Kuwait – WCF Curtain Raiser – Song 3'. YouTube. 22 May 2016. (This can be accessed at https://www.youtube.com/watch?v=cj5A0HU4RuA).

Chanakya

Books

- Khilnani, Sunil. *Incarnations: A History of India in 50 Lives*. Penguin Random House India, 2017.
- Sanghi, Ashwin. *Chanakya's Chant*. Westland, 2010.
- Sri Sri Ravi Shankar. *An Intimate Note to the Sincere Seeker*. Sri Sri Publications Trust, 2021.

YouTube

- *Chanakya*. Written and directed by Dr Chandraprakash Dwivedi.
- ABP News. 'Bharatvarsh: Episode 2: Story of Chanakya, the author Arthashastra'. Youtube. 28 August 2016. (This can be accessed at https://www.youtube.com/watch?v=M5MsYdKoiUE).

Hanuman Uvacha

Books

- Sharma, Jaikanth. *Srimad Valmiki Ramayan* (With Sanskrit Text and English Translation). Gita Press, 2018.

- Misra, Nityananda, ed., *Mahaviri (Hanuman Chalisa Demystified)*. Bloomsbury Publishing, 2018.

YouTube/ TV

- *Ramayan*. Directed by Ramanand Sagar.
- Tilak. 'Ramayan Episode 1. श्री राम भगवान् का जन्म और बाललीला का आनंद'. Youtube. 17 October 2020. (This can be accessed at https://www.youtube.com/watch?v=vIh99bkSc_w).

Narada Diaries

YouTube

- Knowledge Transforms. 'Upanishad Ganga'. Episode 3. YouTube. 20 December 2021. (This can be accessed at https://www.youtube.com/watch?v=iOScYcvRXz4)

Books

- Sri Sri Ravi Shankar. *Narada Bhakti Sutras*, Sri Sri Publications Trust, 2009.

Adi Shankaracharya

Books

- Madugula, I.S. *The Acharya (Shankara of Kaladi)*. Motilal Banarasidass Publishers Pvt. Ltd, 1985.
- Kinkhabwala, Bhavesh. *Adi Shankaracharya, Spirituality and Management (Uncovering Wisdom for Managerial Effectiveness and Workplace Spirituality)*. Notion Press, 2020.

- Varma K., Pavan. *Adi Shankaracharya (Hinduism's Greatest Thinker).* Tranquebar, 2018.

YouTube

- ABP News. 'Bharatvarsh: Episode 4: Watch the glorious story of Adi Shankaracharya'. YouTube. 10 September 10 2016. (This can be accessed at https://www.youtube.com/watch?v=qLdUesiPSb0).
- Acharya Shankar Sanskritik Ekta Nyas. 'Biography of Adi Shankaracharya'. YouTube. 8 December 2017. (This can be accessed at https://www.youtube.com/watch?v=zNI1B9kcVbU).
- Thirumalai, Murali. 'Aadi Shankaracharya Full Movie in Sanskrit'. YouTube. 12 June 2021. (This can be accessed at https://www.youtube.com/watch?v=87wq0lSyebA).
- Study IQ Education. 'Life and Journey of Jagatguru Shree Adi Shankaracharya श्रीआदिशंकराचार्यकीजीवनयात्रा'. YouTube. 19 October 2018. (This can be accessed at https://www.youtube.com/watch?v=OJ3Ei4Bdz7g).

Websites

- Madhaviya Shankara Digvijayam. 'The Biography of Sri Adi Shankaracharya'. *Sringeri.* (Available at https://www.sringeri.net/history/sri-adi-shankaracharya/biography/abridged-madhaviya-shankara-digvijayam#sri-shankara-at-varanasi)
- Nitin Kumar. 'Life of Shankaracharya – The adventures of a Poet Philosopher'. *Exotic India.* 1 February 2005.

(Available at https://www.exoticindiaart.com/article/shankaracharya/)

- Dhandha. 'Two friends: Death and Wisdom'. *Truth Telling*. 29 October 2010. (Available at https://voiceofhappiness.wordpress.com/2010/10/29/two-friends/)

Srinivasa Ramanujan

Books

- Gladwell, Malcolm. *Outliers (The story of success)*. Penguin Books, 2008.
- Kanigel, Robert. *The Man Who Knew Infinity*. Abacus, 2016.

Websites

- Wolfram, Stephen. 'Who Was Ramanujan?'. *Writings*. April 27, 2016. (Available at https://writings.stephenwolfram.com/2016/04/who-was-ramanujan/).

YouTube

- History. 'Ancient Aliens: Ramanujan the Divine Mathematician' (Season 11, Episode 5) History. 22 December 2018. (This can be accessed at https://www.youtube.com/watch?v=_Yn7QAS5Wpw).
- Hollywood World. 'The Man Who Knew Infinity (2015) Full Movie HD||Dev Patel, Jeremy Irons, Devika Bhise'. YouTube. 31 January 2020. (This

can be accessed at https://www.youtube.com/watch?v=8WwLPep9xNg).

- IISER Pune. 'The genius of Srinivasa Ramanujan | Vigyan Prasar | IISER Pune, IISER Pune'. YouTube. 19 September 2017. (This can be accessed at https://www.youtube.com/watch?v=SYBOOjhAMsM).
- Regional Science & Technology Center, Ghaziabad. 'Ramanujan (The Man who reshaped 20th Century Mathematics)'. YouTube. 7 May 2018. (This can be accessed at https://www.youtube.com/watch?v=-5L4Is-VNDI).
- Tibees. 'The letter that revealed Ramanujan's genius'. YouTube. 14 August 2020. (This can be accessed at https://www.youtube.com/watch?v=XFsuRxospbU).
- Universe Inside You. 'Ramanujan—The Man Who Knew Infinity & the Akashic Records'. YouTube. 18 February 2020. (This can be accessed at https://www.youtube.com/watch?v=xGfV80ioA6U).

Rani Abbakka

Books

- Mandana, Kavitha. *The Teenage Diary of Abbakka (The Warrior Queen of South India)*. Speaking Tiger Books LLP, 2020.

YouTube

- Dr Saloni Nandan. 'Rani Abbakka Chowta I The Valiant Queen of Ullal I The First Woman Indian

Freedom Fighter I History'. YouTube. 1 September 2021. (This can be accessed at https://www.youtube.com/watch?v=8QmZoybaP1s).

- Lindybeige. 'Fire-arrows!'. YouTube. 10 June 2016. (This can be accessed at https://www.youtube.com/watch?v=zTd_0FRAwOQ).
- Smithsonian Channel. 'How Medieval Archers Rained Fire Down on their Enemies'. YouTube. 9 March 2020. (This can be accessed at https://www.youtube.com/watch?v=qgUNmuV91ms).

Websites

- 'Abbakka Chowta'. *Wikipedia.* 31 January 2020. (Available at https://en.wikipedia.org/wiki/Abbakka_Chowta).
- 'Battle of Diu'. *Wikipedia.* 24 March 2022. (Available at https://en.wikipedia.org/wiki/Battle_of_Diu).
- Gupta, Archana. 'The Admiral Queen'. 25 October 2015. (Available at https://swarajyamag.com/magazine/the-admiral-queen).
- Hebbar H., Neria. 'The Intrepid Queen, Rani Abbakka Devi of Ullal'. 2 January 2005. (Available at https://www.boloji.com/articles/747/the-intrepid-queen).
- Kr. Mishraa, Kailash. 'Abbakka Rani, The Unsung Warrior Queen'. 13 April 2022. (Available at http://ignca.gov.in/abbakka-rani-the-unsung-warrior-queen/).
- A.V. Murthy, Narasimha. 'Pepper Queen Abbakka'. (Available at https://web.archive.org/

web/20070806161344/http:/www.ourkarnataka.com/Articles/starofmysore/abbakka.htm).

- 'Ullal'. *Wikipedia*. January 17, 2022. (Available at https://en.wikipedia.org/wiki/Ullal).